Collins Revision

GCSE Higher English

Revision Guide

FOR AQA A

Written by Keith Brindle and Kim Richardson

Revision Guide Contents

CONTENTS

Exam Practice Workbook Contents

About your AQA/A English exam

Exam papers

- There are two exam papers, Paper 1 and Paper 2.

- Each paper tests some reading skills and some writing skills.

- Each paper is worth 30% of the total marks you can get in your English GCSE.

See the chart opposite: **GCSE English at a glance**.

> For more on these exam papers, see:
> pages 6–7 (Paper 1, Section A)
> pages 28–29 (Paper 2, Section A)
> pages 48–49 (Papers 1 and 2, Section B)

The skills you are assessed on

- When the examiners mark your answers, they are looking for certain skills. These are called **assessment objectives**. This book covers all the assessment objectives for Reading and Writing.

- Speaking and listening skills are tested in your coursework, along with reading and writing skills.

The reading skills you are assessed on

In the Reading sections of each paper, you need to show that you:

- **understand what the texts are about**.
  This means explaining their content and purpose. You will need to refer to the texts in your answer.

- **can tell the difference between a fact and an opinion**.
  This means identifying facts and opinions in the text, and explaining how and why they have been used.

- **can write about how information is presented**.
  This means saying how effective you think the texts are at doing their job.

- **can follow an argument**.
  This means explaining what a writer is saying, and how they have put their ideas together.

- **understand the techniques that writers use**.
  This means commenting on the language they use, how they organise their texts and the way they present them on the page.

- **can compare texts**.
  This means explaining how one text is similar to, or different from, another. You need to refer to examples across both texts.

These skills are covered in the first two sections of this book: *Reading Media and Non-Fiction* (pages 6–27) and *Poetry from Different Cultures and Traditions* (pages 28–47).

The writing skills you are assessed on

In the Writing sections of each paper, you need to show that you:

- **can communicate clearly and imaginatively**.
  This means writing so that the reader understands what you are saying and is interested in it.

- **have a clear idea of purpose and audience**.
  This means being able to write in a particular form (e.g. a letter or a newspaper article) and for a particular audience (e.g. young people).

- **can organise your writing**.
  This means using sentences and paragraphs, and giving your writing some sort of structure.
- **can use a range of words and sentence structures**.
  This means using a varied vocabulary, techniques such as repetition and contrast, and different types of sentence for different effects.
- **can punctuate and spell correctly**.
  This means using a range of punctuation, such as full stops, commas and questions marks, and showing that you can spell accurately.

These skills are covered in the final two sections of this book: *Writing Skills* (pages 48–61) and *Types of Writing* (pages 62–87).

GCSE English at a glance

GCSE English Specification A

Paper 1   30% of the total marks
1¾ hours

Section A   Reading non-fiction and media   15%

Section B   Writing: argue, persuade, advise 15%

Paper 2   30% of the total marks
1½ hours

Section A   Reading poetry from different
            cultures and traditions   15%

Section B   Writing: inform, explain,
            describe   15%

Coursework   40% of the total marks

Speaking and listening
3 assessed activities   20%

Reading: Shakespeare   5%
           Prose study   5%

Writing: Media   5%
           Original writing   5%

This tests your reading skills. You will be asked about two or three non-fiction and media texts that you haven't seen before. (pages 6–27)

This tests your writing skills. You will be asked to write to argue, persuade or advise. (pages 62–73)

This tests your reading skills. You will be asked about the poems from different cultures in your Anthology. (pages 28–47)

This tests your writing skills. You will be asked to write to inform, explain or describe. (pages 74–85)

These are the pieces of coursework that your teacher has asked you to do. They are not covered in this revision guide.

Paper 1 Section A: Reading media and non-fiction

Key points

- Paper 1 Section A will focus on previously unseen texts. One will be from the **media**. Another will be some form of **non-fiction**. You will have to deal with two or three different texts.

- In an hour, you will have to answer about **four to six questions**.

- This section of the exam counts for **15% of your total mark**.

- The remaining 45 minutes of Paper 1 tests you on your writing skills.

The texts

- At least one text will be a **media text**. You might be given, for instance, an article or editorial, a report, advertisement, web page, obituary, advice sheet or leaflet.

- There will probably also be a **non-fiction text** which might not be from the media, such as an extract from a biography or autobiography, a section from an instructional book or an information text.

The exam paper

Paper 1 consists of two sections. Only Section A of the exam paper is given here.

Paper 1 Section A: Higher Tier

In addition to this paper you will require:
- Text 1: *Need a break? Want a change? Why not try Bognor …?*, from a weekend magazine
- Text 2: *Ancient art of relaxing*, from the *Sunday Express*

These are the texts that you will be given in full in the exam. They are both media texts. They are not reproduced here.

READING: NON-FICTION AND MEDIA TEXTS

Answer all the questions in Section A.
Spend approximately 60 minutes on Section A.

Remember to spend up to 10 minutes of this time reading the texts carefully, before answering the questions themselves.

This question is asking you to identify the purpose and audience of Text 1 – not to write about the text in general.

1 Re-read Text 1: *Need a break? Want a change? Why not try Bognor ....?*

a) What is the intended purpose and audience for this text? Give your reasons. *(5 marks)*

b) How does the writer try to convince us of his argument? Explain:
- the main points of his argument
- how fact and opinion are used
- how other techniques are used. *(9 marks)*

This refers to any persuasive techniques that the writer uses, such as anecdotes, statistics or humour.

This question is asking you to show how well you can follow, and evaluate, the argument. Make sure that you cover all the bullet points in your answer.

2 Next, re-read Text 2: *Ancient art of relaxing*.

a) Why have the presentational devices been included? To what extent are they appropriate for the text? *(5 marks)*

Finally, compare the two texts.

b) How does each writer use language? *(8 marks)*

Total: 27 marks

This question is asking you to think about the use of such devices as headlines, photos, graphics, bullet points and use of colour and design.

The final question usually asks you to compare the texts. In this case, you are being asked to compare only their use of language. To compare, you will need to use material from both texts, and make cross-references between them.

Note how many marks are awarded for each question, and allocate your time accordingly.

The skills you will be assessed on

The questions that you are asked in Paper 1 Section A will be based on assessment objectives. Some questions will test more than one objective, but within the Section you will be tested on your ability to achieve the following:

Assessment objective

1 Read, with insight and engagement, making appropriate references to texts and developing and sustaining interpretations of them

Pages 8–27

2 Distinguish between fact and opinion and evaluate how information is presented

Pages 8–9

3 Follow an argument, identifying implications and recognising inconsistencies

Pages 10–13

4 Understand and evaluate how writers use linguistic, structural and presentational devices to achieve their effects, and comment on ways language varies and changes

Pages 14–21

5 Select material appropriate to your purpose, collate material from different sources and make cross-references

Pages 22–27

What this means in detail

You will be expected to understand **the literal meaning of texts**, so that you can explain their content and recognise their **form**. However, you will also be expected to understand their **purpose** and recognise their **target audience**, and to write about **how far their aims are achieved**. Your views need to be supported by **evidence** from the texts; and your explanations should be **detailed** and range across the texts.

You will be expected to locate **facts and opinions** and be able to explain **how** they have been used by the writer, and **why**. You will be dealing with their **purpose** in the text and their **effect** on the reader. To '**evaluate**' how information is presented, you must give an opinion on **how successfully** any features have been used.

As well as understanding **what** a writer says, and in what order, you are likely to have to explain **how** the argument has been put together: how the writer has used contrasts, anecdotes, humour, exaggeration, evidence and so on. To 'identify implications', you might well have to write about **what the writer is suggesting** rather than clearly stating; and 'recognising inconsistencies' means dealing with any apparent **contradictions in arguments**.

You will be asked about **language**, and how it is used to **create an effect** and further the **writer's purpose**. You will be writing about whether the language used is **appropriate** for a particular **purpose** or **audience**. Similarly, there will be a question on **presentational devices**; and you might also be asked about the **structure** of a text in terms of either general layout, or how it has been organised.

You will have to refer appropriately provide **evidence** of what you have to **compare element** This will mean identifyin **how writers use p** means you could be a or the use of language, presentational devices or la

Fact and opinion

Key points

- In Section A of Paper 1, you will be asked to **distinguish between fact and opinion** in one or more texts and to **evaluate** how information is presented.

- In practice, this is likely to mean you will be expected to:
  - **locate** facts and opinions
  - write about how they are used in relation to **purpose** and **audience**

  and, possibly, to:
  - **compare** the use of fact and opinion in two different texts.

Remember that facts can be used in different ways. Some facts simply present information. Others back up a writer's opinions, so their purpose is more persuasive.

Locating facts and opinions

- **Fact** is what can be proved to be true. Usually there is evidence to back it up.

- **Opinion** is someone's belief. It is likely to be someone's interpretation of events or details.

- Many texts are a **mixture** of fact and opinion.

The article below is from the magazine *Inside Soap*. The facts (and their annotations) are in blue. The opinions (and their annotations) are in orange.

'Flamboyant' and 'mouthy' only in the judgement of the writer.

The spokesperson did make this statement.

But what she said was her own opinion.

> Emmerdale fans had better brace themselves – as another member of the flamboyant Lambert family is about to descend on the village.
>
> Actress Victoria Hawkins – who has previously starred in children's TV show Byker Grove – has been cast as mouthy Sharon Lambert, the estranged daughter of Woolpack landlady Val.
>
> "We're delighted to welcome Victoria to the Emmerdale cast," said a spokesperson for the soap. "Sharon's going to cause a lot of trouble for Val. The pair have a very rocky relationship."

Some people could disagree.

It is true that Sharon Lambert is going to join the cast of Emmerdale.

Purpose and audience

- When you write about the use of facts and opinions in an extract, you should refer to the **purpose** and **audience** of the piece, as in this answer:

The writer's purpose is mainly to persuade viewers to watch the programme, so the facts about the appearance of Sharon Lambert are surrounded by opinions about the characters ('flamboyant', 'mouthy'), [wha]t is going to happen ('going to cause a lot of trouble') and the [eff]ect on the fans (they 'had better brace themselves') ...

Good Points

- The use of fact and opinion is linked to the purpose of the text. This helps you focus on why fact and opinion have been used in a particular way.
- Examples are used to support the ideas.

The next extract is from the *Yorkshire Evening Post*.

- Note how the writer has used facts and opinions to achieve a different purpose.

- The writer does not try to dramatise the situation. The facts outweigh the opinions, and are used to make the opinions believable.

Top Tip!

News articles often include quotations from people who are connected to the story. These words may consist of both facts (things that have happened) and the speaker's own opinions.

The article opens with straight-forward facts. This is because it comes from a newspaper and is reporting, rather than trying to 'sell' something to the reader.

A couple celebrating their 40th birthdays have asked for donations to charity instead of presents.

Graham and Chris Lingard of Ilkley both support Christian Aid, the churches' charity which raises money to help struggling Third World countries.

Their birthdays are close to each other and they decided on a joint party as part of this week's nationwide Christian Aid collection week.

Graham said: 'We both wanted to highlight how unfair our world is, and support a charity that works to help change this injustice.

'The problems facing Africa are hard for us even to imagine. Currently – due to chronic poverty, coupled with recurring drought – 38 million people simply do not have enough to eat. In 2005 AIDS alone killed over 2 million people in sub-Saharan Africa,' he said.

The writer includes opinions from Graham.

Graham has given some facts to encourage people to support them.

Comparing texts

- If you are asked to compare the use of fact and opinion in two texts, the easiest way is to:
  - write about the **first text**
  - write about the **second text**
  - **make comparisons** between the two as you deal with the second one.

If you are comparing the use of facts and opinions in these two articles, you could begin your paragraphs like this:

The first text relies heavily on opinions ...
Whereas the first text relies so heavily on opinions, the second begins with facts ...
The first text makes exaggerated claims, but the second text ...
In conclusion ...

Task

Use the paragraph openers above to complete this task:
Compare how fact and opinion are used in the articles from *Inside Soap* and the *Yorkshire* .

Following an argument

Key points

- At least one of the questions in Section A of Paper 1 will expect you to demonstrate your ability to **follow an argument**.

- This requires more than simply paraphrasing (putting into your own words) what the writer has said. You will probably be asked to consider the writer's **point of view** and **how the argument has been constructed**. This means analysing and commenting upon the **structure, language and techniques** used.

Top Tip!

You need to identify the key points of the argument. These are the steps that lead to the conclusion. Look at the first sentence in each paragraph: it will often summarise the key point in that paragraph.

The writer's point of view

- Initially, you need to decide what the **writer's attitude** to the subject of the text is, i.e. his or her **point of view**. That will help you to clarify the text's **purpose**. You are making a decision about **why** it was written.

- For example, rather than just noting that a text is about the problems facing elderly people, you might need to **explain** that the writer is supporting the need for more medical help for the aged, or for more funding for senior citizens if they live in the country.

Structure

- There are many ways to present an argument, but in most cases arguments have:

  – an **introduction**, which sets out the subject of the argument and indicates the writer's viewpoint

  – **developed points**, designed to prove or justify the writer's case

  – a **conclusion**, summing up the main reasons why the writer's view is correct (and/or why the opposing viewpoint is wrong).

- The writer will take account of the **opposite viewpoint**, because without that there can be no argument.

Look at the article below and on page 11 about sport on TV. Consider how the writer has structured the article. (The middle four paragraphs have been reduced to just their topic sentences.) Read the annotations carefully, which will help you see the structure:

Paragraph 1 sets out the writer's main point – that she feels we are obsessed by sport, and waste much of our lives as a consequence.

What is it that makes people believe that watching sport is the most important activity known to man? Let's face it, we only live for seventy years – eighty if we're lucky – and yet so many people waste so much time watching pretty brainless bodies chasing a ball round a patch of grass; and often spend hundreds of pounds for the privilege. Failing that, they are glued to the game on TV. And when they are dead, what then? A life has been wasted, potential squandered, and nothing has been achieved.

Football fans, of course, see it differently …

This line of argument, however, is nothing short of ludicrous …

How many goals do we remember? How many service aces justify the time we spend watching …?

There must, surely, be more we could be doing …

Paragraph 2 puts the alternative viewpoint.

Paragraph 3 mocks the alternative viewpoint.

Paragraphs 4 and 5 develop the argument presented at the start.

> **Paragraph 6** presents the conclusion – a vision of an improved society, based on the ideas previously stated in the argument. It moves to a final statement of the writer's opinion.

So, what is the solution? In Britain we need to change the consciousness of the nation. Firstly, people need educating to realise that we could do more useful things to develop ourselves and – just imagine! – help others. Secondly, we need to remove the cult of the sport star and, instead, lay much more emphasis on those who do something worthwhile. How much better it would be, for example, if children grew up wanting to be a doctor, rather than Wayne Rooney.

Writing about structure

How could you summarise the way the argument in the article about sport has been put together? You could begin like this:

> The article begins by pointing out that we waste our time watching sport. There is an element of sarcasm (we watch 'pretty brainless bodies chasing a ball') and seem to have no escape at all (we are 'glued', metaphorically, to the game on TV). The message is initially bleak:
>
>   'nothing has been achieved'.
>
> However, we move to a conclusion that suggests ways in which we could improve the quality of our lives – for example, by valuing doctors above sports stars. It all seems perfectly logical:
>
>   'Firstly ... Secondly ...'
>
> In the body of the response, an alternative point of view is offered, but is attacked in a number of ways. It is made to seem crazy ('ludicrous') and a series of rhetorical questions is intended to undermine it:
>
>   'How many goals do we remember? How many ...?'
>
> The repetition makes us imagine the writer shaking her head, as if she is amazed at people's behaviour ...

Grade A

Good Points

- The response shows clear understanding of the structure: beginning, development, ending.
- Significant features are identified and illustrated.
- There is some personal response from the student ('it all seems ...', it 'makes us imagine ...').

READING MEDIA AND NON-FICTION

Language

There are two main ways to examine how language is used:

1 Is it appropriate for the **audience**?

- An argument is unlikely to be successful if the audience is alienated by the language used or cannot understand it. For example:
  - *Hey, guys, don't diss me* is unlikely to impress middle-aged bank managers.
  - *Those on the periphery of society should not be berated* is unlikely to win the attention of the nation's young people.

- In a text, therefore, it is usually possible to identify elements of language which are aimed at the intended reader.

2 Does it suit the **purpose** of the text?

- If the argument is a proposal by a supermarket to build a large out-of-town store, the language will be **serious, logical and restrained**.

- If the writer is aiming to **amuse** the audience as much as persuade them, the language might be more **colourful and exaggerated**.

- When commenting on language, therefore, make reference to the **aim of the writer** and the **context** in which they are writing.

Pages 14–17 (more on language use)

Techniques

- Writers use a range of strategies to entertain and interest the reader. The aim is to persuade the reader to their point of view.

- Some of the techniques for building an argument are described below.

  - **rhetorical questions**: questions asked for effect, that do not expect a reply

  - **exaggeration**: overstating the case, to make a point even more strongly

  - **examples and lists**: details selected to support a point

  - **anecdotes**: brief stories (often personal), used to illustrate the argument

  - **quotations**: usually from people with particular knowledge of the subject

  - **contrasts**: setting contrasting points or images beside each other for effect

  - **humour, such as sarcasm**: used to encourage the reader to agree with the writer's opinion

  - **irony**: when words are used rather sarcastically to say the opposite of what is really meant

Top Tip!

Your analysis will be more effective if you can identify the techniques a writer has used to convince the reader and build the argument. When you identify a technique, use a quotation to make it clear for the examiner. Also, explain what it adds to the text – how it supports or develops the point the writer is making.

Commenting on effectiveness

- To gain a good grade, you need to **analyse** how these techniques have been used and **comment** carefully on their **effectiveness**.

For example, paragraph 2 of the article opposite could be analysed like this:

> The writer makes a good use of contrast to point out the difference between the old-fashioned presenters that he was used to and the new-style presenters. The adjectives 'friendly, reliable, old' are set against 'semi-naked' for good effect.

Good Points

- The response identifies a technique used – contrast.
- It explains why the technique has been used.
- It comments on how the writer has built up the contrast, and how effective it is.
- It quotes appropriately from the text to illustrate the point.

Some convincing techniques are used in this magazine article. A middle-aged man discusses what it is like to grow older.

They say that age is a state of mind. I think age happens when you can no longer watch pop music on TV without cringing. I was brought up on Top of the Pops – in fact I lived for my Thursday evening fix of the latest sounds. I was devastated when the show was axed. What do kids watch now? I decided to find out by sitting with my own children one evening.

Shock and dismay. The channel was called 'Kiss' – that should have been a warning in itself. And instead of some friendly, reliable old DJ fronting the show, there was a continuous stream of what appeared to be semi-naked girls faintly disguised as pop artists.

'How old is she?' I asked my son, aghast, as I watched one of them, who looked as if she should be in school.

'Chill, dad.'

'She just giggles and screams. And she's wearing underwear.'

'So? Don't we all?'

Then, the performances.

'Why do they do that?'

'What?'

'The rappers … Their hands … Why do they do that with their hands? No drier in the toilets?'

'It's what they do.'

'But why?'

It's weird when a whole part of your life has passed you by, but, frankly, you don't care because you are happier with your memories of Tony Blackburn and the Beatles and the Eurovision Song Contest and singers who had hair and sang and didn't have bodies with rings all over, like chain mail.

Of course, it's next stop afternoon bingo. Then a stair lift. And, frighteningly, what comes after that …?

Maybe I'll breathe deeply and try to appreciate the girls and the rappers. While I still can.

contrast

anecdote + quotations

humour

list of examples

exaggeration

rhetorical question

humour + irony

Question

What does the writer of this magazine article have to say about growing older, and what techniques does he use to build his argument?

Language

Key points

- Section A of Paper 1 will ask you to write about the **language used** in one or two of the unseen texts.

- It is not a good idea to try and write about a whole text. You do not have enough time. It is better to write a lot about a little, rather than a little about a lot. Locate **the most obvious linguistic features**, such as:
  - sentences and paragraphs
  - significant vocabulary
  - punctuation
  - similes, metaphors and other linguistic devices
  - the style of the language.

Sentences and paragraphs

- The **length of sentences**, and the way they are **constructed**, can vary enormously and produce different effects. For example:
  - **Short sentences** sometimes suggest speed or excitement, e.g.

  He ran forward. The ball fell at his feet. He shot.

  - They can also indicate surprise or despair, e.g.

  Her inspiration stopped. Her career ended.

  - **Long sentences** can indicate calm, e.g.

  The sergeant reported that right along the river teams of men and women were resting at last and preparing to return to the headquarters for a much-needed break.

  - Or they can build to a climax, e.g.

  The crowds gasped as the top of the mountain blew away, clouds of ash shot hundreds of feet into the sky and rivers of lava, terrifying in the early dawn, shot upwards, then cascaded down into the valley.

- **Paragraphs**, too, can create different effects. A **very short paragraph**, for instance, attracts attention, so that stress falls on the content. Popular newspaper articles are likely to have short paragraphs and contain less detail so that they can be read more easily. Articles in more serious newspapers may have **longer paragraphs**, containing more detail and analysis.

Significant vocabulary

- The sort of words used in a text can also tell you a lot about the **purpose** of the text:
  - Imperative verbs such as 'follow' and 'begin' suggest **instructional** writing.
  - Connectives like 'since' and 'because' may indicate **explanatory** writing.
  - Words such as 'however', 'nevertheless' and 'indeed' may come from **persuasive or argumentative** writing.

- The vocabulary can also tell you about the **audience** for a text:
  - **Longer words** suggest a text is aimed at an intelligent readership.
  - A text containing **modern vocabulary**, for instance dealing with ICT and communications, could be targeting younger people or those in the industry.
  - A text containing **slang** or **colloquial** terms might be aimed at teenagers.
  - Vocabulary associated with a **specific subject** would be used in an article aimed at specialists.

Punctuation

- The punctuation of texts can clearly indicate the writer's intent, as in these headlines:

TEENAGER 'TORTURED TO DEATH'

The inverted commas indicate it may not have happened, but show that someone has offered that opinion.

Let's focus on ... improving your home

The ellipsis (...) suggests that there are many things we could do. The ellipsis can also suggest a fading away.

HOLLY HITS OUT!!

The double exclamation mark is to attract attention and suggest excitement, or even surprise.

Top Tip!

If you can, comment on some elements of punctuation and the purpose they serve. It will make your response more impressive. For top marks, make your comments detailed and develop them as precisely as possible.

Similes, metaphors and linguistic devices

- Most students write about **similes**, **metaphors**, **alliteration** and **onomatopoeia** when dealing with poetry in Paper 2, but many fail to realise that the same devices are used in non-fiction texts.

This extract from an autobiography includes examples of all of them:

similes

alliteration

They held us in a small room. We felt like condemned men and smelt like battery hens. We had no idea of the day or the time and dreaded the dull echoes of sharp boots and the crank of the lock on the door. It was an eternity of torture ...

onomatopoeia

metaphor

You could analyse the use of language in the extract like this:

Grade A*

The writer makes their captivity vivid by using a series of linguistic devices. First, two similes are used: to stress their desperate situation ('like condemned men') and the inhuman conditions in which they were kept ('smelt like battery hens'). Deadly 'd's introduce alliteration as their jailers approach - 'dreaded the dull ...' - and then there is onomatopoeia which captures the sound as the key turns and their horrors are about to begin again: 'crank'. The primitive sound helps us understand their situation. Finally, the metaphor 'eternity of torture' is used to express how long and painful it must have seemed to them at the time.

Good Points

- The analysis focuses on precise aspects of language, rather than generalising.
- Linguistic devices are discussed, not just identified.
- There is an awareness of the way the effects are linked to create an overall impression.

READING MEDIA AND NON-FICTION

Style

- A text may be **formal** and written in standard English, or **informal** if the audience would respond more readily to that style (as in some letters, advertisements and articles).

- You need to start by identifying the **essential features** of each text. For example, if you were asked to compare a formal and an informal text, you might write:

> The first text is formal, using sentences like 'The government has taken a stance which ...', while the second text is less formal and targets drug users: 'Get real ...'

Stylistic techniques

- A variety of stylistic techniques are used depending on whether the texts persuade, argue, advise, inform, explain, describe, review or analyse. For instance:

  - **rhetoric**, especially **rhetorical questions**, used for added impact:

  Can this be acceptable?

  - **emotive language**, which touches the reader's feelings:

  They are tiny and cold and they are starving.

  - **irony** (subtle mockery):

  I have always thought it is a good idea to make the poor starve ...

  - **exaggeration**:

  The royal family eats nothing but caviar for breakfast.

  - **contrast**:

  The seabirds sing, while the fishermen starve.

  - **colloquial language**, as if people are chatting:

  If you want to pull, you have to impress the lads.

  - **ambiguity**, where there can be more than one interpretation:

  Bird watching is a really exciting hobby.

  - **inference**, where things are suggested rather than clearly stated:

  He met the girl of his dreams. He didn't come home that night.

  - **examples** and **quotations**, giving credibility to what is written:

  Only yesterday, a shop assistant said to me ...

  - **humour**, to get the audience on the side of the writer:

  There was more life in my popcorn than in this film.

  - **lists**, for emphasis:

  She packed the potatoes on top of the bananas, the bananas on top of the tomatoes and the tomatoes on top of the eggs.

Top Tip!

Practise finding and analysing these features whenever you read non-fiction. Identifying them and commenting on their effect gets you extra marks in the exam.

This extract from a newspaper article is short, but uses several of the techniques above.

> Who can fail to notice the Prime Minister's excellent track record when it comes to improving all areas of British life?
>
> We all recognise that approach which claims 'I'm a man o' the people', and don't the people just love him? Especially those paying taxes they can't afford, waiting in traffic that never moves, facing ever-mounting debt and an impoverished old age ...

This is what one student wrote about the style of the extract:

Grade A*

> The writer begins with apparent irony. The rhetorical question asks the reader to consider the PM's record, and suggests the track record may not be so good. Later, there is the implication that the people might not actually love him, while the colloquial 'I'm a man o' the people' might be poking fun at him, implying that his 'approach' is a pretence which 'we all recognise'.
>
> Then there is a list of problems, which form a critical commentary on the government. It uses emotive detail ('they can't afford') and exaggeration ('traffic that never moves') as it moves to a cutting climax, with the elderly 'facing ... an impoverished old age.'

Good Points ✓

- Language is analysed to explain the style.
- The writer's point of view is interpreted through the detail.
- Quotations are used to illustrate the points being made.

Question

This extract comes from *Take a Break* magazine.
- What is the text's purpose and audience?
- How is language used by the writer?
- Is the language used successfully?

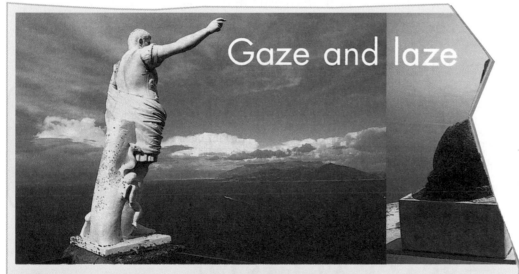

Gaze and laze

Take a break where the sun always shines

All eyes turn to the sea on this 30-mile stretch of Italy's western shore, considered one of the most beautiful coastlines in the world, where Campania gazes out into the Tyrrhenian reaches of the Mediterranean.

It takes in Sorrento, Positano, Salerno and Amalfi – which gives it the local name *Costiera Amalfitana* – and even extends into the sea.

Sitting off the coast like a satellite at the end of the peninsula, the island of Capri is just a 20-minute cruise away from Sorrento. Fram the port of Marina Grande it's a short ride by funicular railway to the labyrinth of narrow alleyways that make up Capri town.

But it is at Anacapri, the island's second town, that you'll find Capri's very own Garden of Eden, where mythological statues sit like sentinels surveying the deep blue waters. Or where classically draped figures from Italy's past appear to hold command over clouds fleeing across the contrasting blue of the sky.

Layout and presentational devices

Key points

- Paper 1 Section A will test your understanding of how layout and presentational devices are used in media texts. **Layout** means the way the page is arranged. **Presentational devices** are the individual features that are used to create the layout, such as pictures and headlines.

- You will be expected to write about **what the writer was hoping to achieve**, and **how** particular devices have been used to **support the writer's purpose**.

Top Tip!

For top grades, you need to use the correct terms for presentational devices. However, it is most important that you show your understanding of these concepts, and that you can relate them to the purpose of the text.

Identifying the features

- Presentation and layout includes the way the **words** are presented and the **illustrations** are used, and the **overall design** of the text.

- Some **common features** used in media texts include:

  – **headings**: what size and style? The main heading in a newspaper story is called a headline.

  – **strapline**: a second, introductory headline, below the main one

  – **subheadings**: how often are they used? Why are they used – to summarise, break up the text, or grab the reader's attention?

  – **font**: style and colour can vary throughout a text. Why has a particular font been used?

  – **capitals**: what is the effect?

  – **captions**: the text under a photograph or diagram which explains it

  – **standfirst**: the introductory paragraph in an article or report, which could be in bold print or with the first word capitalised

  – **pull-quote**: a quotation which is lifted from the article and set apart, in larger or bold type

  – **bold, italics, underline**: different ways of making certain words stand out

  – **slogan**: a memorable word or phrase, designed to create interest

  – **logos**: emblems to represent a product or company

  – **photographs** and **graphics**: how do they relate to the text? What is their purpose?

Top Tip!

As well as commenting on the individual features of presentation, don't forget to comment on the overall design of a media text, such as the colours used and how everything works together.

headine

strapline

capitals

standfirst

subhead

PEACE AT LAST?

PM set to sign treaty at end of historic talks

ONLY LAST YEAR, the prospect of a resolution to the conflict seemed remote. Now, with all parties in agreement, there is a chance of peace.

The Prime Minister faced tough questions yesterday

Last chance

photograph

caption

columns

Analysing how devices have been used

- If you just describe what is on the page, you are working at a very simple level. Instead, you should aim to say **why** the text has been designed in a particular way – what **effect** the writer is hoping to achieve.

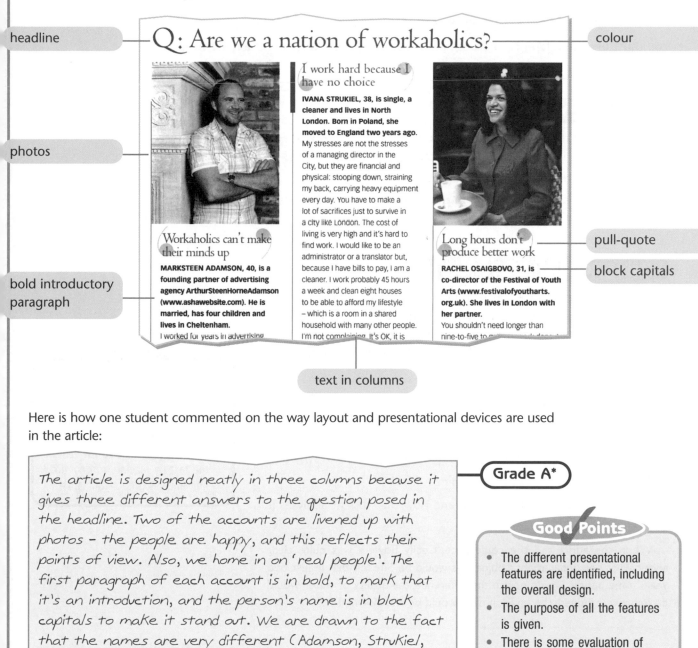

headline · colour · photos · pull-quote · block capitals · bold introductory paragraph · text in columns

Q: Are we a nation of workaholics?

I work hard because I have no choice

IVANA STRUKIEL, 38, is single, a cleaner and lives in North London. Born in Poland, she moved to England two years ago. My stresses are not the stresses of a managing director in the City, but they are financial and physical: stooping down, straining my back, carrying heavy equipment every day. You have to make a lot of sacrifices just to survive in a city like London. The cost of living is very high and it's hard to find work. I would like to be an administrator or a translator but, because I have bills to pay, I am a cleaner. I work probably 45 hours a week and clean eight houses to be able to afford my lifestyle – which is a room in a shared household with many other people. I'm not complaining. It's OK, it is

Workaholics can't make their minds up

MARKSTEEN ADAMSON, 40, is a founding partner of advertising agency ArthurSteenHorneAdamson (www.ashawebsite.com). He is married, has four children and lives in Cheltenham.
I worked for years in advertising

Long hours don't produce better work

RACHEL OSAIGBOVO, 31, is co-director of the Festival of Youth Arts (www.festivalofyoutharts.org.uk). She lives in London with her partner.
You shouldn't need longer than nine-to-five to

Here is how one student commented on the way layout and presentational devices are used in the article:

Grade A*

The article is designed neatly in three columns because it gives three different answers to the question posed in the headline. Two of the accounts are livened up with photos – the people are happy, and this reflects their points of view. Also, we home in on 'real people'. The first paragraph of each account is in bold, to mark that it's an introduction, and the person's name is in block capitals to make it stand out. We are drawn to the fact that the names are very different (Adamson, Strukiel, Osaigbovo), so we register that they might have different backgrounds. The pull-quotes summarise the key points that the interviewees are making; they are bigger because they 'answer' the question posed in the headline. The 'question and answer' format tries to simplify the information for the reader, whilst the use of orange gives a positive effect – which ties in, successfully, with the smiles of those pictured.

Good Points

- The different presentational features are identified, including the overall design.
- The purpose of all the features is given.
- There is some evaluation of how effective the design is.

Top Tip!

If you can evaluate how effective the layout or presentational devices are, you will gain a higher mark. Don't be afraid to give your opinion!

Question

Choose an article from your favourite magazine. List all the presentational devices used, and explain why they are used. Could you improve the overall design? If so, how?

Selecting and using textual references

Key points

- To support the points you make in your answers, you need to **refer directly to the text**.

- You must select references that are **suitable** for the task.

- You must use the references appropriately: **quoting** them briefly and **explaining the effects**.

Selecting references

- To find essential details or quotations, make sure you **read the question carefully** to see exactly what is required. Notice helpful information, such as:

  Read the **opening paragraph** and **explain** ...

  Find **three facts** and say how they **support** what the writer believes ...

  What **techniques** are used to **convince** the reader that ...

Using textual references

- The purpose of making a textual reference is to show the examiner that you have read the text carefully and that any ideas you are putting forward arise from the text itself. In other words, you are **engaging with the material**, rather than just offering random thoughts.

- Put inverted commas around any short quotations and make sure they are contained within fluent sentences. Indent longer quotations, starting on a new line.

- Make at least one comment on each quotation, to explain why you have included it.

Look at this extract from *Africa Today*, and how the student analyses it.

Top Tip!

Examiners always reward the development of ideas:
- Explain what the material is saying, why and how.
- Link the reference to the rest of the text by placing it in context and analysing its significance.

> When she addressed the conference, Cecily Bowers was quite clear about what her department's objectives would be. She felt that in just two years' time people would notice the difference: the quality of water would be improved; indeed, the environment would be transformed ...

The writer makes Ms Bowers seem confident from the start. He says she: 'was clear' about her objectives. The 'clarity' suggests she has thought through her ideas, and can put them across forcibly. Then, he goes on to indicate some of the improvements she is intending. The description builds up from the quality of water to a complete transformation of the region, which emphasises how wide-ranging and effective her plans are.

Good Points

- The candidate has used a textual reference to support each point. In one case this is a quotation, in the other a textual detail.
- The significance of the textual references is explained.

Task

Improve the student answer on page 19 by adding another textual reference to it.

Analysing text types

Key points

- There are a number of different **text types** within media and non-fiction. Each is targeted at a particular **audience** and is written for a particular **purpose**.

Page 6

- Each text type uses particular devices – in **language**, **layout** and **presentational devices** – to achieve its purpose and to reach its audience effectively.

- To be successful in your exam, you need to recognise what the writer **wants to achieve** and the **methods** used.

- This demands a **careful reading** of the text.

News reports

This is a news report from *The Sun*. The annotations describe the devices that have been used.

Strapline tells you more about the story: 'Protest' gives immediate impression of conflict.

Grey-fill gives dismal effect.

Catchy **headline** put in block capitals.

Picture – ship appears old/ready to scrap and needs a tug.

Alliteration – 'toxic time bomb' gives ticking effect.

Short paragraphs (one sentence each) make text easy to read.

Emotive language makes ship sound dangerous.

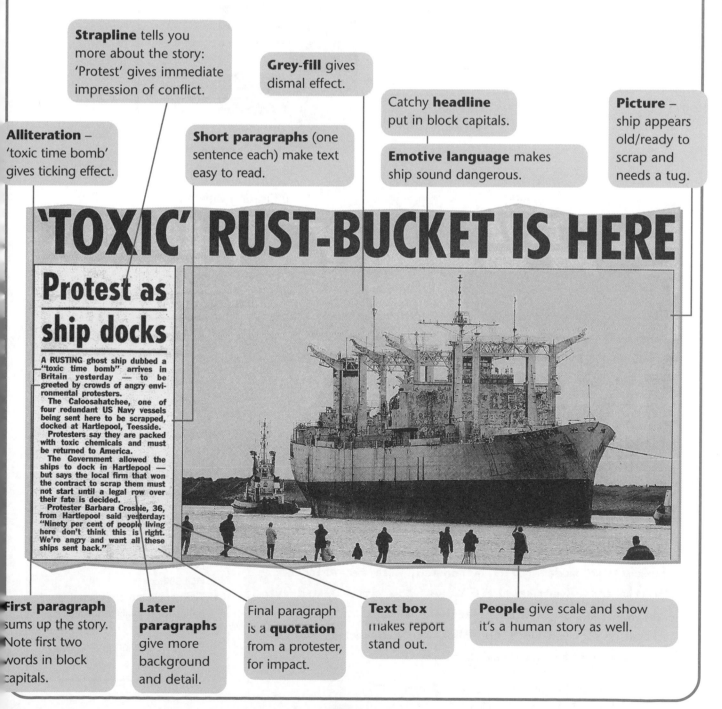

'TOXIC' RUST-BUCKET IS HERE

Protest as ship docks

A RUSTING ghost ship dubbed a "toxic time bomb" arrives in Britain yesterday — to be greeted by crowds of angry environmental protesters.

The Caloosahatchee, one of four redundant US Navy vessels being sent here to be scrapped, docked at Hartlepool, Teesside.

Protesters say they are packed with toxic chemicals and must be returned to America.

The Government allowed the ships to dock in Hartlepool — but says the local firm that won the contract to scrap them must not start until a legal row over their fate is decided.

Protester Barbara Crosbie, 36, from Hartlepool said yesterday: "Ninety per cent of people living here don't think this is right. We're angry and want all these ships sent back."

First paragraph sums up the story. Note first two words in block capitals.

Later paragraphs give more background and detail.

Final paragraph is a **quotation** from a protester, for impact.

Text box makes report stand out.

People give scale and show it's a human story as well.

Web pages

- Look at these different features and devices, which are often used on web pages.

website provider indicated

indication of content

main photo to attract attention: deep blues and greens dominate

solving dilemmas over choice; sounds exciting

for further searches

main navigation bar showing range of content in website

links provided

short snatches of text to tempt the reader in for more

logo stands out

variety of links

range of linked topics

alliteration to link with phrase above

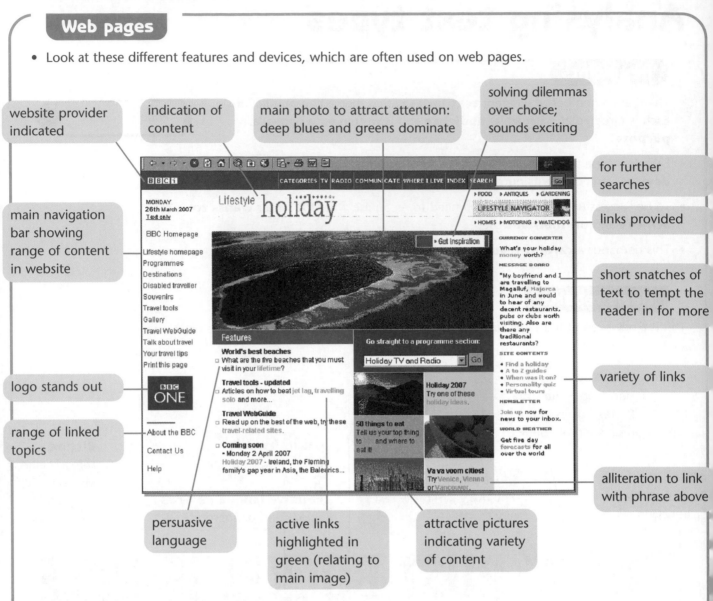

persuasive language

active links highlighted in green (relating to main image)

attractive pictures indicating variety of content

Here is one student's analysis of this web page:

Grade A*

This is a successful web page, designed to interest those considering a holiday and tempt those who had not previously considered taking one. The main picture looks breathtaking and will attract any potential traveller; the smaller pictures are varied and make us want to travel (there is the romance of the sunset, the succulence of the fruit and the beauty of Venice). The text also demands attention: there are the imperatives – 'Try ...', 'Tell us ...', – and a range of associated topics, all clearly highlighted in blue, with green links, both to stand out but also to link with the main title and the colours in the main photo. A sense of humour and modernity is introduced, with the reference to the car advertisement ('Va va voom cities'), and even the punctuation is used effectively: ellipses to suggest there is so much more to follow and exclamation marks to emphasise the excitement of it all ...

Good Points

- The student has dealt effectively with both purpose and audience.
- Precise details from the text are included.
- The details are considered critically, to analyse the text's success.
- Both presentation and language are analysed.

Autobiographies

- This extract is from an **autobiography** by Sir Robin Day. Sir Robin used to interview politicians on television, and this is about his first ever time in front of the cameras – in the 1950s, when television was less technical and there were no autocues!

- There are no presentational devices used in a text of this sort, so your focus must be on the **language**.

short, dramatic first sentence →

tension building →

dialogue adding variety and human interest →

countdown moving text towards the climax →

> I was ready to go. But there was a little more delay. The lighting was causing trouble with my spectacles – reflection flashes from the lenses and shadows from the heavy hornrims. An engineer climbed up ladders to adjust the arc-lamps until the director in the control room was satisfied. It seemed to take a very long time. I began to sweat under the heat of the lights.
>
> We had been asked to memorise our material so that we would not have to look down. They wanted to see us looking full-face into the camera. I took a final look at my notes. The phrases which last night were crisp and bright seemed limp and dull, but it was too late to make any changes.
>
> 'Are you ready?' called the floor manager. I nodded.
>
> 'Stand by.' He stood to one side of the camera, and raised his arm above his shoulder.
>
> 'Thirty seconds to go ... Fifteen seconds.'
>
> Suddenly the floor-manager jabbed his hand down towards me. A red light glowed on top of the camera. This was it.

← detail brings scene to life

← fear that material is not good enough: threat of disaster

← short sentence – dramatic ending

Here is one way to start analysing the language used in the extract:

The text sets out to illustrate to Robin Day's fans just what he had to cope with. It begins with a short sentence and ends the same way. It seems tense, as if Sir Robin is taking short breaths ...
The problems with the glasses and the lights are mentioned to show how everything seems to be going wrong, making Sir Robin more worried ('I began to sweat ...'). Obviously, it is all building up inside him, so he seems very human and doubts even the quality of his material: 'The phrases ... seemed limp and dull'...

Good Points ✓

- The whole of the text is covered.
- The purpose of this part of the text is taken into account.
- Relevant quotations are used to support the student's ideas.
- This is likely to develop into a Grade A answer.

Top Tip!

To achieve top marks, you need a clear understanding of particular text types.
Always bear in mind purpose and audience.
Try to respond to the whole text, and be aware how individual features fit into the whole text.

Task

Write two paragraphs describing how the newspaper story on page 21 sets out to attract the reader and keep their attention.

Comparing texts

Key points

- One question on Section A of Paper 1 will probably ask you to **compare two texts**. This could be a simple comparison, for example comparing the writers' use of language. However, you might have to write about a number of features in the texts, such as layout, language and presentation.

- Make sure you provide the **right details** and make all **cross-references** clear.

Providing the right details

- Read the question carefully to make sure that you provide the right information. The wording of the question will show you exactly what you should be comparing in the texts. For example:

The **main question**, which asks you to compare the texts. The focus of your answer should be on how **successful** they are …

> Which text is more successful?
> Compare the texts by writing about how the writers have used:
> - fact and opinion
> - argument.

… and not just how successful in general, but how successfully the writers have used **these features**. Your mark would be reduced if you analysed the features but did not evaluate their success and say which works better, and why.

Making clear cross-references

- The vital element is to **compare the texts**. It is not enough to write an analysis of one, then an analysis of the other.

- In making references to the texts, you must clearly **link one text to the other**. Notice how the second answer below does this successfully, while the first one simply refers to the two texts in turn:

> The first text concentrates on giving advice to old people and uses lots of facts and figures. The second text encourages relatives to invest in security for senior citizens.

✗

> The first text concentrates on giving advice to old people. However, the second text …

✔

- It is useful to have a stock of words and phrases to make comparisons clear, such as:

similarly	in contrast	while the first text …,
just as …	whereas	the second text …
likewise	on the other hand	when we turn to …
also	but	in comparison
so …	however	the second text, though …

Top Tip!

To get top marks:
- make detailed comparisons between the texts
- provide an imaginative response, giving your own opinions.

For example:

The first text [short quote] treats old people as if they are …
whereas the second text has a tone that is softer, suggesting that …

Two texts to compare

Read the texts below, then look at the annotated student's answer to the question on the right:

Compare these texts by saying whether they will appeal to their audience. Write about the use of language in both texts.

Text 1

This is from an obituary for the poet Charles Causley in the *Times Educational Supplement*, a teachers' newspaper.

> At Launceton voluntary primary he discovered by accident the power of the ballad – a form he later made his own – to quell unruly eight and nine-year-olds.
>
> In a TES interview to celebrate his 70th birthday, he told Neil Philip: 'I used to have a double class of boys every Thursday afternoon. There were 50 or 60 of them, quite a horror, and I had the wrong books with me. At the top of the pile I had a selection of English and Scottish ballads … I opened it in desperation … Stop a riot with a ballad.'
>
> The boys were transfixed, but Mr Causley never forced poetry on anyone. He simply made it a natural part of the school day.

Text 2

This newspaper article offers a somewhat different view of young people.

> ### A pensioner's life made a misery by 'young vandals'
>
> Frank Blackburn, 78, who lives on the Albany Estate, has been a prisoner in his house each evening for over a year. Groups of children, many as young as 7 or 8, have made him fear for his life and the safety of his property.
>
> 'They gather every night,' says Frank. 'The police don't do anything about it.'
>
> Stones have been thrown through his windows, excrement has been pushed through his letter box and he cannot sleep. Gangs roam the area, shouting and drinking. Other older residents are just as fearful.
>
> A police spokesman said they are currently dealing with the matter.

This is the start of an A* response:

Grade A*

Answer addresses focus of question directly by discussing the appeal of the texts to their intended audience.

Precise quotations are used, which are integrated smoothly into the sentences.

'In contrast' makes a further clear comparison. The focus here is on facts and opinions in the second article.

The audiences for these texts are different. The piece on Charles Causley is written for teachers, and therefore presents a positive image of Causley in the teaching situation, whereas the other article is for a more general readership and concentrates on the pensioner's suffering, to get a sympathetic response.

The facts in the TES obituary show how difficult Causley's situation was ('50 or 60 of them'; 'I had the wrong books with me'). However, the wonder of what he achieved relies on his own opinion of what they were like. Originally the situation was 'quite a horror' but then 'The boys were transfixed'; the book of ballads was opened 'in desperation' but soon became 'a natural part of the school day'. We rely on Causley's interpretation for the final impression of how poetry managed to 'quell' the children.

In contrast, the second article's vision of young people seems much more immediate and believable. The facts are grim: stones through the windows, and excrement; gangs 'shouting and drinking' and Frank fearing for his life. What is worse, this is happening to a 78-year-old, persecuted by 7- or 8-year-olds. The opinions give a further impression of the children ('young vandals and thugs'), of the effects (his life is 'a misery', whilst the 'other older residents are just as fearful'), and of the police who 'don't do anything about it'…

'whereas' links the texts by contrasting them.

Focus on how facts and opinions are used in the obituary.

The student's personal response. This shows a keen understanding of the text.

Task

Complete the answer to the question above. Write.
- a paragraph on the use of language in Text 1
- a paragraph on the use of language in Text 2
- a final paragraph to summarise the ways the two texts are similar/different, referring to the main focus of the question (appeal to audience).

Raising your grade

If you want to raise your grade to A or A*, you need to show these skills.

Show a thorough understanding of the text

- Make sure you refer to the **purpose** of the text, as this shows that you understand why it has been written or presented in the way it has, e.g.

  The article describes prisons as 'waste-paper baskets' and 'cess pits'. These are negative and unpleasant images <u>which reinforce the writer's argument that prisons should be abolished</u>.

- Make sure you refer to the **audience** of the text as well. This shows that you appreciate how the words have been chosen to suit a particular group of people, e.g.

  <u>The writer is appealing to an intelligent readership. We know this because</u> he uses long sentences and quite difficult ideas. The article is very text-heavy, <u>which would not appeal to someone thumbing quickly through the newspaper</u>.

- Give an **overall interpretation** of the text to show that you grasp the text as a whole. Arguing for a particular view of a text from start to finish will earn high marks.

Show that you can analyse and evaluate, not just comment

- **Analyse** the writer's use of language, presentation and structure. This means explaining in some detail how certain features have been used, e.g.

  The writer suddenly throws in a short sentence, 'No good'. <u>This reflects how the runaway has come to the end of the road and has nowhere to turn. He is stopped short, just as the reader is.</u>

- Say **how successful** the writer has been, giving **reasons** for your evaluation, e.g.

  The final paragraph of the article is <u>less successful because</u> we are expecting a full-scale conflict, whereas Martin just backs down and disappears into his office. The writer could have chosen a more powerful example to illustrate bullying in the workplace.

- **Read between the lines** of the text, so that you are interpreting it. Exploratory responses are rewarded as long as they are backed up with evidence, e.g.

  The style of the second extract is softer, which suggests that the writer has some sympathy for the children in the unit. For example …

Make good use of the text in your answer

- Make a **variety of points** that cover the **whole of the text**. Don't just focus on one part of it, unless the question asks you to.

- **Choose your quotes carefully**, and integrate them into your sentences. The quotations should be brief and relevant, e.g.

  Davidson is presented as a rather pathetic figure: <u>he 'waves ineffectually' at the taxi and gets splashed as it passes him.</u>

- **Link texts** together when you are comparing them, e.g.

  The second text <u>also</u> uses strong language, but this time for a different purpose. <u>Whereas the first text is aimed at selling a product, the second is …</u>

Read the question and the student's answer below. The annotations show why the examiner awarded it an A grade.

What impression of Nivea for Men moisturiser is this advertisement trying to create? In your answer, explain the use of language, layout and presentational devices.

BDF ●●●●
Beiersdorf

NEW

NIVEA FOR MEN SENSITIVE

EXTRA SOOTHING MOISTURISER

Moisturises & Protects against irritation

Sensitive skin

THEY'VE RUN OUT OF HALF-TIME PIES.

Life has enough irritations. Don't let your skin be one of them.
NIVEA FOR MEN® Extra Soothing Moisturiser soothes and calms your skin.

Grade A

The answer begins by dealing directly with the question. It gives an overview of how the advert is intended to work.

The advertisement is trying to make the product attractive to men. Since many men would think skin products are made for women, the advertiser has tried to create an advertisement that avoids features which are stereotypically feminine.

The answer is well structured – here the student moves on to discuss the text.

To begin with, most of the advertisement is blue, and blue is 'for a boy'. Also, it is not just any shade of blue – it is dark and a far remove from 'girly' pink. Perhaps it is meant to suggest the colour of a deep sea: that would fit with the idea of cleansing.

The student is not afraid of making their own suggestion or interpretation.

The actual moisturising product is displayed in a clear, unfussy way on the right of the advert. It looks straightforward and functional, not at all flashy. Again, this may be to appeal to an average man who might be reluctant to buy a beauty product.

Good use of textual reference. The student does not need to quote the text in full, but integrates references to the text in the answer.

It's the writing that dominates in this advert. It dominates not just in the way that it takes up most of the space, but also because it catches the eye: what on earth have pies got to do with skin cream? This is obviously what the reader is meant to think – it draws them in to read more. Also, the idea of half-time pies summons up a very male picture. The double meaning of 'irritations' is clever and funny, and another way of getting the reader on side.

The purpose and audience of the text are referred to throughout.

The design of the text is solid and 'basic', to match the product. Colours are simple white against the blue, to match the design of the product; and the block capitals are well chosen as they suggest stability, firmness and a lack of feminine curves.

The conclusion sums up the student's opinion, which has been consistent throughout. An overall interpretation has been offered, with another reference to the audience of the text.

Each feature of the advertisement, therefore, is designed for men and it is hard to imagine it having any sort of attraction for women.

Good analysis of the features – the student always gives a good amount of detail, and comments on how successful the features are.

Paper 2 Section A: Reading poems from different cultures and traditions

Key points

- Paper 2 Section A will test how well you understand and can write about two poems from different cultures and traditions.

- There will be two questions, but you will only have to answer one of them. In both questions you will be asked about a named poem, and you will have to compare it with another poem of your choice.

- One question will target the first Cluster of poems in the Anthology. The other question will target the second Cluster.

- This section of the exam counts for 15% of your total mark.

- You will be expected to spend about 45 minutes on your answer. The remaining 45 minutes of Paper 2 tests you on your writing skills.

Top Tip!

Focus on your reading skills when answering the Reading questions. You won't get any marks for your spelling, punctuation and grammar.

The exam paper

Paper 2 consists of two sections. Section A is Reading poetry. Section B is Writing to inform, explain, describe. Only Section A of the exam paper is given here.

The first question focuses on the first Cluster of poems in the Anthology. One poem is named and you choose another one to compare it with.

Paper 2 Section A: Higher Tier

READING: POEMS FROM DIFFERENT CULTURES AND TRADITIONS

Answer **one** question.

You are allowed to refer to a copy of the Anthology in the examination.

EITHER

1 Compare *Night of the Scorpion* with any other poem of your choice. How do the poets present relationships in the poems? *(27 marks)*

OR

2 How is language used to reveal the speaker's situation in *Not My Business* and in any other poem of your choice? *(27 marks)*

You are given two questions, and you have to answer one of them.

You will be given a clean copy of the Anthology in the exam. You can't refer to your own marked-up copy.

The second question focuses on the second Cluster of poems in the Anthology. One poem is named and you choose another one to compare it with.

The skills you will be assessed on

The questions that you are asked in Paper 2 Section A will be based on assessment objectives. The table shows what examiners will be looking for, and what that means in detail.

Assessment objective	What this means in detail
1 Read, with insight and engagement, making appropriate references to texts and developing and sustaining interpretations of them. *Pages 30–47*	You will be expected to understand **what the poets are saying**, hopefully moving beyond the obvious meaning and examining the **deeper messages** that the poets offer. You will think about **why** the poems have been written. Your views need to be supported by **evidence** from the texts (quotations from the poems) and your explanations should be **detailed** and range across both poems.
2 Understand and evaluate how writers use linguistic, structural and presentational devices to achieve their effects, and comment on ways language varies and changes. *Pages 36–47*	You will be expected to show **how the poets have used language**, what **effect** it has and **why** the poets have used it in particular ways and for particular purposes. You will be writing about how the language is used appropriately to convey a particular **message**. If you can **evaluate** the usage – say how successful it is – you will be rewarded with a high mark. You will also need to consider other presentational elements such as the **structure**, including how the poem begins, develops and ends, as well as the way it is set out on the page.
3 Select material appropriate to your purpose, collate material from different sources and make cross-references. *Pages 32–47*	References to the poems need to be **relevant**, so you need to focus on the question that is asked, avoid irrelevancies and select ideas and quotations that are apt. It is not enough simply to write about two poems; for top grades, you need to make **clear and developed comparisons** of messages, poetic techniques or whatever is required by the question.

Question

It always helps to revise poems in pairs, since you will have to compare two poems in the exam itself. Which two poems from the list on the right would you use to answer a question on each theme given, and why?

Themes	Poems
Suffering	*Nothing's Changed*
Poverty	*Limbo*
Inequality	*Island Man*
Man and Nature	*Night of the Scorpion*
Contrasting cultures	*What Were They Like?*
	Two Scavengers in a Truck...
	Blessing
	Vultures

Different cultures and traditions

Key points

- The questions on Paper 2 Section A will focus, in part, on the different **cultures** or **traditions** identifiable in the poems.

- The cultures and traditions are revealed by various things, such as the **language** that is used, the **setting**, the **people**, and their **situations and problems**.

- You need to show that you understand **how** the poems reflect these different cultures and traditions.

Language

- Language plays a significant role in setting the poem within a particular culture.

  - It can show how people speak:

    munay hutoo kay aakhee jeebh aakhee bhasha

      (*from Search For My Tongue* by Sujata Bhatt)

    Explain yuself
    wha yu mean

      (*Half-Caste* by John Agard)

  - It gives us names: Oya, Shango and Hattie (*Hurricane Hits England*).

  - It introduces items unfamiliar to many people in Britain, e.g. yams in *Not My Business*; a salwar kameez in *Presents from my Aunts in Pakistan*; paddies and water buffalo in *What Were They Like?*

- It is very important to show that you understand **how** the poets use language, and **why**.

Look at this extract from a student's answer about the language used in *from Unrelated Incidents*.

> thi reason
> a talk wia
> BBC accent
> iz coz yi
> widny wahnt
> mi ti talk
> aboot thi
> trooth wia
> voice lik
> wanna yoo
> scruff...
> yooz doant no
> thi trooth
> yirsellz cawz
> yi canny talk
> right.
> *(from Unrelated Incidents)*

Grade A

In 'from Unrelated Incidents', Tom Leonard uses a regional voice to criticise BBC English and all it represents. We appreciate his accent and the pronunciation because it seems ordinary – and, arguably, more honest than the manufactured television version of 'trooth'. When the newsreader says we would not want him to talk 'lik wanna yoo scruff', we are presented with an image of Glasgow, peopled by ordinary folk; but we are left to wonder whether they are people that we would trust more than someone who uses 'received pronunciation'.

Good Points

- The focus is upon how and why the language is used.
- The use of language is explained ('we are presented with ...').
- The reaction of the audience to the use of language is explained ('We appreciate his accent ...').

People and settings

In most of the poems, the people and the places where they live are different from those we would find in Britain:

> *peasants; their life*
> *was in rice and bamboo.*
>
> (*What Were They Like?* by Denise Levertov)

> *a bright yellow garbage truck*
> *with two garbagemen in red plastic blazers*
> *standing on the back stoop...*
>
> (*Two Scavengers in a Truck, Two Beautiful People in a Mercedes* by Lawrence Ferlinghetti)

This poem is set in America. It is closer to our own world, but still different.

Situations and problems

Many of the poems address problems that arise from being in or coming from a different culture:

- **Being in an alien environment**

  In *Island Man*, by Grace Nichols, the central character has left his home, with its surf, seabirds and fishermen, and is now coping with life in a huge city. He has to drag himself out of bed to face its challenges:

  > *island man heaves himself*
  >
  > *Another London day*

  The final line, separated, shows the significance of 'another London day', which seems heavy and depressing.

- **Slavery**

  In *Limbo*, by Kamau Brathwaite, we are presented with the world of slavery and the suffering of the Africans. The plight of the slaves is desperate:

  > *stick is the whip*
  > *and the dark deck is slavery*

  though the ending suggests there might be salvation of some kind:

  > *and the music is saving me.*

- **Endless evil**

  Some poems are very dark, and appear to offer no solutions. We are faced with 'the perpetuity of evil' (*Vultures*, by Chinua Achebe) and we are told in Tatamkhula Afrika's poem that *Nothing's Changed*.

- **The struggle for existence**

  In many poems, people just have to struggle on. In *Night of the Scorpion*, Nissim Ezekiel describes his mother's suffering, then reveals his mother's reaction, which indicates that her only thoughts were for her children:

  > *My mother only said*
  > *Thank God the scorpion picked on me*
  > *and spared my children.*

- **Hope for the future**

  At other times, there are some flashes of hope, such as when Imtiaz Dharker conjures a positive vision and excitement:

  > *This is the time and place*
  > *to be alive.*
  >   (*This Room*)

  Also, Derek Walcott demonstrates how we can come to a peace within ourselves and how our lives will be richer because of our understanding:

  > *You will love again the stranger who was yourself.*
  >   (*Love After Love*)

Task

Compare *from Search For My Tongue* with any other poem of your choice, explaining the problems revealed in the poems and how the poets feel about the situation.

Content, message and attitude

Key points

- When you write about poems from different cultures and traditions, you may have to comment on:
  - the **content** of the poems
  - the **messages** in the poems
  - the poets' **attitudes** to the subject.

What the poem is saying

- For each of the poems you are studying, you need to understand exactly **what the poem is about**. You should be able to answer the questions: who? what? where? when? why?

- Precise **details of language** tell the reader a bit more – they add some **meaning** to the bare details.

This student has annotated the opening of *Vultures* by Chinua Achebe to help her understand what is going on in the poem. Red annotations identify the basic facts. Purple annotations add comments on the meaning.

> **Top Tip!**
>
> When you write about a poem, you need to go beyond the surface meaning. You need to 'interpret' the poem, which means using the language as clues to its deeper meaning.
>
> When you comment on the poem, refer to the language to back up your points, e.g.
>
> *The word 'charnel-house' is unusual and draws attention to the extent to which creatures can be indifferent to even horrors when they are in love.*

Dawn scene – it's depressing, which sets the tone for the poem.

The vulture nestles up to mate – the 'affection' is surprising for birds described as so ugly.

They sit on a branch after eating – the description of their eyes makes them unfeeling.

> In the greyness
> and drizzle of one despondent
> dawn unstirred by harbingers
> of sunbreak a vulture
> perching high on broken
> bone of a dead tree
> nestled close to his
> mate his smooth
> bashed-in head, a pebble
> on a stem rooted in
> a dump of gross
> feathers, inclined affectionately
> to hers. Yesterday they picked
> the eyes of a swollen
> corpse in a water-logged
> trench and ate the
> things in its bowel. Full
> gorged they chose their roost
> keeping the hallowed remnant
> in easy range of cold
> telescopic eyes...
>   Strange
> indeed how love in other
> ways so particular
> will pick a corner
> in that charnel-house
> tidy it and coil up there,
> perhaps
> even fall asleep – her face
> turned to the wall!

A vulture on a tree – 'broken bone' and 'dead tree' are images of death.

They ate a corpse – gruesome details add to our disgust.

Poet comments on how creatures behave when in love – love makes us ignore appalling things.

The message of the poem

- Poems always have a **message** underlying the surface meaning. A message is a general observation about life, or rights and wrongs, that the reader can draw from the specific examples described in the poem. For example, in the first part of *Vultures* we are led to consider how strange it is both to feed on death and to love.

This is how one student analyses the first part of Achebe's poem:

Grade A*

> The vultures of the title are described in some detail by the poet. They are a couple, part of nature ('a pebble on a stem') but unpleasant to look at, the male with a 'bashed-in head'. The 'cold telescopic eyes' are frightening and the atmosphere around them is similarly depressing. There is drizzle, no appreciation of sunbreak, and the situation is compared to a 'charnel house'.
>
> This is because death is part of the description, for although the birds are lovers (he has his head 'inclined affectionately to hers'), they have gorged on a corpse, eating its eyes and what was in the bowel – grim details about a quite frightening pair.
>
> The final section of the extract comments on how those in love can overlook unpleasantness in their proximity, metaphorically turning their face to the wall. They can live and cope in what is, in truth, a vile situation.

Good Points

- The student goes beyond the factual meaning of the poem to discuss the underlying meaning.
- The extract is considered as a whole.
- References to the language of the poem are used to show the meaning.
- All the ideas are supported with precise textual detail.
- There are three clear sections: the birds, their behaviour and the general point (the message) to conclude.

- Our understanding of the message of *Vultures* deepens as we continue reading the poem. The Commandant of Belsen is another example of an extremely unpleasant creature, surrounded by death:

> *Thus the Commandant at Belsen*
> *Camp going home for*
> *the day with fumes of*
> *human roast clinging*
> *rebelliously to his hairy*
> *nostrils …*

- However, even the worst offenders can show some 'tenderness'. In this case, the man in charge of the death camp is also a loving 'Daddy' who lavishes treats on his child:

> *… will stop*
> *at the wayside sweet-shop*
> *and pick up a chocolate*
> *for his tender offspring*
> *waiting at home for Daddy's*
> *return …*

- In the final lines of the poem, the poet asks whether we should be grateful that tiny acts of love can exist alongside horror, or whether we should despair:

> *for in the very germ*
> *of that kindred love is*
> *lodged the perpetuity*
> *of evil.*

Content, message and attitude

The poet's attitude to the subject

- Sometimes you are asked to comment on the **poets' own feelings** about the situation in the poems.

- You can determine their attitude by studying the **language** they use, and how the situation is described.

  Sometimes the poet's **attitude is clear**. For example, Niyi Osundare shows his attitude right from the start in *Not My Business*. We are shown what is happening in the society and how people react to it. They ignore the suffering of others and think only of themselves.

Top Tip!

Don't assume that, if the poet writes in the first person (using 'I'), she or he is speaking directly to the reader. Here, Niyi Osundare is adopting another personality (or persona) to make his point.

'Stuffed' suggests rough treatment, 'belly' suggests they fed him to an animal or monster – another frightening image.

> They picked Akanni up one morning
> Beat him soft like clay
> And stuffed him down the belly
> Of a waiting jeep.
>   What business of mine is it
>   So long they don't take the yam
>   From my savouring mouth?

The simile shows that Akanni was beaten to a pulp. He was powerless.

The speaker's actual words are quoted – it is clear that he doesn't want to be involved. 'Savouring' suggests that he is only concerned about his own satisfaction.

However, the fact that the speaker has tried not to get involved does not save him. His turn comes too:

He is frozen with fear – just as others have been fearful.

> And then one evening
> As I sat down to eat my yam
> A knock on the door froze my hungry hand.
> The jeep was waiting on my bewildered lawn
> Waiting, waiting in its usual silence.

He was more interested in his yams than in his neighbours' problems.

He is bewildered – how could this happen to him?

He was silent when others were taken, so it is fitting there is silence when they come for him: silence represents the lack of opposition.

- Sometimes the poet's attitude **may be unclear**, because he or she has mixed feelings. In *Two Scavengers in a Truck, Two Beautiful People in a Mercedes*, the poet is doing opposite things:

  – contrasting pairs of people from opposite ends of society ('scavengers' … 'beautiful')

  – saying that in American democracy it may be possible to bridge this gap (all four are held together by the red light, and there are similarities between them).

  These mixed feelings are summed up in the phrase 'small gulf' between them: (a gulf is usually wide, not small).

Writing about attitude and message

- It is vital to **explain exactly what you mean** and to **support your comments** with close reference to the poem. In this example, a student was asked:
  - to explain the poet's attitude to what happens in *Not My Business*
  - what the reader can learn from the poem.

Grade A*

From the opening stanza, the poem is based on a contrast. We have four lines of persecution, then three lines in which the speaker dissociates himself from what is happening around him.

The suffering is personalised by the use of names (Akanni, Danladi and Chinwe), and intensified by the use of detail. Akanni, for instance, is beaten 'soft like clay', whilst, when they come for Danladi, they 'booted the whole house awake'. Violence is foremost in both incidents. At the same time, there is a frightening sense of mystery: Danladi goes for 'a lengthy absence' and Chinwe's job is taken for no clear reason.

Such happenings grab our attention and sympathy; yet the speaker seems callous, and continues to eat yams, look after himself and ignore the injustice around him. His 'savouring mouth' should be speaking out, not eating comfortably and well. The way he is presented makes him seem almost as bad as the jeep which 'eats' those who are being persecuted.

However, the poet shows us that hoping to avoid trouble does not lead to escape from oppression. The 'knock on the door' at the end is terrifying and even stops the speaker eating. The frozen moment is accompanied by silence, which is perhaps fitting in this case, because this is where our silence leads: to the jeep for us all. The final stanza is not broken into two parts, because there is no longer any difference between the speaker and the victims - his time has come.

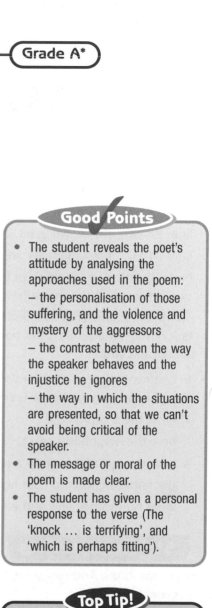

Good Points ✓

- The student reveals the poet's attitude by analysing the approaches used in the poem:
  – the personalisation of those suffering, and the violence and mystery of the aggressors
  – the contrast between the way the speaker behaves and the injustice he ignores
  – the way in which the situations are presented, so that we can't avoid being critical of the speaker.
- The message or moral of the poem is made clear.
- The student has given a personal response to the verse (The 'knock … is terrifying', and 'which is perhaps fitting').

Top Tip!

One key to a top grade is to focus on the poet's message by analysing three elements:
- **what** is said
- **how** it is presented
- **why** it is presented in that way.

Question

Read *Blessing* by Imtiaz Dharker.
- What happens in this poem?
- What is the poet's attitude to it?
- What message can we take from the poem and in what way is it different from the message in *Not My Business*?

Structure

- You might need to write about the **structure** of two poems. This would mean analysing:

  – how each poem is **organised**: how it opens, develops and concludes, or how the ideas are put together. You might need to show how the structure is appropriate for the poet's message, and explain how the structure affects the reader's understanding.

  – how each poem is **set out on the page**: its layout (stanzas, line length and so on).

How the poem is organised

- Lawrence Ferlinghetti's *Two Scavengers in a Truck, Two Beautiful People in a Mercedes* could be broken into five sections:

  lines 1–9   a description of the truck and the Mercedes caught together at the stoplight

  lines 10–15   the 'elegant' couple in the Mercedes are described

  lines 16–25   the 'grungy' couple in the garbage truck are described

  lines 26–30   the 'scavengers' looking down at the couple

  lines 31–37   message: they are close yet far apart.

  Note the clear organisation of the ideas. We are led from step to step, ending with the poet's thoughts (the message).

  The poem opens with mention of the stoplight, and ends with a similar reference. This lack of movement binds the poem together and emphasises that this is a snapshot of American culture.

- In contrast, *Night of the Scorpion* by Nissim Ezekiel is a **narrative**. The poem describes what happens to Ezekiel's mother over 20 hours. It tells:

  – what the scorpion did

  – how the neighbours react

  – how the incident is given a religious significance (*May the poison purify your flesh*)

  – the father's efforts to cure her

  – what his mother says at the end.

Structural devices

The poems in the Anthology use a variety of **structural devices**:

- **refrain** – a repeated chorus

  The refrain in *Limbo* suggests a kind of performance, as in the limbo dance:

  > *limbo*
  > *limbo like me*

- **stanza** – a fixed number of lines arranged in a pattern

  In *Not My Business*, the stanzas break into two parts: what is happening to others, then how the speaker is reacting.

  - **repetition** – of words or phrases

  Half-Caste relies heavily on repetition to challenge the listener's/reader's preconceptions:

  > *Explain yuself*
  > *wha yu mean.*

- **pattern** – a repeated movement that gives shape to the poem

  Vultures has a stanza about the birds, followed by a stanza generalising about what this shows of life. This is mirrored by a stanza about the Commandant, followed by another which again generalises, linking clearly the birds and the man.

Top Tip!

When you identify any structural devices, make sure that you consider their effect upon the reader. They will have been chosen to support or emphasise the poet's message.

How the poem is presented

- In some cases, the visual impression created by a poem is striking. For example, *from Unrelated Incidents* by Tom Leonard is set out as a television autocue, as if the poet is reading from it – an ironic activity for someone who would not be allowed to read the news on television.

- The **different line lengths and indentations** which are a feature of Lawrence Ferlinghetti's *Two Scavengers in a Truck, Two Beautiful People in a Mercedes* suggest the movement in the travellers' lives and a shifting modern existence:

> At the stoplight waiting for the light
> > nine a.m. downtown San Francisco
> a bright yellow garbage truck
> > with two garbagemen in red plastic blazers
> standing on the back stoop
> > one on each side hanging on
> and looking down into
> > an elegant open Mercedes
> with an elegant couple in it

Note the **enjambements** (lack of punctuation at end of lines), so the sentence runs on, like life itself. Also, there is the uneasiness of the shifting nature of the lines on the page:

> > across that small gulf
> in the high seas
> > of this democracy.

If you had to comment on the layout of this poem, you could write:

> The poem gives the impression of someone speaking, with their pauses indicated by the breaks in lines and continuity. In places, the enjambements and indentations give emphasis to what follows:
>
> > 'and looking down into
> > > an elegant open Mercedes
> > with an elegant couple in it'.
>
> The reader's eye drops to the next line, as does the gaze of the garbagemen, noticing first the car, then, standing out from it, the 'elegant couple'.

Note how the presentational features are explained, rather than just identified, e.g. 'The reader's eye drops to the next line …'.

- *Night of the Scorpion* is presented in **solid blocks of text**, which emphasises the narrative drive of the poem. The mother's words are contained in their own short stanza at the end, to emphasise their significance:

> My mother only said
> Thank God the scorpion picked on me
> and spared my children.

- The **shape of the lines** in *Limbo*, with no punctuation until the very end, mimics a limbo dance which keeps flowing until the end.

Question

Read *What Were They Like?* by Denise Levertov.
- How is the poem structured?
- Why has it been structured in this way?
- How successful is this structure?
- Compare the structure with that of another poem you have studied.

Language

- No matter which question you decide to answer, you will need to write about language. You need to comment on:
  - **poetic techniques**, e.g. similes, rhyme and rhythm
  - **language use**: how the poet uses words, sentences and punctuation.
- You will also need to **explain what effect** the language has on the reader.

Poetic techniques

- Most poems employ a range of poetic techniques, such as **similes**:

  The peasants came like swarms of flies
  (Night of the Scorpion)

  The comparison of the peasants to flies makes them seem irritating, like pests.

  trees / Falling heavy as whales
  (Hurricane Hits England)

  Comparing the trees to whales makes the winds appear incredibly strong. The image of whales also makes the reader think of the Caribbean background.

- This extract from *Limbo* by Edward Kamau Brathwaite contains a range of other techniques:

rhythm – suggesting the beat of the limbo dancers, and the chanting of the slaves

assonance – repeated vowel sound ('stick', 'hit', 'ship') suggests the sounds of the ship

alliteration – the repeated 'd's suggest footsteps in the dance and the blows of punishment

metaphor – where something is compared directly with something else: the limbo stick here is also the slave-drivers' whip

And limbo stick is the silence in front of me
limbo

limbo
limbo like me
limbo
limbo like me

long dark night is the silence in front of me
limbo
limbo like me

stick hit sound
and the ship like it ready

stick hit sound
and the dark still steady

limbo
limbo like me

long dark deck and the water surrounding me
long dark deck and the silence is over me

limbo
limbo like me

stick is the whip
and the dark deck is slavery

stick is the whip
and the dark deck is slavery

limbo
limbo like me

drum stick knock
and the darkness is over me...

enjambement – lines not ended with punctuation, because the dance is on-going and the slaves' suffering has no end

repetition – suggesting the chorus of a song to go with the limbo dance; also to create the mesmeric effect of the dance

rhyme – repetition of the word endings emphasises the song-like nature of the poem, and perhaps the repetitive nature of life on the ship

symbol – where something represents something else: here, the stick symbolises the repression of the slaves

onomatopoeia – where the sound of the words represents the sound of the action being described

- It is never enough just to **identify** poetic techniques. The examiner is looking for an **explanation** of why they have been used and the **effect** they are creating.

If you were analysing the poetic techniques used in *Limbo*, you might write:

Top Tip!

Reading poems aloud to yourself will help you hear the rhythm, rhyme and other sound effects.

Grade A*

In 'Limbo', Brathwaite sets out to show the situation and suffering of the slaves, as they are transported to America. Underpinning the whole poem is the rhyme and the rhythm of the dance; the slaves, perhaps, dance and chant to remember their homeland; or maybe they are just dancing to the white man's tune. There is the repeated refrain:

'limbo
limbo like me'

as if the dance – and, perhaps, their suffering – simply goes on and on. This is further suggested by the repetition in the poem, and by the general lack of punctuation: we feel the horror is unremitting, until the very end of the poem, with its one full stop.

The poem also relies on metaphor and symbol. The 'stick' represents the way in which the slaves are repressed and, no doubt, beaten. The stick is their master. The 'dark deck' stands for their metaphorical slavery – it suggests a deck packed with the slaves, or even a deck stained with blood. The darkness also implies that light and joy have gone from their lives. The alliteration of 'd's makes it sound dismal and depressing.

As well as the rhythm and the refrain, the reader is also presented with other sounds from the ship. There is the onomatopoeia as the stick provides the beat:

'drum stick knock'.

These three sounds do not stand alone, though. We also hear the swish of a beating:

'stick is the whip'.

The hardness of 'stick' – a word repeated throughout the poem, for emphasis – is transferred, using assonance, to the whisking of 'whip' ...

Good Points

- The use of poetic techniques is linked to the poet's overall purpose.
- There is explanation of how the techniques have been used, rather than just simple identification.
- An interpretation of the poem is offered: the student gives an overview, then shows how she interprets the poem's features.

Other language use

You need to judge the effect of particular vocabulary, punctuation and sentences in poems. These language features will have been chosen by the poet to create meaning, develop ideas or add significance.

Top Tip!

To gain the highest mark:
1 Identify the language features.
2 Explain their relevance within the context.
3 Explore the different layers of meaning – what is stated and what is implied.

• Individual words are used for a reason. For example, they might have **associations**:

> *fumes of human roast*
> (*Vultures*)

'Roast' suggests a meal, which adds to the disgusting image.

• Or the words might create a **particular effect**:

> *My mother cherished her jewellery –*
> *Indian gold, dangling, filigree.*
> (*Presents from my Aunts in Pakistan*)

The detailed description of the jewellery, especially the unusual word 'filigree', makes it seem foreign and fascinating.

• The **length of the sentences** should be noted:

In *Not My Business*, each stanza is made up of two sentences – one a description and the other a comment by the speaker.

• Look closely at the **punctuation** as well:

Island Man has no punctuation other than capital letters, suggesting the dreamlike state the man is in.

• The **position** of the words on their lines can be important:

> *This is the time and place*
> *to be alive*
> (*This Room*)

Putting 'to be alive' on its own line suggests this is a key idea in the poem.

• Some of the language features in *Love After Love* are analysed here.

'own' is repeated to emphasise 'yourself'. (Central idea of poem is coming to terms with yourself.)

Simple language (with repetition of 'and') emphasises the peace and simplicity of the action.

List of what must be done to love again: sentences begin with imperatives (commands).

'elation' emphasises the joy from the start. Commas make you pause, to highlight the feeling.

'Eat': the simple pleasure is indicated by one-word sentence.

Wine and bread have religious (Christian) significance.

Repetition of 'heart' – appropriate in this love poem.

Love After Love

The time will come
When, with elation,
You will greet yourself arriving
At your own door, in your own mirror,
And each will smile at the other's welcome,

And say sit here. Eat.
You will love again the stranger who was your self.
Give wine. Give bread. Give back your heart
To itself, to the stranger who has loved you

All your life, whom you ignored
For another, who knows you by heart.
Take down the love-letters from the bookshelf

The photographs, the desperate notes,
Peel your own images from the mirror.
Sit. Feast on your life.

Sentences get shorter as the old complicated life (complex sentences) changes into simple acceptance.

Idea of celebrating, enjoying life again – refers back to wine and bread earlier.

Analysing the language use

If you had to analyse the use of language in *Love After Love*, you could write this:

> Walcott is writing a poem intended to give the reader confidence that, as life goes on, each of us will be happy with our own self and what we really are. From the beginning, he focuses on happiness ('elation', 'smiling'), stresses that we are in our 'own' environment and can enjoy the experience.
>
> It is as if we are returning to simple pleasures. 'Eat' is a one-word sentence, but stresses the fact that we can feed ourselves - we do not need others. In fact, there is a kind of religious communion, with the mention of: 'Give wine. Give bread'. This notion is repeated later ('Feast on your life'). It is as if we have enough memories and knowledge to sustain us as long as we live.
>
> The sentences the poet uses help to support his message. In the last two stanzas, there are relatively complex sentences, as the old life is dismantled, and one line lacks the necessary punctuation at the end, as if to suggest it should be carried out quickly and we should move rapidly to the next action:
>
> 'Take down the love-letters from the bookshelf'.
>
> The list of which this is a part, along with:
>
> 'The photographs, the desperate notes ...'
>
> forms a clutter of activities which contrast with the simplicity of the ending:
>
> 'Sit. Feast on your life.'
>
> This is all showing that everything will be easier and simpler when we have come to terms with what we really are.

Grade A*

✔ Good Points

- Language features are analysed to show how they help the poet achieve his purpose.
- There are precise references to the poem.
- Comments on vocabulary, sentence forms and punctuation have all been integrated into the answer.

Comparing language use

- When you compare two poems in the exam, part of your answer will compare the way the poets use language.

Look at how language is used in these two extracts:

vocabulary of hatching

enjambements

vocabulary of upward movement

contrast: dark, shift to open sky

This room is breaking out
of itself, cracking through
its own walls
in search of space, light, — **list**
empty air.
The bed is lifting out of
its nightmares.
From dark corners, chairs
are rising up to crash through clouds.

(This Room)

onomatopoeia and alliteration

first person

alliteration

I tried each satin-silken top –
    was alien in the sitting-room.
I could never be as lovely
        as those clothes –
    I longed
for denim and corduroy.
    My costume clung to me
        and I was aflame,
I couldn't rise up out of its fire,
    half-English,
        unlike Aunt Jamila.

(Presents from my Aunts in Pakistan)

emotive use of 'alien'

simile

everyday vocabulary

metaphors

image of the phoenix

Task

Compare the use of language in *This Room* and *Presents from my Aunts in Pakistan*. Include the points identified above, and think about the overall mood that the poet wants to convey.

Comparing two poems

- The questions on Paper 2 will expect you to **compare two poems**. The question itself will highlight what aspects of the poems need to be compared.

- There are **two main ways** of comparing poems. Each needs a brief **introduction** and **conclusion**.

- You need to support your views with **clear references** to the poems.

Making a comparison

- The **focus of the comparison** will be given in the question. Examples are:

  - comparing the different cultures, situations or settings

  - comparing the message of the poems or the attitude of the poets

  - comparing the language and structure of the poems.

- There are two main methods of comparing poems:

Top Tip!

Use whichever method of comparison you prefer, but do not mix the two. Be very clear about the structure of your answer.

Method 1	Method 2
Introduction: Introduce both poems and relate them to the subject of the question.	**Introduction:** Introduce both poems and relate them to the subject of the question.
Detailed comparison: • Write in detail about one poem, bringing out the details of theme, language and style that relate to the question. • Then write in detail about the other poem, referring back to the first where appropriate to make your comparisons.	**Detailed comparison:** • Write in detail about each aspect of the question in turn, referring to both poems together and bringing out the comparisons as you go.
Conclusion: Summarise the key points, and perhaps consider the success of the poems.	**Conclusion:** Summarise the key points, and perhaps consider the success of the poems.

- Method 1 is more straightforward and allows you to focus on one poem at a time. However, it is less effective at bringing out points of comparison.

- Method 2 (examining the two poems together) is a very thorough way of analysing and comparing poems as it fully integrates the ideas and features. However, it is a more difficult skill, especially if you have not revised the two poems as a pair. It is likely to mean directly comparing elements of language – setting the structures side by side, and so on.

Referring to the poems

- Make sure that you refer to **both poems** in your answer.

- Provide the **right details**. The wording of the question will show you precisely what you have to compare.

- You should **compare the texts**. It is not enough to write an analysis of one, then an analysis of the other.

- In making references to the texts, you must clearly **link one text to the other**. Words such as 'however' or 'similarly' are useful when you do this.

Page 24

Using quotations and examples

Always support your ideas by referring to the text of the poems. There are different ways of doing this:

- You can refer to the poem **without quoting** it directly:

> Agard goes on to consider whether music is half-caste as well. He refers to the composer Tchaikovsky mixing black and white Keys on the piano – which of course he had to do to produce a symphony.

- You can include **brief quotations** from the poem in your sentences. Quote the exact words and enclose them in inverted commas:

> Tom Leonard's words are spelt as they would be spoken by someone with a strong Scottish accent, for example 'wanna you scruff' and 'yi canny talk right'.

- If you are referring to a **longer passage**, and you need to quote it to make your point, set the passage out on a new line, after a colon:

> The language used to describe water cleverly portrays the sound it makes:
> 'Imagine the drip of it,
> the small splash, echo
> in a tin mug'

Top Tip!

Don't waste time by copying out long quotations from the poem. When you are commenting on longer passages, it's better to write about them than to copy out chunks of text.

Sample question

> Compare *Nothing's Changed* with another poem from a different culture or tradition. Show how the people in the poems react to their surroundings.

This part of the question outlines the precise point of comparison. You need to focus your comparison on this point, not compare the two poems in general terms.

One poem is always named; make sure that you can relate the second poem to it with reference to the focus of the question. In the answers on pages 44–45, the student has chosen to compare *Nothing's Changed* with *Island Man*.

***Nothing's Changed* by Tatamkhulu Afrika**

Small round hard stones click
under my heels,
seeding grasses thrust
bearded seeds
into trouser cuffs, cans,
trodden on, crunch
in tall, purple-flowering,
amiable weeds.

District Six.
No board says it is:
but my feet know,
and my hands,
and the skin about my bones,
and the soft labouring of my lungs,
and the hot, white, inwards turning
anger of my eyes.

***Island Man* by Grace Nichols**

(for a Caribbean island man in London
who still wakes up to the sound of the sea)

Morning
and island man wakes up
to the sound of blue surf
in his head
the steady breaking and wombing

wild seabirds
and fishermen pushing out to sea
the sun surfacing defiantly
from the east
of his small emerald island
he always comes back   groggily groggily

READING POETRY

Sample answer

- In answer to the question on page 43, you could write an **opening paragraph** like this:

First poem summarised briefly.

Further detail relates poem to focus of question: how the man reacts to the situation.

> In 'Nothing's Changed', we are presented with a picture of South Africa after the end of apartheid. The poet is suggesting that life has not improved, and has produced a protest poem which shows the inequalities and unfairness in that country. The situation in 'Island Man' is different, because Grace Nichols reveals how a Caribbean island man still thinks of his home, but has to get up and cope with existence in the country to which he has moved. He may not be happy, but has chosen this way of living.

Grade A*

Further detail relates the situation in the poem (the focus of the question) to the poet's purpose.

Second poem summarised briefly, and a clear comparison made.

Top Tip!

Make sure your opening paragraph:
- refers to both poems
- refers to the focus of the question
- is brief and clear.

Good Points ✓

- The student **focuses on the question**.
- The poems are **summarised briefly**.
- From the start, the student **compares the poems**.

- You could use **Method 1** to write a **detailed comparison** like this:

Page 42

(Note: In this answer, the student has already written about *Nothing's Changed*. These paragraphs, therefore, focus on the second poem, *Island Man*. Only the beginning of the detailed comparison is shown.)

Clear signal that the student is now turning to the second poem.

Backs up points by close reference to the text, and by giving comments on the passages quoted.

New paragraph for new point, but focus is still on the second poem.

> When we examine 'Island Man', we see that his situation is similar in that he, too, can imagine a better life. In his case, though, it is a beautiful life he has known already. Details such as 'the sound of blue surf' and 'fishermen pushing out to sea' give a vivid picture of the sound and sights of his homeland, brought out by the repeated 's' sounds, which suggest the sound of the sea.
>
> Grace Nichols shows us Island Man apparently accepting his situation ('he always comes back...'), even though perhaps reluctantly, as suggested by the heavy last line 'Another London day'. This contrasts with the first poem, which can see no hope for black people in South Africa and where the speaker feels like turning to violence.

Grade A*

Focus is on the 'better life' in the second poem, though a point of comparison is made with the first poem.

Cross-reference to the first poem to show comparison.

- You could use **Method 2** to write a **detailed comparison** like this:
  (Note: This is an extract from the middle section of such a response.)

Page 42

Island Man comes from a culture which seems close to nature, calm and relaxed:

'wakes up
  to the sound of blue surf'.

This romantic image of the sea, supported by the soft onomatopoeia of 'breaking and wombing', makes the memory a treasure. It is very different from the harsh realities of life in South Africa. The verbs used by the poet at the start of that poem sound sharp, and make the environment appear desolate, whilst the mood is one of despondency or aggression: 'click', 'thrust', 'trodden on', 'crunch'.

In the second stanza, Afrika uses a list and repetition of 'and' to build to what seems a climax of rage at the unfairness in the country:

'and the hot, white, inwards turning
  anger of my eyes.'

The whiteness suggests his emotions have become molten; whilst Nichols captures a much more relaxed scene by using 'blue surf' and 'small emerald island'. Here, we have warmth, not heat, and the use of 'emerald' shows the island is a jewel to be treasured ...

Grade A*

Good Points ✓

- The two poems are set side by side and compared. Each paragraph focuses on a different aspect, and both poems are discussed.
- The points made are relevant to the focus of the question.
- The response is detailed, with precise quotations and explanations.

Top Tip!

The weaving together and comparison of different elements of two poems is a skill rewarded by examiners with a high mark.

- You could write a **concluding paragraph** like this:

The way people react to their surroundings, therefore, is treated very differently in each poem. Tatamkhulu Afrika seems to consider violence as the only answer: the final stanza leaves the reader with the image of a bomb smashing the glass. The last line effectively returns us to the start, because, as we learnt in the title, 'Nothing's changed'. 'Island Man', however, seems resigned to his life, accepts the traffic noise because he must and leaves behind his dreams for 'Another London day'. The contrast between his life as it was and his life as it is, though, has been made very clear, and there does not appear to be the energy in him there once was.

'therefore' signals a summing up. Note the student still has the focus of the question in mind.

Overview of the first poem's message, and mention of technique. There is some evaluation of the poem's success ('effectively').

Overview of the second poem's perspective. There is some evaluation of the poem's success ('very clear').

Task

Show how *Half-Caste* and one other poem from a different culture present the feelings of people who do not feel part of the society around them.
Write about:

- the problems the people have
- their feelings
- how successfully their feelings are shown.

Raising your grade

If you want to raise your grade to A or A*, you need to show these skills.

Give a convincing and imaginative personal interpretation of the poems

- An '**interpretation**' is a fully argued response that analyses the poems' meanings. '**Convincing**' means that you should write as persuasively as you can, and back up your points with evidence from the text. '**Personal**' means that you are not afraid to put forward your own view, even if it is an unusual one.

- Your interpretation should **explore the poet's ideas and attitudes** – not just state them, but discuss them in detail.

- You should **present your ideas coherently** – that means organising your response so that the introduction sets out your point of view, the main body of the answer goes into a detailed analysis, and the conclusion sums up your argument.

Analyse a variety of techniques

- Don't just show that you understand the poet's techniques: **analyse** them. This means explaining in detail how they work, offering alternative interpretations where appropriate.

> The Gujerati script shows the problems of dealing with a foreign tongue. ✗

> The Gujerati script, even when translated, is alien to us. It makes us realise how difficult it must be for the speaker to cope with two languages. ✔

- Refer in detail to a **variety of techniques**. This means addressing the language, structure and presentation of the poems.

- Provide a **sophisticated evaluation** of the poets' use of language. This means showing how effective the poets' language is.

> The couple in the car seem totally unreal to the scavengers - the simile 'as if they were watching some odorless TV ad' emphasises well how they seem to come from another world and is an effective and critical comment on the couple, making them seem unfeeling and removed from everyday reality. ✔

Make good use of the poems

- Compare the poems **throughout** your answer.

> Whereas in 'Two Scavengers' everything freezes into a picture, highlighting the contrast, in the other poem it is different ...

- Make sure that your references are **well chosen** and **developed effectively**.

- **Integrate** the references **with your argument**. This means choosing references that back up your overall interpretation, and making it clear how they do this.

Overall argument/ interpretation.

> The rhythm of 'Presents from my Aunts' is reflective and lacks the pace and energy of 'This Room'. Whereas Dharker is 'clapping', Alvi is 'staring'; as Dharker enjoys the 'excitement', Alvi stares through fretwork and is, undoubtedly, fretting.

Short but relevant references from both poems to support the interpretation.

Read the practice question and an extract from the student's answer below. The annotations show why the student was working at Grade A standard.

> Compare how language has been used in the endings of *This Room* and *Presents from my Aunts in Pakistan*.

This Room

Pots and pans bang together
In celebration, clang
Past the crowd of garlic, onions, spices,
Fly by the ceiling fan.
No one is looking for the door.

In all this excitement
I'm wondering where
I've left my feet, and why

My hands are outside, clapping.

Presents from my Aunts in Pakistan
Sometimes I saw Lahore –
          my aunts in shaded rooms,
screened from male visitors,
    sorting presents,
        wrapping them in tissue.

Or there were beggars, sweeper-girls
    and I was there –
        of no fixed nationality,
staring through fretwork
        at the Shalimar Gardens.

Grade A

The response is well organised – she deals with each poem in turn, and signals to the reader where the discussion is going.

A sophisticated evaluation of language, showing how effective it is.

Throughout, the student argues persuasively for her interpretation of the poems – that one is calmer and reflective, the other has pace and energy.

Even while discussing the second poem, she refers back to the first, and integrates the reference with her overall argument.

The extract from 'This Room' begins with bustling noise. There is an alliteration of 'p's and the onomatopoeia of 'pans bang', followed by an echoing rhyme: 'clang'. There is metaphor, too, because the items do not really 'fly by the ceiling fan'. However, the idea of wonderful change is reflected by these perceptions, and it is so dramatic there are even spectators, a metaphorical 'crowd of garlic, onions, spices.' This list and the sense of loud movements stretch through the first sentence, but it is all shown to be anything but frightening because of the brief but straightforward reflection to end the stanza:
    'No one is looking for the door.'
  Dharker feels as if everything is suddenly out of her control, and this is reflected in the enjambements that follow, which make her thoughts stretch out – yet, as we read the lines, the thoughts seem broken, as if she cannot concentrate. He is happy, though, as signified by the final line, ended with 'clapping'. The commas before the word makes the reader pause, giving the word extra emphasis.
  'Presents from my Aunts in Pakistan' is much calmer. It begins with an internal rhyme ('saw Lahore'), which seems slow. It also seems to stretch out, perhaps like the girl's life. The description of her aunts' existence has none of the energy of 'This Room.' The poet uses the language of seclusion ('shaded' and 'screened') to describe how they are hidden quietly away. Instead of encountering the sharpness of 'garlic, onions, spices', which we can taste and smell and which affect the senses, in Alvi's poem the women are covering things and packing them away:
    'wrapping them in tissue.'
  This world seems safer, but lacks the 'excitement' that Dharker highlights.

Explaining in detail how the poet's techniques work.

Sensitive exploration of the poet's ideas and attitudes.

A personal response is given.

Paper 1 Section B and Paper 2 Section B: Writing

Key points

- Section B of both English papers tests your writing skills.

- In each paper you have to choose one question from the four offered.

- Paper 1 requires you to write to argue, persuade, advise. Paper 2 requires you to inform, explain, describe.

Pages 62–85

- Section B of Paper 1 counts for 15% of your total mark. Section B of Paper 2 counts for a further 15% of your total mark.

- You should spend about 45 minutes on each answer. That means covering about two sides of paper. The first part of each paper tests you on your reading skills.

The exam paper

- Both papers will test the general **quality of your writing**: the way you generate and use ideas, your structure and paragraphing, the variety of your sentences and vocabulary, and the accuracy of your punctuation and spelling.

- The **purpose** and **audience** will depend on the type of writing you are asked to do.

This is an example of Paper 1 Section B. Paper 2 Section B is organised in exactly the same way.

Each paper consists of two sections. Section A (not given here) is the Reading questions.

Paper 1 Section B: Higher Tier

WRITING TO ARGUE, PERSUADE OR ADVISE

Answer **one** question.

You are advised to spend about 45 minutes on this section.

EITHER

3 Write an article for your local newspaper, **arguing** that there is too much pressure on teenagers and that they should be allowed to enjoy 'the best years of their lives'. *(27 marks)*

OR

4 Writing as a celebrity chef, produce a newspaper column to **persuade** parents to encourage their children to eat healthily. *(27 marks)*

OR

5 Write an article for your local newspaper, **advising** residents how to protect their homes against burglars. *(27 marks)*

OR

6 Write a letter to **advise** a relative about how to spend money they have inherited recently and **persuade** them to spend some of it on other members of the family. *(27 marks)*

In Paper 1 Section B (here) you have to write to argue, persuade, advise. In Paper 2 Section B (not given here) you have to write to inform, explain, describe.

Two-thirds of this mark are awarded for your communication and organisation; one third for your sentences, punctuation and spelling.

What you will be assessed on

The questions that you are asked in Section B of each paper will be based on assessment objectives. Examiners will be assessing your ability to achieve the following:

Assessment objective	What this means in detail
Ideas Communicate clearly and imaginatively, using and adapting forms for different readers and purposes.	This means you must know how to write for a specific **purpose** (e.g. to advise), and in a specific **form** (e.g. a letter), as well as how to target a specific **audience** (e.g. younger people). You must be able to produce ideas **relevant** to the task and **varied** and **imaginative** enough to keep the reader's interest.
Structure and paragraphing Organise ideas into paragraphs and whole texts, using a variety of structural features.	It is not enough to have a number of ideas. The way you **structure** them is important – including a good **opening**, a clear sequence of paragraphs for the **main section** and a powerful **conclusion**. Your ability to write paragraphs of appropriate and effective **lengths** will also be assessed and marks awarded accordingly.
Sentences Organise ideas into sentences, and use a range of sentence structures effectively.	The **quality** of your sentences is vital. They need to be **varied and effective**, which means using sentences of different **length**, **type** (e.g. questions, commands, statements) and **complexity**, and they must be **appropriate** for the purpose.
Vocabulary Organise ideas using a variety of linguistic features.	The **quality** of your vocabulary is often a clear indicator of your overall English ability. Your vocabulary must be **suited to the form of writing**, and the **purpose and audience**. It must be **varied** to demonstrate your range and to avoid repetition and cliché. You should use **linguistic techniques** where appropriate, such as imagery, repetition, contrasts and lists.
Punctuation Organise a range of sentences with accurate punctuation.	It is not enough to rely on full stops and capital letters. Producing 'a range of sentences' involves using a **range of punctuation** correctly. This will include commas, apostrophes, exclamation marks and question marks, as well as quotation marks, colons and semi-colons.
Spelling Use accurate spelling.	Incorrect spelling will affect how your writing is perceived and understood by the examiner. You will be rewarded for spelling accurately a **range of words** – if you can spell regular and irregular words from a wide vocabulary, your marks will be higher.

Ideas and planning

Key points

- The exam paper will advise you to spend at least **five minutes planning** your response for Section B.

- The first stage in that process is to **generate ideas** that you can use in your writing.

- When generating ideas, you should always have the **purpose and audience** of the task in mind.

- You should then **structure** your ideas and **develop** them.

Generating ideas

- Your first priority is to identify the **essential elements** in the question title. It is useful to highlight the important words, to help you focus on them and identify the purpose and audience.

- The **purpose** of your writing will be to argue, persuade, advise, inform, explain or describe. You will also be expected to produce the **form** of writing that has been requested. This might be quite specific, especially for Paper 1. For example, you might be asked to write a letter, article or speech. For Paper 2, it is more likely that you will be asked to produce a standard 'essay'. In each case, the style you use must fit the task.

- The **audience**, the person or people for whom you are writing, may be of a certain age or from a certain background, e.g. senior citizens or school governors. For Paper 2 in particular, you may be writing for the examiner. Again, it is essential that you use language and content that are suitable.

Top Tip!

In Paper 2, questions often have no stated audience. In this case, assume that you are writing for the examiner. Your approach should still be relatively formal.

This is how you could make notes on a question from Paper 1:

purpose: formal writing

Write a section for a school booklet to be sent to teachers applying for a job at your school. Offer them advice on how to cope with any problems they might encounter.

audience: will need clear but relatively basic advice, since they will be just starting the job

purpose: to identify the problems and tell the new teachers exactly how they might cope with them

Structuring ideas

- Now you should assemble your ideas, first of all as **brief notes**.

- You could produce your ideas as a **spider diagram**, like this:

SCHOOL BOOKLET: FIRST IDEAS

Difficult students   State of the school

Marking ——— Problems ——— People not
                                in uniform
Finding your
way round
the building   Large student numbers

- Alternatively, you could **list your ideas** in the order you might deal with them in your actual response:

Developing your ideas

- Now develop the basic ideas by adding **further detail** to your plan.

- Although planning time is brief, you will benefit later from doing this. It will be easier to write the response itself, because you will know **exactly what details to mention** in each section.

You could begin to develop the ideas for the school booklet like this:

> School booklet
>
> Difficult students:
> Problem: aggressive attitude to teachers - regular fights during breaks - exclusions increasing
> Advice: try listening and being understanding; don't be too strict but apply the rules
>
> State of the school:
> Problems: needs renovation - old desks - leaking roof - suffers vandalism
> Advice: set an example by keeping your classroom tidy/get any graffiti removed that you see; set up after-school litter patrols
>
> People not in uniform:
> Problems: trainers worn - Mrs Miller's crusade against nose studs! - regular detentions issued
> Advice: give one chance, then issue detention; apply rules fairly; explain the reasons for uniforms

> School booklet
> Difficult students - problems (e.g. fights, exclusions) and advice to help
>
> State of the school - problems (old buildings, etc.) and advice
>
> Uniform - problems (e.g. wearing trainers) and advice

Here's another example. The writing task is 'Describe the person you most admire in the world.'

> 1. Uncle Frank: age, kind of person he is, how others see him, why he is my hero -
>   (1) someone talking about him?
>   (2) or anecdote?
> 2. How he found out about his illness. The effect it had: job/home.
> 3. Aunty Jane's situation. What she said. What they did. The outcome. Family involvement.
> 4. What he has been like since: with other people and on trips to the hospital.
> 5. Fund raising: his pain and his gains, reports in local paper, award from Queen.
> 6. His future plans: ending with hope
>   (1) quotation from U.F. or
>   (2) view of Aunty J.

Good Points

- The notes are broken into sections which, in most cases, will also represent the paragraphs you produce. (You might sometimes choose to turn one of the sections into two or three shorter paragraphs.)
- There is a 'core idea' for each section, then further detail on what could be included.
- The student has more than one idea of how to use the detail in the introduction and ending.

Task

Collect the detailed ideas you would use for this task:

Write the text of a speech to be given to your year group, in which you attempt to persuade them to show more interest in what the school offers out of lesson time.

You might wish to mention:

- sports teams
- clubs and societies
- trips.

Structure and paragraphs

Key points

- You will be awarded marks for your ability to **structure** your writing.

- That means writing an effective **introduction**, developing the ideas logically in the **main section**, and ending with a memorable **conclusion**.

- It also means **organising and linking your paragraphs** in an appropriate and creative way.

Top Tip!

The five minutes or more you spend on planning are crucial. Place your ideas in the order in which you intend to deal with them, and aim to write one or more paragraphs on each main idea.

Pages 50–51

The introduction

- Your first paragraph should **grab the reader's attention**.

- There are **many ways** to do this, for example using a description, a conversation, a moment of high drama, an anecdote or a series of rhetorical questions. Think hard about which might be most **effective**.

If your task was 'Describe the person you most admire in the world', you could begin like this:

Relevant opening sentence – it gives an immediate sense of a hero.

> Even our mayor admires my Uncle Frank, and hosted a dinner in his honour last year: 'What Frank has done,' he said, 'is show just how much a person can achieve when they set their mind to it. He has overcome incredible disadvantages to work tirelessly for others, even though most people in his position might expect others to look after them. In the eyes of this town, he is a great man.'

Quotation makes Frank seem real, and brings response to life.

Establishes Frank's qualities and situation, and shows how highly Frank is regarded by all.

Another idea would be to tell an anecdote about Uncle Frank, which puts him in a real setting and allows the reader to see him in action.

The conclusion

- Your final paragraph should **round off** your piece of writing.

- Ideally, it should be **memorable** and, whenever possible, **link with the opening**.

- Here is a possible ending to the piece of writing on Uncle Frank.

> 'I'm not great, like that mayor said,' Uncle Frank once told me, laughing. 'It was kind of him, but I'm just a stubborn man who does what he thinks is right. I've always lived like that, and I always will. I won't give in, but that's not special, it's just the way I am.' But he is special, of course. And that is why I admire him so much.

Good Points

- The ending refers back to the opening paragraph.
- The spirit of Frank is captured, to conclude the response.
- The final sentence links directly to the title.

Organising and linking paragraphs

- Begin each paragraph with a **topic sentence**. This presents an idea which the paragraph goes on to develop in more detail, e.g.

   The government has its priorities wrong … – to be followed by what is wrong or what should be the real priorities.

   There are seven steps to perfect happiness … – which will then be identified.

   You need to take care if your flight is to be without incident … – the paragraph will deal with safety requirements or the incidents which could occur.

- Link your paragraphs by using **connectives** – words or phrases that show the reader you are **linking ideas**, e.g.

   – chronological: *At first, Then, Later*

   – logical: *Therefore, Consequently, As a result*

   – contrast: *On the other hand, In contrast*

   – a simple ordering of ideas: *Firstly, Secondly, Finally*

   – an extension of ideas: *Because of this, What is more, In addition*

> **Top Tip!**
> Using topic sentences, connectives and different paragraph lengths will boost your marks.

Look at how this student organises and links her paragraphs in a piece about an eventful holiday.

Topic sentence introduces feelings about holidays.

Grade A*

My holidays used to be boring: long mornings spent pretending to do the list of jobs my mother left me before she went to work; long afternoons in front of the television watching repeats and the dross of daytime television; and evenings gazing out of the window, wishing that something would happen - that anything would happen! It even seemed crazy to me at the time, but I wished school would start again, so that I could be back with friends. There is nothing more lonely than having to talk to a goldfish and trying to take a tortoise for walks round the garden.

Long opening paragraph, with list of boring activities, captures the mood.

chronological connective and next topic sentence

Then I met Garth and my life was transformed. He smiled over the hedge and the sunshine beamed - he wasn't just a new neighbour, he was perfect.

Short dramatic paragraph: contrasts to what went before and suggests life and change.

Connective links to previous paragraph and short topic sentence introduces more lively ideas.

Suddenly, I had a purpose. It was no longer a matter of filling the hours, it was all about trying to find enough time to get ready and to be with Garth and even to say goodnight. It was about looking my best and looking out for Garth and being half of a whole …

Last paragraph is built on a list which refers back to the topic sentence at the start, but contrasts with it: items are shorter, reflecting a more dynamic mood.

Task

Find a detailed article in a magazine. Identify the topic sentences and the connectives. Notice how they help you follow the stages of the article.

If there are very few topic sentences and connectives, does it make the article harder to follow?

Note: Reading widely will improve the quality of your own writing.

Sentences

Key points

- Your sentences should make your **meaning clear**; but they must also have a **tone** which is suited to the needs of your **purpose** and **audience**.

- Use a **range of sentence lengths**, and a **range of types**: simple, compound and complex sentences, questions and exclamations.

Simple sentences

- Simple sentences are usually **short** and contain a **subject** and a **verb**:

  He walked in.

  The woman in the hat smiled at me.

- They can produce a **feeling of simplicity**, but that does not mean they convey no emotion. For example, this moving incident from Ernest Hemingway's *A Farewell to Arms* is mostly made up of simple sentences (see right):

> 'Mrs Henry has had a haemorrhage… The doctor is with her.'
>   'Is it dangerous?'
>   'It is very dangerous.' The nurse went into the room and shut the door. I sat outside in the hall. Everything was gone inside of me. I did not think. I could not think. I knew she was going to die…'

- Simple sentences can rush, one after the other, to provide **excitement**:

  He began to run. The man followed. His heart was racing.
  The man was catching him. He had no choice. He dived into the icy water.

- A short sentence after a series of longer sentences can make a **quick but powerful point**:

  The situation right across the country is one that leads many to despair. Hospitals struggling with under-funding and short of both staff and resources are trying to keep our aging population on its feet whilst billions are being wasted on defence contracts and over-spending. It makes me angry.

- A single word sentence can create a **particular effect**, though be careful not to overuse it.

  We waited for more information from the governors. Nothing. What a waste of time!

Compound and complex sentences

- **Compound sentences** are created when simple sentences are linked together by a conjunction:

The Prime Minister has not told the truth.
He must resign.

*The Prime Minister has not told the truth **and** he must resign.*
*The Prime Minister has told the truth **but** he must resign.*

- **Complex sentences** have a main clause and a subordinate clause or clauses, which would not make sense alone:

  Because the Prime Minister has not told the truth, he must resign.

  The Prime Minister must resign, if he has any sense of honour.

Creating effects

- Compound and complex sentences can produce a **variety of effects**.

- They are useful for **explaining ideas** in explanatory or argumentative writing:

  We cannot overlook the effect on the local wildlife and the countryside, which are bound to suffer. On the other hand, we know how poor the local people are and they must have a say in their own future.

- They provide **more detail** in descriptive writing:

  I see the old lady every summer, sitting at the bottom of the steps with her wise eyes and wide smile, and she seems unchanged by the years.

This is an extract from a descriptive response:

> At dawn, I woke to the lightening of the sky and the sound of distant crows in the woods behind the house. There was no traffic, just the animals in the fields and the lightest of breezes, rattling the window occasionally and shifting the curtains, which moved as if touched by faint ghosts. The house itself was otherwise silent, like a ship in a harbour. Then the children were about. The boards started to creak. There were loud voices down the hall. I stretched and began to think of pulling myself from the bed, settling my mind to face the day, whatever it might bring.

Grade A*

Good Points

- The first three lengthy sentences create an impression of lethargy. Life seems unhurried, as if the narrator has the time to concentrate on exactly what is going on around her.
- The next three short sentences create more urgency as the house begins to wake up.
- The last long sentence mirrors the time taken to become fully awake.

Questions and exclamations

- Questions and exclamations should be **used sparingly**, so that they have an impact.

- They should fit the **form**, the **purpose** and the **audience** of your writing.

- **Rhetorical questions** don't expect an answer from the reader. Instead, they are making a statement:

  Do you know any school that has all the facilities it really needs?

  This implies: 'There are no schools that have all the facilities they need.'

- You could begin or end an 'argue/persuade/advise' response with a rhetorical question:

  Is it ever acceptable to value animals more than humans?

  This implies: 'It is never acceptable to value animals more than humans.'

- **Exclamations** show emotional reactions and aim to make the reader react in the same way:

  What a disgrace!

  The results were stunning!

Top Tip!

Different effects suit different purposes and audiences.

Task

Change these simple sentences into complex and compound sentences, so that the text sounds as if it comes from a speech made by a politician. You can alter the order of the ideas and add extra words as necessary.

We knew nothing about the plans. The intelligence services told us nothing. They are very secretive. We could have issued warnings. It is all very sad. We apologise. We wish we could turn back the clock. That is simply not possible.

Vocabulary

Key points

- Whichever question you choose in Section B, your vocabulary will need to be **appropriate**.

- If you can also use language **imaginatively**, so that it seems original, you will be rewarded with high marks.

- Focusing on your use of **connectives and imagery** can gain you marks.

Top Tip!

Reading widely is really the only way to produce the breadth of vocabulary that you need for the highest marks.

Appropriate vocabulary

- The vocabulary you use must be suited to **purpose and audience**.

- If you are asked to write a letter to inform your school governors about problems, the language should be **formal**:

  It is with considerable reluctance that I have to bring this serious matter to your attention ...

- On the other hand, a letter describing problems to a friend might be **informal**:

  You'll never guess what happened to me. It was some big deal at the time ...

- However, never use text language!

Wide vocabulary

An **extensive vocabulary** is required for a top grade. You should, therefore:

- avoid repetition and **aim for variety**, e.g.

  – In your letter to the governors, instead of repeating 'serious', you might use 'grave' or 'important'.

  – The letter to your friend might use a range of words to describe something bad, e.g.

  terrible, awful, tragic, shattering, criminal, drastic, mind-numbing, cataclysmic

- **avoid slang and colloquialisms** generally, though they can be used occasionally, e.g.

  – It would not be appropriate to tell the governors that some of the dinner ladies are 'minging'; but that might be fine if you were writing to a friend.

  (Be careful, though: the examiner wants to see a range of standard English words. Using slang might lose you marks.)

- use words **appropriate to the context**, e.g.

  If you are writing about care for the elderly, you might use terms like 'social services' and 'primary care'. A response dealing with educational matters might include phrases like 'continuing education', 'tertiary provision' and 'vocational courses'.

Connectives

- Use connectives to join paragraphs and ideas together. These might be:

  – to order your ideas, e.g. *Firstly, Finally, To begin with, Then, And to top it all*

  – to give reasons, e.g. *Consequently, Therefore, As a result*

  – to offer alternatives, e.g. *On the other hand, Yet, Meanwhile, Nevertheless*

  – to develop a train of thought, e.g. *What this means is, Taking this one stage further, Because of this*

Page 53

Using imagery

Page 15

- A **striking use of imagery** will attract the examiner's attention. It can be used in descriptive writing as well as the other forms of writing.

- **Similes** make a comparison using 'like' or 'as':

  Although your father seems <u>as old-fashioned as a sideboard</u>, in this case he is right ...

  Your opportunity to work for that company might seem <u>like a ticket to paradise</u> right now, but ...

- **Metaphors** state things that are not literally true, but the comparison has a strong effect:

  Even though your teachers <u>come from the age of the dinosaurs</u>, they can teach you many things ...

  You <u>exploded</u> when I last suggested this, but, at the risk of causing another <u>full-frontal attack</u>, I must tell you again that ...

Top Tip!

You can also impress by using sound effects such as **onomatopoeia**, where you capture sounds in words:

Imagine the <u>dull thud</u> as the university's door to opportunity closes behind you.

and **alliteration**, where words that are close together begin with the same letter:

<u>W</u>hat a <u>w</u>eary <u>w</u>ay you <u>w</u>ill have to tread, <u>w</u>ithout further qualifications.

Page 38

Notice how this A grade student uses a variety of vocabulary, imagery and sound effects:

> My life in the hospital kitchen is very different from my existence at school. As I slave in the pan room, over sinks of boiling water, there is no window. There are cooking pots to scrub and I am like an automaton: wash the pan, sterilise it, leave it to drain, move on to the next. Whereas in school a teacher might occasionally encourage me back to reality, in the steam of my nocturnal hell I am generally alone. There is just the intense heat, the sweat from my brow and the clashing of aluminium for hours on end. I feel like I am working in the bowels of existence.

Grade A

simile + advanced vocabulary

connective linking the ideas by contrasting them

an original metaphor which would impress the examiner

onomatopoeia

a particularly striking image with which to end the extract

Task

This is an extract from a student's description of his uncle. Rewrite it to:
- use more interesting and precise words
- avoid repetition (e.g. 'spends a lot of time').

Can you include some imagery?

> At home, Uncle Tom spends a lot of time in his study. That's not because he likes marking school work ... it's to get away from Aunt Sylvia. He spends a lot of time in school as well, which is 3 miles down the road.

Punctuation

Key points

- To obtain top marks, you need to use a **range of punctuation**.

- The examiner **will expect you to use** any of the following, as appropriate: commas, apostrophes, question marks, exclamation marks, speech marks, brackets, dashes, ellipses, colons and semi-colons.

Commas

- Use commas to:

  1 separate the **items in a list**:

  We have a first-class health service, education system, defence force and parliamentary system.

  2 add clauses or phrases to a main sentence:

  Although we sometimes doubt politicians, they are working, slowly and carefully throughout the years, to make our lives better, so we should respect them.

  3 add extra detail to a noun or pronoun:

  The Prime Minister, a man of great integrity, is supported by his ministers.

Apostrophes

- Use apostrophes to:

  1 indicate **possession**:

  – If the 'owner' is singular, the apostrophe goes before the 's', e.g.

  Europe's problems, my aunt's car

  – If the 'owner' is plural, the apostrophe goes after the 's', e.g.

  schools' problems, footballers' wives

  2 show where there is an **omission**. The apostrophe goes where a letter, letters or even a word has been removed, e.g.

  Is not it? becomes *Isn't it?*; *You are losing* becomes *You're losin'*.

Question marks and exclamation marks

- Use a **question mark** at the end of every question.

- Don't use too many **exclamation marks**. They should only be used to highlight humour, or register strong or sudden feelings like anger, surprise or delight.

Page 55

In this extract, a doctor explains how he struggles with difficult patients:

Comma separates the phrase that adds information to the main clause.

Question mark clarifies how he said the sentence.

> You have to be firm with them. On one occasion, an old lady complained so much that I could stand it no longer. 'Problems?' I said. 'You think you have problems? You should try doing my job!'

Emotion is registered by the exclamation mark.

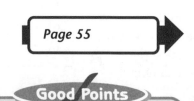

Good Points

- The question marks indicate the doctor's voice rising, so that we sense his frustrations.

- The final exclamation mark suggests he has reached the end of his tether.

- Without the punctuation, it would not be possible to know how the doctor wants us to read the text. He could appear quite calm if only commas and full stops were used. (Try reading it that way!)

Speech marks

- When punctuating speech:
  - The speech marks go around the words actually spoken.
  - Punctuation at the end of speech is placed before the final speech marks.
  - There can be only one speaker per paragraph.

If the speaker follows the words spoken: punctuate, close the speech marks, then use a lower case letter to continue.

'Are you well?' asked my mother.

'He looks strange,' said my father.

I replied, 'I'm as well as could be expected, under the circumstances.'

'In that case,' said my mother, 'we can proceed.'

'But I don't want to go to the dentist,' I said. 'Can't it wait until next week?'

If the speaker comes first: put a comma, then open the speech marks and start with a capital letter.

If the speaker comes in the middle of an interrupted sentence: for the second half put a comma, open the speech marks, then use a lower case letter to continue.

If the person speaking is placed between two complete sentences: put a full stop before the second one, open the speech marks, then re-start with a capital letter.

Top Tip!

Although you will not be producing a narrative in your exam, you might want to include some direct speech in any Section B response, so you need to be aware of the rules about its punctuation.

Colons and semi-colons

- Use a **colon** to:

  1 introduce a quotation:

  As the Queen said only yesterday: 'The commoners are not what they were in my father's time.'

  2 introduce a list, following a general statement:

  This town can be proud of its heritage: the cathedral, the castle and its famous men and women who fought for what was right.

- Use a **semi-colon** to:

  1 separate two closely-related sentences, giving a shorter pause than a full stop:

  I know we can win the cup; we have the talent and the ambition.

  2 separate the sections of a complicated list:

  I love John because he's so good-looking; I love Zack because he's kind; and Ryan is especially special because of the size of his wallet.

Brackets and dashes

- **Brackets** are usually used to offer some **additional information**, as in this extract from Norman Mailer's book about Mohammed Ali:

> His hands lost no speed, his hands looked as fast as Ali's (except when he got hit) and his face was developing a murderous appetite.
>
> *The Fight*

- Sometimes brackets make the words in them seem like **an actor's 'aside'**, used to suggest a reaction or emotion to the reader. Here, Mailer describes Ali with one of his followers:

> While he spoke, Ali put his hands on Bundini's head as if a crystal ball (a black crystal ball!) were in his palms; each time he would pat Bundini's bald spot for emphasis, Bundini would glare at the reporters like a witch doctor in stocks.

Good Points

- The repetition of 'crystal ball', with the addition of 'black' the second time, gives an impression of humour or wonder.

- **Dashes** can be used in the same way as brackets, but they can also **make information stand out**. In this extract from *The Sun*, the sums of money are made to seem particularly significant:

> Billionaire Chelsea owner Roman Abramovich has bought himself a new toy – a £72 million yacht.
>
> The Russian oil tycoon – worth £3.5 billion – stunned onlookers when the 378ft craft put into the South of France last night.
>
> *Martin Wallace*

Ellipses

- An **ellipsis** (…) can be useful to provide a number of effects:
  - to create the idea that the situation will **run on for ever**:

  And so, the dynasty seems set to continue …

  - to give an **air of mystery**:

  Who can say what terrors they must have witnessed … ?

  - or simply to allow the readers to **decide for themselves** what might fill the space:

  They laughed, they cried, and sometimes, when the night was dark, there were other, wilder emotions …

Task

Punctuate this extract so that it is
(a) correct
(b) more effective and interesting.
You will have to replace some of the full stops.

The problem for most single parents men and women is that they have so little time to do anything but care for their children and work. Days are all the same make what seem like endless meals clean and tidy the house work in an attempt to pay for next weeks food and get as much sleep as possible. Its a limited existence.

But what can be done. There must be ways that these people can make their lives a little easier.

As far as I am concerned said Mr Grayson who works for a government agency all we can do is make clear the benefits they can claim and offer wherever possible support workers to help them through. Then, it depends how the individual reacts.

Spelling and accuracy

Key points

- In Section B, **accurate spelling** is expected from Higher level students.

- Your writing also needs to be **legible**.

Accurate spelling

- Where words **follow a set pattern**, remember it so that you can spell other related words, or words affected by the same rule, e.g.

  - Words ending with a single vowel and single consonant double the consonant if you add an ending beginning with a vowel:

    sit – sitter – sitting; ban – banned – banner

  - Remove the final 'e' from a verb before adding 'ing':

    love – loving; have – having

> **Top Tip!**
>
> Don't be afraid to make alterations. As long as the end result is legible, you won't lose marks. However, if the examiner can't make sense of what you have produced, that will let you down.

- Although you should never copy text from Section A, it often contains vocabulary that is useful for Section B. Always carefully check your spelling of **words included in the stimulus materials** or on the exam paper itself.

Common errors

- There are some words which are used frequently but which cause spelling problems. You need to **avoid the most common errors**. In particular, know the difference between:

  your (belonging to you) and **you're** (you are)

  their (belonging to them), **they're** (they are) and **there** (any other use)

  where (place), **were** (verb) and **we're** (we are)

  too (as well or very), **two** (the number) and **to** (any other use)

Make sure you can spell these words which are frequently used and frequently misspelt:

argument	conscience	emphasise	metaphorically	prejudice	symbol
atmosphere	definitely	empathise	naïve	professional	unnatural
beautiful	develop	environment	necessary	psychological	vicious
beginning	disappear	favourite	occasionally	sense	
business	dynamic	immediately	parallel	stereotype	
character	embarrassed	independent	persuade	suspense	

Checking and correcting

- Spend five minutes at the end of the exam **checking** and **improving** your writing.

- Failure to do so can affect your mark considerably, because vocabulary, punctuation and spelling **can all be improved**.

- Ideally, read through your response very slowly, as if reading aloud, and be prepared to **alter** your work whenever necessary.

- With regard to spelling, check for:

  - words **spelt differently** in different parts of your answer: decide which version is correct

  - words which are clearly **spelt incorrectly**: try to apply spelling rules.

Writing to argue

Key points

- One of the questions in Section B of Paper 1 lets you **write to argue**.

- When you write to argue, you **present and develop a point of view** about something, and try to convince the reader that the view is correct.

- Your answer should:
  - refer to the **other point of view**
  - be **well structured**
  - use appropriate **techniques** to convince the reader.

Including two points of view

- Your main task is to present your **point of view** about the issue. Make it clear from the start.

- However, an argument must have **two (or more) sides**. If there is no alternative viewpoint, there can be no argument. When you write to argue, you must always be aware of the opposite point of view and include it in your response.

- You can **refer to the opposing point of view** in a variety of ways:
  - Present one side of the argument briefly, then argue at length for the alternative. The alternative side of the argument will be your point of view.
  - Put one idea, then contradict it; present another, and contradict it, and so on until you reach your own point of view.
  - Make passing references to another viewpoint as you develop your own ideas.

This extract is from a response in which a student is arguing for more funding for schools.

Writer's own view is clear.	**Grade A**

Anyone who knows anything about schools is aware that more money is needed, and that the extra books and equipment it can buy help teaching to improve and results to rise. If this were not the case, independent schools would charge less and do without their excellent facilities. The fact that they invest in the latest books and technology implies that such spending is necessary if they wish to maintain their reputation.

Of course, as the government points out, the quality of teaching is the most important element of any school. Yet, teaching must be better when every student has a book and does not have to share, or has a PC on which to access the internet. Adequate funding is vital if these goals are to be achieved.

Example of independent schools proves the point.

Writer's own beliefs are stated strongly again.

Reason for view is explained.

An alternative viewpoint is put very briefly.

It is immediately attacked through 'yet' connective.

Good Points

- The student's view is clear from the start.
- There is a brief mention of the other side of the argument.
- The opposing viewpoint is immediately dismissed so that the writer's views can progress.

Top Tip!

For top grades, it is vital to link ideas smoothly. Here, the connective 'yet' shows the reader that the opposing viewpoint is about to be criticised.

Pages 53 and 56 Connectives

Structuring your response

- When you write to argue, you will be expected to include:
  - an **introductory paragraph** which presents the topic and probably suggests your attitude to it
  - an **argument which develops** logically and progressively
  - a **conclusion** to sum up your opinion.
- You should follow this approach **whatever you are asked to write**. This could be a letter, an article or even an argument with no specific audience (which means you are writing for the examiner).

Introduction

Compare these two introductions, from responses which have been given different grades. The students are writing an article for an employers' magazine, to argue for or against work experience.

A simple introduction: the student's point of view is clear, but the comments are very general.

> In my opinion, work experience is a good thing. Some people argue that it is a waste of time, but I am going to show that it helps students get to know what real life is like. There are many things in its favour...

Grade C

short and effective opening sentence

sense of personal involvement, even in an argumentative response

change of viewpoint – and writer's point of view made clear

> I am not afraid to admit that the idea of work experience terrified me. How would I cope with new people, a new working environment and having to get up at six o'clock each morning? Would the fortnight even be worthwhile? I guessed not, and feared I would be bullied, put upon and, frankly, bored for most of my time. I felt certain I would be better off learning maths in a classroom, rather than draining oil in the local garage.
> However, that was before I arrived; and how wrong I was ...

Grade A*

touch of humour

challenging questions

Good Points

- A lively and imaginative introduction, both personal and gently humorous, which captures the reader's attention.
- The style is appropriate for the purpose and audience: entertaining yet setting out to argue.
- The subject of the article – work experience – is mentioned immediately, giving focus to what will follow.
- The use of the writer's fears presents one side of the argument, but that aspect is soon discounted.
- The writer's viewpoint changes at the start of the second paragraph. This will introduce the arguments in favour of work experience.

TYPES OF WRITING

Development

- As part of your **planning**, you should decide:
  - what arguments you intend to deal with
  - in what order
  - in what depth.

Pages 50–51

For example, the A* student who worked at the garage might decide to write about:

PLAN

Para 2: what I learnt about working in the team
        co-workers / responsibilities / support and development

Para 3: how I enjoyed the range of tasks
        opportunity to dismantle engines / jobs in office /
        breakdown outings

Para 4: what I learnt that I would not have learnt at school
        dealing with real problems / longer hours / few breaks
        of any kind

Para 5: minor problems I encountered
        health and safety / some exploitation? / butt of humour

Para 6: problems encountered by my friends
        bad bosses / boring work / unfriendly workmates /
        treated as children

Para 7: why it is an invaluable experience
        school is too protected / we will soon be in these
        environments / will have to work for 40-50 years

Conclusion: back to the start
        why it was so beneficial

Good Points ✔

- There is logic in the development of the argument:
  - what the student got out of it
  - some of the problems
  - others' problems
  - why, nevertheless, it is valuable.
- Different viewpoints are included.
- The student is aware of an overall structure, as s/he links the conclusion with the opening.

Conclusion

- The **conclusion** should summarise the views you have expressed. Try to provide an **original** ending, which will stick in the memory and which **links clearly** to the tone and style of the beginning.

Here is the conclusion to the A* response:

summary of the experience

linking back to opening

summary of argument

still a personal response

enthusiasm to back up the point of view

So, incredibly, in just two weeks it was all over. I had no fears left and I had made good friends I was sorry to leave – even though I did have a lot of sleep to catch up on! Any problems were only minor. I loved almost every minute, learnt a great deal, and they have offered me a Saturday job. I now believe that work experience is a vital part of the KS4 curriculum. If it comes to a choice between doing maths or cleaning out a filthy sump, I've learnt there is no real comparison. After all, as Mick the manager said: 'You're better off with oil dribbling down your nose than getting square roots drilled into your head.' I can only agree. Roll on next Saturday!

Grade A*

additional thought: humour again – and quotation

main point stated

Top Tip!

The conclusion is the last thing the examiner will read before awarding your mark, so if you can make it memorable you should benefit!

Using a range of techniques

- Use a **variety of techniques** to present your argument effectively, e.g. giving reasons, evidence, examples, anecdotes, quotations, facts and figures, rhetorical questions, direct address, lists, sentences of varying type and length.

This letter to the local council includes many of these techniques. It argues that more needs to be done for hard-pressed local residents.

Grade A*

rhetorical questions to challenge the reader

topic sentence for each paragraph, indicating what it will be about

the council's different viewpoint

opposing viewpoint dismissed

connectives ('Of course', 'Ironically') used to link ideas

link with opening

strong statement of the writer's viewpoint

quotation to illustrate exactly what the council is saying

a touch of sarcasm/humour

extended list of complaints: long, well-controlled sentence for variety

memorable last sentence

Dear Sir,

Does our city have to suffer from graffiti and litter and heaps of junk in the streets? Is there nothing that can be done? You collect our taxes and say you are concerned about our problems, but nothing ever seems to improve. I am tired of living in what amount to slum conditions on my housing estate, and I know that you can do something about it, if only you develop a will to fight for improvement and a positive drive to improve our quality of life.

Ironically, on a regular basis we receive your leaflets, telling us how our neighbourhoods are safer and cleaner and how new action schemes are making our lives better. But we do not recognise what you describe. When the mayor writes:

'We can celebrate, because independent studies have confirmed the improvements in the state of our environment ...'

we are simply amazed. He seems to have no idea of what it is really like.

Of course, if you ever set foot outside the town hall and visited us, you would see the truth for yourself. We have bins unemptied, then tipped all over the pavements; there are abandoned cars, which often rust for months before they are removed, and which local teenagers delight in torching; and the walls are covered in obscenities which will not scrub away.

That is why I am writing directly to you to say it is time to act. The people in this city deserve better and it is up to you to provide it. You won our votes: it is time you set about winning our hearts.

Good Points
- The writer has introduced two viewpoints, structured the letter logically and linked the opening and ending.
- Sentences and vocabulary are varied.
- A range of techniques is used, such as rhetorical questions, quotation and sarcasm.
- The reader is guided through the text by topic sentences and connectives.

Task

Write an article for a local newspaper, arguing that your town, village or city needs improvement. Remember to:
- use an effective structure
- refer to different viewpoints
- include suitable techniques.

Writing to persuade

Key points

- One of the questions in Section B of Paper 1 lets you **write to persuade**.

- When you write to persuade, you try to get the reader to **do something or believe something**.

- You should **structure your ideas** appropriately.

- You should also use a range of **persuasive techniques**, which may include:
  - emotive language
  - examples and anecdotes
  - rhetoric.

Structuring ideas

- There are different ways of persuading people. You might, for example, persuade readers by presenting a **logical argument**. This is like writing to argue, and you could use similar techniques to those in the previous section.

Pages 62–65

- However, unlike argument, persuasion does not necessarily need to include more than one point of view. Rather than balancing contrasting ideas or ensuring that another viewpoint is included, persuasive writing often presents just **one, subjective view** of a subject. This section will focus on that approach.

- For example, if you were writing a letter to persuade an elderly relative to protect herself against dangers in the home, all you need to do is stress the need for more protection, rather than suggesting that she may already be well protected.

- First, you need to put your ideas into a **sensible order**, so that one idea **flows logically** from the previous one:

> PLAN
>
> <u>Intro: the need to be secure</u>
>
> She is an important part of the family; her home is not as safe as it should be
>
> <u>Para 2: new measures needed to give protection against burglars</u>
>
> Not even a chain on the door; needs modern locks, an alarm, etc.
>
> <u>Para 3: what the other problems are and how they can be solved</u>
>
> Old gas appliances; no wiring checks for years; gas service can be arranged annually; local, friendly odd-job man will do the wiring
>
> <u>Para 4: the benefits which will come from greater protection</u>
>
> She can be more relaxed; cheaper home insurance – and improvements are likely to cost very little in total
>
> <u>Conclusion: how everyone in the family will feel better knowing she is safe</u>
>
> She has to be there to cook me tea whenever I'm passing!

need outlined

↓

current problems

↓

benefits from taking action

Top Tip!

Even when planning, remember that **original ideas** will improve the quality of the final response. In this plan, there are already some original touches, such as the final comment about popping in for tea. This suggests that the writer will be appealing to her particular audience (an older relative) in a way that is likely to 'win her round', and persuade her to make changes.

Good Points

- The plan sets out ideas in a sensible order. It details the current problems and then moves on to the benefits which would come from taking action.
- The main points are given (underlined), then developed by adding detail and examples.
- The introduction stresses the dangers but the conclusion celebrates 'feeling better', so the persuasion has a clear direction.

Emotive language

Emotive language – language which touches the reader's emotions – is a most **effective technique** when writing to persuade. It can often be a more powerful tool than cold logic.

On the right is part of Nelson Mandela's speech when he was sworn in as the first black president of South Africa. Note the emotive language.

> We dedicate this day to the heroes and heroines in this country and the rest of the world, who sacrificed in many ways and surrendered their lives so that we could be free. Their dreams have become reality. Freedom is their reward.

A Grade C student producing an opening paragraph to persuade Grandma might write:

Grade C

Dear Grandma,

I have been thinking about the fact that you are not as safe in your home as you might be. I do not want to worry you, but I am concerned that someone could break in or that you could be harmed by a fire. I am not even certain that your gas fires and cooker have been checked recently. If you follow my suggestions, though, I can guarantee you will be perfectly safe.

An A* student might persuade Grandma to take the situation seriously by using an emotive approach:

humorous opening, but appropriate for this audience

emotive details

touching feelings expressed

Grade A*

Dear Grandma,

I hope you are really well and not getting too involved in snowball fights this winter! I like to think of you safe in your flat, comfy in your armchair with the heating on, protected from the howling wind outside. In fact, we need to know you are secure and away from everything dangerous, because you have a wide family that loves you and needs you. Who could we find to make us special Christmas cakes if anything happened to you?

Good Points ✓

- It uses emotive language.
- It uses a tone which is appropriate for the audience: humorous and caring.
- It includes persuasion from the start: Grandma must become more secure so that the family feels better. Rather than worrying her, the letter is persuading her to do this for others.

humour to balance the strong feelings and the suggestion of possible dangers

Examples and anecdotes

- You can use **examples** to illustrate any point you are making.

- **Anecdotes** are really extended examples – short stories which can be used to enrich your writing. The reader is more likely to be persuaded if you can write about what has actually happened.

When writing about how Grandma's current security measures offer only limited protection, this A* student added detail and a persuasive anecdote:

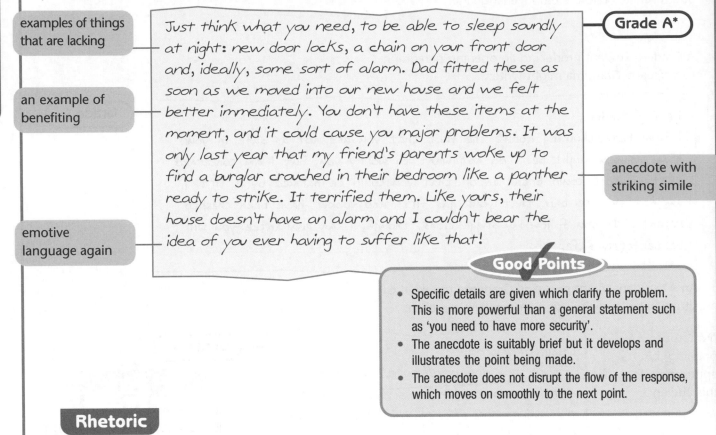

examples of things that are lacking

an example of benefiting

emotive language again

> Just think what you need, to be able to sleep soundly at night: new door locks, a chain on your front door and, ideally, some sort of alarm. Dad fitted these as soon as we moved into our new house and we felt better immediately. You don't have these items at the moment, and it could cause you major problems. It was only last year that my friend's parents woke up to find a burglar crouched in their bedroom like a panther ready to strike. It terrified them. Like yours, their house doesn't have an alarm and I couldn't bear the idea of you ever having to suffer like that!

Grade A*

anecdote with striking simile

✔ Good Points

- Specific details are given which clarify the problem. This is more powerful than a general statement such as 'you need to have more security'.
- The anecdote is suitably brief but it develops and illustrates the point being made.
- The anecdote does not disrupt the flow of the response, which moves on smoothly to the next point.

Rhetoric

- **Rhetoric** is 'language used for effect'. It can transform a promising response into one which deserves a top grade.

- This is the conclusion of the same student's response:

Figurative language – the simile emphasises how precious she is.

rhetorical question – to challenge the reader

humour again to conclude

> As far as the family is concerned, you are as valuable as the Koh-i-noor diamond and should be protected with even more care. We want you safe from burglars; we want you safe from all other dangers; we want you safe and with us for a very long time to come. It makes sense, Grandma: when we consider the range of horrendous accidents and appalling assaults on people and property that take place daily, it has to be wise to take every available precaution. And, after all, is there any reason why you should not make all these improvements straight away? Don't forget, you have to be perfectly safe so you can cook me my tea whenever I'm passing!
> All my love . . .

Grade A*

Repetition hammers home the points.

powerful adjectives, nouns and **verbs**; also **alliteration** (*appalling assaults on people and property*)

Using a range of techniques

Try to use all the techniques dealt with in this section, as in the answer below.

Write an article for a national newspaper persuading more people to vote.

Grade A*

Rhetorical questions and repetition create a powerful opening.

Elaborate language suggests a knowledgeable writer.

Alternatives are trivialised.

emotive language

direct address

Links back to opening.

Clear point of view is hammered home by short sentences.

examples: emotive images and simile

Anecdote highlights main point of article.

Why everyone should vote ...

How many times have you heard people criticise the government? How many times have you heard someone at the bus stop moaning about taxes or transport or wars? And how many times have you heard people saying they don't vote anyway, because it does no good? As far as I am concerned, if they do not vote, they do not have any right to complain. More importantly, they are wasting a right. It is as simple as that.

Consider those who are oppressed around the world. They would give almost anything to be allowed to cast a vote for what they believe in. They are sent to prison for having an opinion, are tortured because they speak out, and often die like slaughtered animals because they do not have our democracy.

In contrast, so many people in the western world choose, blindly, to ignore the ballot box, claiming that it is a pointless exercise. They say their cross is meaningless, as if the very act of voting fritters away the time when they could be watching television or playing darts over a pint. Martyrs have given their lives so that we might have a say in our own futures, but that means nothing to so many.

A recent television programme looked at two different democracies. It focused on a man in Africa who queued for ten hours to vote – it was the first time he had ever been able to. It also interviewed a Scottish man who said he had never voted. The contrast was glaring. In our comfortable world, we seem to have lost our sense of values.

Yet we must vote, because nothing is more important than the society in which we live. So when the next election comes around, you should find the time to add your cross because it represents your right to choose. You should vote if you care about our country, and it will also help you justify your protests afterwards.

✔ Good Points

- The text is persuasive throughout.
- The full range of techniques is used effectively.
- There is a powerful opening and the conclusion links back to it.
- Sentences and vocabulary are varied.

Task

Write the script of a talk to be given on radio, to persuade the listeners to become more involved in helping charities.

Structure your talk effectively, and include:
- emotive language
- at least one example and anecdote
- rhetoric.

Writing to advise

Key points

- One of the questions in Section B of Paper 1 lets you **write to advise**.

- When you write to advise, you are helping someone **to do something** or **to behave in a particular way**.

- You should **organise your ideas** appropriately.

- You should also be **logical**, adopt the **right tone**, offer **solutions** and use **examples**.

Organising your ideas

- There are **two methods** you can use when organising your ideas on any particular subject. You might decide to:

1 First set out the **problem** in a lot of detail.

Then offer **advice** in the later part of the response.

For example, in a magazine article for teenagers:

– Page 1 explains how problems with parents can become very serious.

– Page 2 gives advice about how to avoid or minimise any such problems.

OR

2 Set out the advice **in sections**. Offer advice as you go, so that the **advice is interspersed with the problems**, e.g.

The first thing you mention in your letter is …	*I think that you need to tackle this in three different ways …*
You then go on to explain that …	*In this particular case, you might consider …*
Then, there is your concern about …	*If I were you, I would …*

- The way you decide to structure your advice will obviously influence your **planning**.

> ### Top Tip!
>
> Sometimes, your advice can be made more effective by explaining what might happen if nothing is done:
> *If you just turn up and expect everything to be fine, you will struggle. If you do not adopt a positive attitude …*
> You could also explain what might happen if your advice is ignored:
> *Others may tell you to just follow what your friends do. However, that can lead to disaster …*

Being logical

- Your advice won't be convincing if it isn't logical. That means you need to:

1 show exactly **what the problem involves**

2 explain **what can be done about it**.

You could end by showing **what the benefits will be** if your advice is followed.

- Make sure that your ideas are connected. They should develop sensibly from the problem(s) you have set out.

- Look at the plan on the next page, produced by an A grade student in response to the following question:

> Write a section for your school brochure, offering advice to new students about how best to settle in at the school.

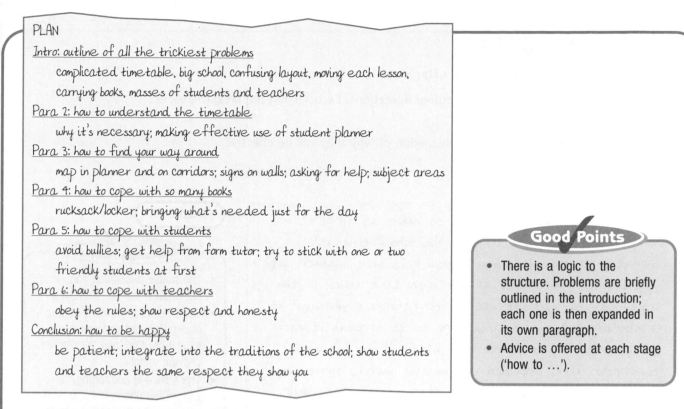

PLAN

<u>Intro</u>: outline of all the trickiest problems

complicated timetable, big school, confusing layout, moving each lesson, carrying books, masses of students and teachers

<u>Para 2</u>: how to understand the timetable

why it's necessary; making effective use of student planner

<u>Para 3</u>: how to find your way around

map in planner and on corridors; signs on walls; asking for help; subject areas

<u>Para 4</u>: how to cope with so many books

rucksack/locker; bringing what's needed just for the day

<u>Para 5</u>: how to cope with students

avoid bullies; get help from form tutor; try to stick with one or two friendly students at first

<u>Para 6</u>: how to cope with teachers

obey the rules; show respect and honesty

<u>Conclusion</u>: how to be happy

be patient; integrate into the traditions of the school; show students and teachers the same respect they show you

Good Points

- There is a logic to the structure. Problems are briefly outlined in the introduction; each one is then expanded in its own paragraph.
- Advice is offered at each stage ('how to …').

The appropriate tone

- As with any other response, adopt a tone that suits the **purpose** and **audience**.

- You are more likely to be asked to write a **formal response**, for example a letter to a newspaper, than an **informal response**, for example a letter to your best friend.

- You need to **address the reader** from the outset.

- This Grade C response chooses to **tell the reader directly what to do** (note the commands, 'musts' and 'shoulds'):

> <u>Don't worry</u> when you come to our school. <u>You must</u> get to grips with a whole new situation, including the crowds, the size of the school and all the new people. <u>You should</u> take a deep breath and <u>must not</u> panic. <u>Keep</u> your cool. <u>You will</u> soon get used to it all.

Grade C

- However, this A* student blends the direct, more aggressive approach with a **gentler approach**:

> When you first arrive at our school, <u>the best thing to do</u> is to try not to panic. Everyone has been new at some stage. <u>If you can stay calm</u>, then <u>you will be on the way to</u> coping with your new world. <u>See</u> the long corridors as a challenge; <u>see</u> the complex timetable as a puzzle; and <u>see</u> the students and teachers as friends-to-be. <u>Don't worry</u> if your bag is too heavy or you have no idea what to do next. <u>Think back to</u> how frightening your primary school seemed at first. You soon got used to it and <u>the same will happen here</u>.

Grade A*

Good Points

- The less aggressive approach will make the newcomer more confident. The tone implies throughout that the writer understands the situation of the newcomer and is clearly sympathetic ('everyone has been new at some stage').
- The imperatives (commands) also offer clear advice.
- The A* response is more detailed and, therefore, more convincing.

Writing to advise

Offering solutions

- As part of your advice, you need to **offer solutions** to the problems.
- The plan on page 71 has been structured in sections. Each section requires, therefore:
  - an **explanation** of the problem
  - suggested **solutions**, with an explanation of why they will be effective.

This extract deals with the problem of understanding the school timetable:

> Because the lesson times vary so much, at first it is difficult to know exactly how the school timetable operates. I recommend you always keep your planner with you, because that lists all the important times in the school day, so you can use it for reference whenever it is needed; and, in addition, try to go through it each evening, to remind yourself of what will be happening tomorrow. Then, provided you wear a watch, there should be few serious problems: check the planner, check your watch, and you will be able to arrive where you need to be – on time and with no stress at all.

Grade A*

Good Points ✓

- The problem, solution and explanation are all made clear.
- What needs to be done seems straightforward and appears a logical solution: use the planner and the watch.
- The advice is comforting, suggesting this is not a serious problem and that, if the advice is followed, the problem will disappear.

Using examples

- You can make your advice more convincing by **using examples**:

  Consider what happened when …

  It is worth remembering …

  In a similar situation …

- Relating your advice to what has happened before **reassures the reader**. The advice seems easier to trust.

This is how you could **conclude** the response:

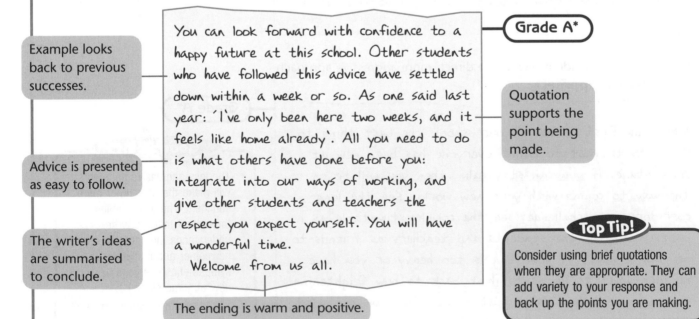

Example looks back to previous successes.

> You can look forward with confidence to a happy future at this school. Other students who have followed this advice have settled down within a week or so. As one said last year: 'I've only been here two weeks, and it feels like home already'. All you need to do is what others have done before you: integrate into our ways of working, and give other students and teachers the respect you expect yourself. You will have a wonderful time.
>   Welcome from us all.

Grade A*

Quotation supports the point being made.

Advice is presented as easy to follow.

The writer's ideas are summarised to conclude.

The ending is warm and positive.

Top Tip!

Consider using brief quotations when they are appropriate. They can add variety to your response and back up the points you are making.

Using a range of techniques

Try to use all the techniques dealt with in this section, as in the answer below.

Write an article for a travel magazine, to advise travellers on how to cope with foreign languages.

Grade A*

Appropriate tone is used for this sort of magazine article: to interest/ entertain.

Why you will benefit.

first definite advice

Positive results are shown.

advice again

Persuasive conclusion, to make the advice more acceptable.

Traditionally, the British speak English and expect the rest of the world to adapt accordingly: if some foreigner does not speak English, then shout at him, and he will get the idea! However, although that has often been the attitude in the past, the world has moved on; and, thankfully, so has the British attitude to travel and languages.

Most of the British who go abroad now realise that, to get the most out of their time, they need to be able to 'speak a de lingo' – or, at least, some of it. They can then get on better with the locals, pick up a clearer flavour of the culture and feel as if they have really been somewhere foreign, not just a Brighton with endless sunshine. They can feel less like holidaymakers and more like travellers.

Of course, it is hard to suddenly just be there and 'talking the talk', so sensible travellers do a little work at home. Language guides, in either book or CD form, give an excellent start. It is amazing how your attitude can change when you realise it is so simple to ask for bread or to order a drink in the language of your choice. My brother, who is only seven, loves being in Paris because he can go out each morning to the bakery with his 'Je voudrais une baguette, s'il vous plaît.' He hands over his euro and comes back smiling, having done himself good and also having done something positive for Anglo-French relations.

So we should be learning from the signs around us, from menus and just from what we hear in the street. Also, your hosts will be delighted if you ask what they call knives and forks or lipstick. They will even teach you whole sentences once you show an interest – and it is incredible how swiftly you will 'pick it up'. Kein problem, as we say in German.

It is simply a matter of making the effort and then appreciating the results. Travel broadens the mind and, if the experience can also extend your language skills, the journey has been doubly worthwhile.

Logical organisation of ideas. The old situation is described in paragraph 1, the new approach in paragraph 2.

Positive comment: benefits are pointed out.

Anecdote/example proves the point.

appropriate examples

Good Points ✔

- The response presents situations, offers advice and suggests likely outcomes.
- The tone is light but presents some serious points.
- French and German are used for illustrative purposes.
- The examples and anecdotes give the advice more credibility.
- The introduction is memorable, with the image of 'traditional' British behaviour.
- The response develops logically, leading to a positive conclusion.
- Language is used effectively.

Task

Your school has been given a grant of £100,000 from the government. On behalf of your year group, write a letter to your headteacher to offer advice on how the school should spend it.

Writing to inform

Key points

- One of the questions in Section B of Paper 2 lets you **write to inform**.

- The information you provide should be **clear, detailed, relevant** and **organised logically**.

- You should include **facts** and **opinions**, and a **personal response** if possible.

Top Tip!

To achieve a high grade you need to show that you can write in depth about the subject given. Try to focus on the most significant points and include as much detail as possible.

Choosing the information

- Information texts aim to tell someone about something, so **provide information**!

- Begin by planning. Collect a range of relevant ideas, as below.

Write a letter to a pen friend who is about to visit, to inform them about the area in which you live.

famous residents · recent developments · provision for young people
local historical sites · Kinds of people
life on the estate · employment
surrounding attractions · sports facilities
shopping · local politics · main buildings · schools

Barlington

- There are too many points here. Decide which are the most significant and focus on those.

- The ideas need to be organised so that similar ideas are covered at the same time.

Logical organisation

- Whenever you produce a written response, your ideas should develop logically, so that one point appears to develop from what has gone before. Look at this detailed plan:

PLAN
<u>Intro: general details</u>
   looking forward to the visit, much to find out
   about, many things to see
<u>Para 2: immediate vicinity</u>
   neighbours, the estate – shops and houses
<u>Para 3: the town</u>
   employment, schools, facilities
<u>Para 4: what's worth seeing</u>
   historical sites, buildings, attractions
<u>Para 5: other points of interest</u>
   youth culture, recent improvements
<u>Conclusion: summary of Barlington</u>
   some fun, some interest

Good Points

- Most of the ideas in the spider diagram have been blended into this detailed plan.
- They have been organised into particular topics, one per paragraph.
- There is a logical development: overview – nearby – town itself – famous features – other interest – personal response.

Facts and opinions

- The information you supply is likely to be a mixture of facts and opinions:
  - The **facts** provide the basic detail.
  - The **opinions** provide an assessment of the material, and can give it a more personal focus.

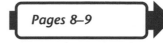*Pages 8–9*

This student has provided a mixture of facts and opinions in the introduction to her response:

> Dear Gabbi,
>
> I imagine you are starting to worry about what your two weeks with us might bring. So, to set your mind at rest, I thought I would tell you all about our little community, so there will be no unexpected surprises when you arrive. There are many positives: we are surrounded by bits and pieces of history, which can be quite fascinating. Also, there are some unusual aspects: some of the families who live around us lead very odd lifestyles - but they aren't dangerous!

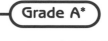 Grade A*

Good Points

- The student includes some facts – what she is going to do, the fact that the community is full of history.
- The opinions give it a lot of colour – 'positives', 'fascinating', 'unusual aspects', 'odd lifestyles'.

Making the information clear

- When you write to inform, it is essential that you make the **information clear**. Usually, the reader will not be aware of the situation, place or whatever is being described.

- The **more detail** you can give, the clearer the picture you provide.

The letter to Gabbi needs to be absolutely clear, because she probably has no knowledge of the local area. Compare these two extracts:

Some information follows.

Unclear – what is the connection between the pillars and the courts?

> There are many things worth seeing locally, if you are interested in things like history. There is a civil war castle that is still just about standing and the town hall and the county hall are both in town and quite grand. They have big pillars outside and are next to the law courts. We might also go to the boating lake, where we will be able to hire a canoe, and there is a reservoir, if you like walking round in a circle, just to get back where you started.

Grade C

Information lacks detail.

Links with previous paragraph.

Details make information clear and interesting.

Language is assured and gives further detail.

> We do, though, have some attractions which you are likely to find genuinely interesting. For a start, my parents intend to take us to the castle, which is only a couple of miles away and in all the history books. It was the site of a famous battle during the Wars of the Roses (1460) and was besieged several times during the Civil War (1642-48). From the top, you get panoramic views of the countryside around, and can imagine the clashing of swords and cries of the dying men as the relatively primitive armies struggled, fought hand to hand and wreaked massive devastation. The museum on site exhibits many of the weapons and has detailed charts of how the battles were organised ...

Grade A*

personal opinion

Personal response creates a vivid picture of the castle.

Good Points

- The detail, personal response and mature language bring the attraction to life.
- The paragraph has been linked to the one before.

75

TYPES OF WRITING

Personal response

- Try to include a **personal response** with the information you are giving. This lifts the material from being just a list of details. For example, you could say whether things are of value and why.

- A personal response may be a significant feature of the conclusion to your writing. At this point you are summing up for the reader and, hopefully, giving your own perspective on the information.

- The personal response might be relatively simple, as here:

> **Grade C**
>
> You should now have a good picture of what it is like here, and we hope you will have a wonderful time whilst you are with us. You will be able to experience the things I have told you about, and give us your opinions on them. Personally, I am certain you will enjoy the sports facilities best – but we will see whether I am right.
>
> Best wishes ...

On the other hand, it could be made more striking, as here:

A personal response runs throughout.

There is a cluster of informative detail, with opinions included ('exhausting', 'hysterical').

Final example of what the area has to offer.

> **Grade A***
>
> The one certainty is that you will be given the warmest of welcomes and I can promise you a variety of experiences: fascinating guided tours of our historical heritage; exhausting afternoons playing squash at the sports centre; and hysterical evenings with my crazy friends.
>
> I am intending to give you a thoroughly 'English' experience. In fact, whatever else happens, before you go home you will be treated to a huge helping of local fish and chips, which we can eat out of newspaper - and that should give you something to remember when you return to your bistros and cafes!
>
> Best wishes ...

Personal opinion included on the effect it will have.

Good Points ✔

- The response is still informative.
- The writer's opinion gives a positive slant on the information – suggesting it will all be enjoyable.
- The sentences are varied and the use of language is imaginative (e.g. 'historical'/'hysterical').
- The letter draws to an effective ending, introducing fish and chips as the climax and then imagining the guest returning home.

Using a range of techniques

Try to use all the techniques dealt with in this section, as in the answer below.

Write an article for one of the more serious national newspapers, to inform the readers about the problems faced by modern teenagers.

Grade A*

Immediately links with title.

Complex sentence informs reader of the range of problems.

Paragraph linked.

Problems are apparent.

Paragraph linked again.

'designer': repeated modern word emphasises modern problem.

Paragraph linked once more.

Impressive vocabulary: suits a serious newspaper.

Rhetorical finish puts all the information into perspective.

Rhetorical question implies personal response.

Detailed information on home life.

A personal 'slant' is given.

Vocabulary is impressive throughout.

Personal comment added.

Detailed information given on problems of school life.

Cluster of problems to conclude.

It has never been easy to be a teenager, and it is particularly difficult today. The world expects us to be grown up but rarely treats us like adults; we are part of a society in which drugs are readily available but extremely dangerous; our education consists of examinations and more examinations; and, on top of that, we have the perennial problems of adolescence, as we cope with so many changes and try to come to terms with our new selves. Is it any wonder we struggle at times?

One of the biggest problems is that parents and teachers demand mature and intelligent behaviour from us, yet usually think of us as still being children. We help clean the house, do a range of chores and care for sickly grandparents, but cannot watch adult movies on television. We are expected to show an interest in current affairs and get a part-time job to begin to support ourselves, but are not even allowed a say in where we go for the family holiday – never mind being allowed to holiday with our friends!

Outside the home, we have to make sure our dissatisfaction does not lead us to outright rebellion and to the dealers who are just waiting to sell us a myriad of drugs. Older generations had to come to terms with alcohol and cigarettes; that was easy, by comparison. We go to a club, to dance, then are faced with temptation, peer pressures and our own desire to fit in with the crowd. There is always someone there with a designer drink, a designer smile and the latest designer drug to tempt us. Being a teenager has never been harder.

Of course, it has never been so grim in school either. We have so many examinations, it is difficult to keep track: SATs, GCSEs, A/S levels ... and the practice tests that accompany them. Homework is never-ending. No teacher seems aware of how much work the others are setting, and, anyway, would not care, because they are all under orders to improve results or their own careers will suffer.

Through all this, teenagers are suffering from raging hormones, relationship problems, changes in their bodies and their minds and the fear of suddenly being alone. They are no different, in that sense, from their parents and grandparents. But would previous generations have wanted all the other modern pressures? I imagine they feel fortunate to have been born at another time, in another world.

✔ Good Points

- The writer presents organised and detailed information.
- The facts are supported and illustrated by opinions.
- The language and style are mature and appropriate for the purpose and audience.

Task

Write informatively about a pastime you enjoy.

Note: In a task of this kind, you should assume your audience is the examiner.

Writing to explain

Key points

- One of the questions in Section B of Paper 2 lets you **write to explain**.

- If you choose that title, you need to be aware that explanation is **different from straightforward information**.

- Writing to explain requires:
  - a response which answers the **precise demands of the title**
  - content which sets out **how or why** something occurs, rather than just what happens
  - **appropriate language**.

Many students fail to explain properly the subject they are writing about. Don't lose focus and just write to inform, without including the explanation that is required.

Responding to the title

- When you write to explain, you are giving reasons, saying **why** or **how** something happens (or happened). Rather than just providing information, you need to add commentary and explanation **throughout**.

Think about this title:

> Most people have memories of a particular holiday or trip. Choose one that you have experienced, and explain why it was so memorable.

- For a high level response, you need to **limit the points** you write about. It is better to explain a few points at length, rather than trying to include too much material.

- Your plan might look like this:

This question does not ask you to:
- write about trips in general
- describe what happened on one special trip
- write informatively about the place you visited.

It does require you to:
- decide what made one particular trip special and say why
- select memorable features of the trip and explain why they are memorable.

```
PLAN
Intro: where we went, when, why memorable
        Turkey, highs and lows
Para 2: first part fun
        different culture, beaches, food, friends: show why
Para 3: dad's nightmare
        drunken evening, people complaining, wrestling with red monster:
        explain what happened
Para 4: mum bitten by cat
        rabies fears, doctor and hospital, injections: how the horror unfolded
Para 5: leaving
        friendliness: doctor and nurses: explain it still didn't take
        away the horror
Conclusion: never going back!
        problems outweighed pleasures
```

Good Points

- This plan shows clear organisation. The introduction sets out to show two sides to the holiday – these are developed further in the sections which follow. The conclusion weighs the two sides in the balance.
- There is a focus on explanation throughout: 'why', 'explain', and 'how' are all important words in this plan.

- It is a good idea to **explain from the beginning** of the response. It establishes your focus, which is then easier to maintain.

Look at how these students approach the task differently in these introductions:

> About six years ago, I went on holiday with my family to Turkey. We stayed in a place called Datca, and there were not many British people there. I am sure we could have had a good time and then it would have been 'just another holiday'. However, there were also some seriously bad moments which made the holiday especially memorable.

Grade C

> When it comes to memorable holidays, our family's package expedition to Datca in Turkey will take some beating. We had a beautiful place to stay in a resort which is lovely, and all of that is captured in our photographs - yet that summer stands out because of one particular experience, which we did not record on camera but which we will never forget. It has haunted us ever since.

Grade A*

✓ Good Points

The A* opening:
- is more detailed
- immediately introduces more vivid explanation – the experience which 'has haunted us ever since'
- has more varied sentences.

'How' and 'why'

- Good explanatory writing presents a **situation**, then says **why** it came about and the **effect** it had.

- Sometimes, depending on the title, it might explain **how someone feels** about what has happened.

- Throughout, it **gives reasons**.

Look at how the middle section of the response can be improved from a Grade C to an A*.

Informs about what happened and the consequences.

> My mother had a real problem. One night, she was bitten by a cat. She had to go to see the doctor and then to the local hospital, where she was told she had to have an injection into her stomach every two days. They thought she might have rabies. This was terrible, and made our holiday a nightmare. My mother was really frightened, and cried quite often. The injections really hurt her, and it is not something we will ever forget.

Grade C

Explains the effect on the family.

Links to title – explains why it has made such an impression.

Links clearly with previous paragraph about father (see plan).

This clearly explains the incident, and focuses on how it came to affect the family and the holiday so much.

> Incredibly, though, something even worse happened to my mother. My father's problems caused us unforgettable embarrassment, but my mother's misfortune turned our holiday into a nightmare - one from which we could not wake up.
>
> It all started when my mother was bitten by a cat. She was eating in a restaurant and moved her arm suddenly and a cat, which was beside her chair and must have thought she was going to harm it, struck first. The doctors feared she might have rabies. This meant she had to have a series of six injections directly into her stomach - one every two days. As you can imagine, our holiday was wrecked. The injections caused agony, she spent much of the day in tears, her stomach became black and swollen and all we could do was watch her suffer. It was no longer a holiday but a daily torture for everyone.

Grade A*

Explains why these incidents were memorable, with an echo of 'haunting' from the introduction.

79

Using appropriate language

- The explanation must be **clear**, so that the reader understands it perfectly.
- Some **explanatory phrases** you may find useful include:

1 terms to explain **cause and effect**, e.g.

As a result of this …

This meant that …

This is because …

The reason for this …

As a consequence …

Therefore …

2 modal verbs, when something is uncertain, e.g.

It could be …

It may be / might be that …

- Some of these phrases have been used in this conclusion:

Modal verb – suggests possible explanation.

Cause and effect identified.

It might be that what happened to my mother has coloured my impressions of Turkey for ever. It is certainly a beautiful country, I know that; and it has wonderfully friendly people. However, my mother had a terrible time, my father was distraught for her, and the rest of us just felt helpless. This meant that things we might have enjoyed, like the beach, were just stops along the way to the next injection; and things we might have laughed at, such as my father's experience, pale into relative insignificance. My mother was in pain, and therefore we remember that above all else. It is a holiday we cannot forget - but for many of the wrong reasons.

Grade A*

Explains again why it was so memorable.

Continues to explain how they were affected.

Top Tip!

The examiner is looking to reward language skills, so sentences with varied length and structure – such as these – will create a positive impression.

Good Points ✓

- The holiday is effectively summarised in the conclusion.
- The effects of the misfortune are explained: we know why it was so memorable and how the family reacted.
- 'It might be' and 'This meant that' helpfully support the explanation.

Using a range of techniques

Try to use all the techniques dealt with in this section, as in the answer that follows.

Explain what you most dislike about television.

Begins with positives, which then highlight what is wrong.

Lists the three problems with TV that he is going to explain in more detail.

I am sure that television is not all bad. It has educational uses, brings top sporting events into the living room and has the potential to enliven dark winter evenings. However, the diet that is drip-fed into my house does anything but stimulate the brain or delight the senses: it could cause premature ageing and certainly hardens the arteries. I am sick of soaps, reality television and almost all things American.

Grade A*

Contrast: explains what he dislikes most; exaggeration for effect; 'sick' continues imagery of food and eating.

I am going to ignore daytime television, since it is beneath contempt – but even in the evening there seems to be no originality at all in most of the programming. The soaps drip on, like some twenty-first century water torture. Everyone spends each evening in the pub; every community is afflicted by ever more incredible calamities; and we sit on our settees drinking our tea, eating our crisps and lapping up such rubbish, because there seems to be no alternative.

Actually, that is not totally true, of course. The twenty-first century has brought something new and different. Unfortunately, it is even more dire: the reality show. Because they are starved of anything better, and because the newspapers comment on these day after day, people sit and watch has-been semi-celebrities swearing at each other in the jungle and gossiping about who might fancy who. On the next night, they watch youngsters who are locked in a house together, in the hope a couple might decide to have sex or, second best, a row.

At times, it makes you think that, comparatively, it must have been riveting to live in a time when families gathered round a piano to sing hymns for their entertainment. At least there must have been some sense that life was real, back then. Also, we were all British then, not an extra branch of the American dream. Now, we suffer 'The Simpsons' night after night (and the American way of speaking) and 'Friends' repeated and repeated. Consequently, we are starved of anything that improves us or genuinely moves us.

The worst thing about so much of this type of television is that it crushes our imagination and limits our horizons. I see it all the time in my family: my brother has become so acclimatised to soaps and reality television that he no longer makes the effort to watch anything more stimulating or intellectually demanding. My sister is so addicted to 'Friends' that life for her stops between 8pm and 9pm. For me, an early night with a book is usually the best move that can be made.

Annotations (left):
- arresting simile
- Explains why we act as we do.
- Introduces cause and effect.
- sarcasm
- Explains his dislike of American shows.
- cause and effect
- Explains how this affects the family, and why it upsets him.

Annotations (right):
- Explains problems with evening TV.
- Second problem explained.
- Implies why he does not like the shows – criticism is suggested through such words as 'gossiping'.
- Explains it is the unreality of reality shows that he dislikes.
- Conclusion includes the writer's response.

Good Points

- The introduction introduces three aspects of TV which he dislikes.
- The dislikes are then explained in detail in separate paragraphs.
- The response concentrates on 'why' and 'how' rather than just 'what'.
- The language is entertaining – including imagery (food and eating) and sarcasm ('comparatively, it must have been riveting').
- Sentences, punctuation and paragraphs are assured, effective and varied.

Task

Explain how you have dealt with difficult situations that have arisen in your life. You might wish to write about:
- relationships with parents
- friends and their expectations
- problems at school
- any other difficult situations you have encountered.

Writing to describe

Key points

- One of the questions in Section B of Paper 2 lets you **write to describe**.
- The question will probably ask you to describe **a person or place**.
- When writing to describe, you should concentrate on:
  - giving it an **effective structure**
  - writing a **striking introduction and conclusion**
  - using the **five senses**, as appropriate
  - including **imagery**.

Describe what you know

- It makes most sense to describe something or someone **you really know about**. Although it can be a temptation to describe a town in the United States or a mysterious individual from Siberia, unless you have precise knowledge of these subjects your response probably won't be convincing.

- However, if you do decide to describe a **person** you have invented, make sure their characteristics are based on **people you know well**, so that he or she comes across as a real person.

- If you are describing a **place**, choose one where you have lived, or one you have visited.

An effective structure

- **Group relevant** ideas together and link them effectively. Unless you plan carefully, you run the risk of writing a rambling description that lacks direction.

- This is a **detailed plan** for a response to the question below. Note that the question is not asking for a story, but a detailed picture of what the beach is like.

> Describe a beach in August.

PLAN
<u>Intro</u>: the atmosphere on the beach
     sounds, colours, sights, weather, people and games
<u>Para 2</u>: families
     dads red, mothers looking after babies and children;
     wind breaks and deck chairs
<u>Para 3</u>: children
     on sands, in sea, digging and games, ice cream and
     sunburn
<u>Para 4</u>: sea
     sandy grey waves, seaweed, inflatables
<u>Para 5</u>: entertainments
     donkeys, volleyball, cricket, football, watching the
     girls/boys
<u>Conclusion</u>: view from the pier
     congested; tide coming in; movements, people drifting
     to steps and home

Good Points ✓

- The plan is clearly divided into sections.
- The ideas are connected: there is a movement from arriving to leaving.

Introduction

- A **vivid opening** will immediately attract the attention of the examiner. Unusual or inventive approaches can gain you marks.

- For example, when describing the beach, you could open by focusing on:
  - one family or individual, then broadening out the description (see student extract below)
  - one particular area or feature of the beach
  - your personal reflections on arrival at the beach.

Focuses on one family for a striking opening. The quotation grabs the reader's attention.

Grade A*

'Tommy! Tommy! You stop that right now! She's got sand in her eyes ... I told you, didn't I? You wait till I get hold of you!' The beach was a heaving mass of families determined to enjoy themselves and banish the problems that plague them throughout the rest of the year ... and failing. Everywhere across the drying sand, children laughed and cried, and parents rubbed on sun screens and screamed at errant sons and daughters. I had arrived on the hottest day of the year, and it seemed that people's tempers and tantrums matched the temperature.

Picture of packed beach painted immediately, with focus on sounds, sights and behaviour.

Personal response to end paragraph, which sets the weather and tone of the piece.

Include all five senses and imagery

- Good descriptive writing of a place will appeal to **all five senses**. Write about what you (or other people) are seeing, hearing, touching/feeling, smelling and tasting.

- **Imagery** is another essential element. **Similes** and **metaphors** can capture what is happening in an original phrase, and illuminate a scene or the description of an individual.

Page 57

- **Descriptions of people** involve less use of the senses. Instead, try to include some description of background, as well as physical description.

Note how this response appeals to all five senses and includes imagery:

sight

metaphor

sight (simile)

feeling

sound

The windbreaks and T-shirts were bright, but everything else was just as loud. The air was rich with the smell of sun-tan cream and fried onions from hot-dog stalls, and lips tasted of sea salt and sand. All along the beach, fathers were ripening like red apples. They sat uncomfortably in deck chairs, reading their papers with sweat trickling down their necks or lay on towels, huge bellies rising like sand mounds from the waists of rolled-up trousers. Mothers, meanwhile, endeavoured to keep the children in check: shouting at boys and girls alike, who moaned back, 'It wasn't me, you always pick on me ...' Babies looked hot and uncomfortable; the rough sand was scrubbing their sore arms and faces raw.

Grade A*

smell

taste

sight (simile)

feeling

Top Tip!

- Good descriptive writing often includes features that are found in poetry. Note the alliteration here ('sea salt and sand'), capturing the hiss of the water on the sand.
- Sentence control also impresses the examiner. The student makes good use of a colon, semi-colon, quotation marks and commas.

Good Points

- The senses heighten the seaside experience.
- Similes and metaphor are used to help the reader picture the fathers and imagine the atmosphere.

Conclusions

- Effective conclusions not only round off the response, but usually **link back** clearly to the introduction.

Look at how the A* student concludes her response:

> The sun is lower in the sky and the tide is creeping up the littered beach. Families retreat, then pack and go. Tommy and Sarah are tired and complain about carrying the ball and spade; father is burning bright, a deckchair in one hand and his newspaper still in the other; and mother struggles with the push chair, laden with bags, over the sand. The heat has taken its toll, so now they are all drained, but calm. There is a queue by the steps from the beach and they join the shuffling masses, dutifully: a British end to a British day by the sea.

Grade A*

Good Points ✔

- A vivid description, which describes the general scene as well as the original family.
- This final paragraph links back effectively to the introduction: time has moved on and the same family is reviewed.
- The movement from the start of the day to going home is handled effectively: the sun is sinking, and things have changed (the people's energy levels, the increase in litter and sunburn).
- Effective control of sentence structure and vocabulary ('creeping up the littered beach', 'laden with bags', 'join the shuffling masses, dutifully').
- There is a touch of humour about the British willingness to queue.

Using a range of techniques

- Try to use all the techniques dealt with in this section, as in the answer that follows.

> Describe the person you find most inspiring.

Grade A*

Contrast makes an effective introduction.

> Some people choose sportsmen as their heroes; others choose men who have climbed mountains or won the Victoria Cross. However, the person who inspires me most is not famous or wealthy, lives just down the road from me and goes to the same school. His name is Jonathon and he is paralysed from the waist down. But he is amazing.

Short sentences have dramatic effect.

> One thing he has taught me is that being unable to walk does not make you a suitable case for sympathy. And if anyone might welcome sympathy, you would have thought it might be him: according to most girls, he was the Brad Pitt of Year 11. He captained the football team; he was Head Boy of the school and looked set for the brightest of futures . . . then, just before his mock A levels, he went downhill on a sledge in the snow, backwards. And hit a tree.

Adds physical description, and description of his abilities.

> When he woke up, he was in intensive care, still on his back, and was told he might never regain any movement below his neck.

Short, powerful paragraph emphasises severity of injury.

Describes his attitude.

Describes how he was injured – complex sentence followed by startling short sentence.

Description of qualities and attitude – note control of sentence length and structure.

mature vocabulary

Describes intellectual abilities.

simile

appropriate metaphor

Conclusion returns to idea of being an 'everyday' hero.

He did, of course. Stoke Mandeville Hospital – and the most incredible will to get better and be mobile – saw him through. From the outset, he would not be patronised and did not want to be looked after for the rest of his life. He had too much living still to do.

Now, he motors round in his wheelchair like some sort of demented Lewis Hamilton and does wheelies in the discos that make you want to cheer and weep – yes, he even has that effect on boys. He has also demonstrated that physical incapacity is no restriction on intellect, which is something we all know but sometimes find difficult to accept. Despite missing so many months, he looks set to pass all his exams with A grades, and should eventually get to a top university. He might not ever be able to row for Oxford, but he will make an excellent doctor, which is his ambition.

One can only imagine the suffering he feels, when he is alone and unable to sleep, but it is not an emotion he reveals to the world. Like the airman Douglas Bader, who lost his legs in World War II but continued to fight, he will not accept his life has been ended by injury. He tells you he will fly again.

Because of all this, Jonathon is greater than Wayne Rooney or Neil Armstrong or anyone else I have ever heard of. He is so normal, but also so incredibly different. He convinces you that he can do anything he sets his mind on – and makes you re-examine your own existence and values. If he can overcome such hurdles, there should be nothing to stop any of us.

humorous simile

Describes effect he has on others.

Metaphor returns to idea of 'inspiration' mentioned at the start.

Top Tip!

When describing someone, you could add variety and interest by including:
- a conversation with them
- an anecdote about them
- someone else's view of them
- a newspaper report about them.

Good Points

- The response is well structured.
- There is description at every stage.
- When imagery is used, it creates an effect on the reader.
- The introduction and conclusion include memorable ideas.
- The writing is sensitive and touching.

Combining types of writing

- An option in Section B for both Papers is to write a response which involves more than one kind of writing. For example:
  - A question on Paper 1 might ask you to argue, persuade and advise.
  - A question on Paper 2 might require an answer that describes and explains.

- Any combination of writing skills is possible. You can use the skills you have learnt for each type of writing to cover all the types of writing that are required by the question. For lots of practice questions, you can use the *Exam Practice Workbook* which starts on page 97.

Task

Describe a place where you spend much of your time, for example:
- a swimming pool
- a club
- your bedroom.

Raising your grade

Key points

If you want to raise your grade to A or A*, you need to show the following skills. All the extracts are from a response to the question on the right:

> Write an article for your school magazine in which you:
> • argue in favour of good role models
> • seek to persuade the readers to accept your own suggestions about people we should admire.

Purpose and audience

• Show that you are aware of the **purpose** and **audience** throughout your response.

• Make sure the **form** of the writing suits the purpose, e.g. a letter, speech, advice leaflet.

• Make sure the **style** and **tone** suit the purpose and audience.

• Make sure the **content** is relevant and interesting.

> Why should we not hold up and admire someone who spends time raising money for charities rather than liberating cash from their parents to spend on the latest designer jeans?

Shows awareness of audience, as readers will be students and parents. Style and tone are formal, but the informal 'liberating cash' shows awareness of the context.

Shows awareness of purpose, as a rhetorical question is a persuasive device.

Communication

• Present **ideas** in a **convincing and original** way, e.g. by providing a striking introduction and conclusion.

• Use irony and imagery and other **techniques** as appropriate.

• Use **impressive vocabulary** wherever possible – go back and change words if necessary when you are checking your work.

• Show that you have complete **control over your sentences**, by varying their length, type and structure.

> Even though these sickeningly over-paid footballers are rich and these silky-thighed models have the world at their feet (which are beautifully pedicured, naturally), it does not mean that they make good role models.

Contrast of model and role model is an interesting idea.

interesting and unusual vocabulary

heavy irony, with humour

Structure of sentence is controlled and clear ('Even though … it does not mean …').

Structure and organisation

• Think carefully about the **overall organisation** of your response, e.g. referring back to the introduction in your conclusion.

• Make the structure crystal clear by using **paragraphs** accurately and effectively.

• **Link the text** within paragraphs by devices such as connectives, repetition and contrast.

> After all, why should we not revere the boy who goes through school with an excellent record? Why should we not cheer the girl who spends time helping out in an old people's home?

Repetition gives the sentences pattern and structure.

Connective links with previous paragraph.

Contrast (with boy) also used to link sentences.

Punctuation, grammar and spelling

- Show precise control of a **full range of punctuation**, including colons and semi-colons.
- Show ambitious **grammatical structures** in your sentences, e.g. by including strings of subordinate clauses.
- **Spell** a wide range of vocabulary **extremely accurately**.

> We should admire and seek to emulate those who have bravery or intelligence; or, indeed, those who help others needing support and comfort.

Sentence shows grammatical accuracy and control.

good use of semi-colon

mature vocabulary and accurate spelling

Read the question and an extract from the student's answer below. The annotations show why the examiner awarded it an A* grade.

Write an article for a magazine that is sold abroad, **informing** the readers about how most Britons spend their leisure time, and **explaining** why.

assured style and mature vocabulary

Grade A*

The British, then, enjoy complaining, and wallow in the national characteristic of self-criticism. Perhaps it all has to do with their colonial past, and a feeling that they can never enjoy themselves: it is more important to suffer – and if nothing is currently imposing torment, they must torture themselves.

ironic style, continued throughout the extract

interesting sentence structures, perfectly controlled

Ironically, they are also extremely patient in some ways, not least when they have the opportunity to queue. Whereas a Greek old lady will consider it a matter of pride to burrow to the front of any group waiting for anything and a Frenchman will shrug nonchalantly and wander off for a coffee until things subside, the Briton sighs with satisfaction and waits indefinitely for all those claiming priority to go before him. It has to do with school uniforms and standing for hymns and prayers in school assemblies for many centuries – the British constitution has been based on respect for order and understanding your place in the great scheme of things. So, the British wait. And wait. And if there is a line to queue in, so much the better.

light, mocking tone

assured control of style/content

sentence originality and variety

more irony

Oh, the satisfaction to be gained from a good long queue! The sense of community with those around you, the excitement as the line edges forward! These are joys that foreigners will never understand . . .

- This is a mature response. The student displays skilful control in all aspects:
  - the form, with the development of ideas, all linked by the ironic tone
  - the content, appropriate and subtly presented
  - the style, maintained throughout.

- The expression is always original, the sentences and the punctuation are varied and demonstrate a high level of technical expertise. There is a full range of appropriate sentence structures. For example, the waiting is emphasised by the sentences: 'So, the British wait. And wait.'

Answers

Reading media and non-fiction

Remember that there are no 'right or wrong' answers in English, as there are in Maths, for example. The answers below, therefore, are examples of the kind of responses that get high grades. Compare them with your own answers and decide if yours too contain the features needed to achieve a top grade.

page 9

Grade A*

The first text relies heavily on opinion. It wants people to watch *Emmerdale*, and implies that the new character is really going to stir things up ('Sharon's going to cause a lot of trouble'). In fact it even suggests that the fans are going to be so shocked that they 'had better brace themselves'. The alliteration here adds to the impact but also injects some humour. Two colourful and emotive adjectives are used: the Lambert family is described as 'flamboyant' and the particular member of the family herself is described as 'mouthy'. All these opinions, which make the show seem exciting, are backed up by the spokesperson for the soap. Such opinions, of course, are grounded in facts, such as details about the actress and how her character fits in with the story.

Whereas the first text relies so heavily on opinions, the second text begins with fact. As a newspaper report, it sets out exactly what is happening: who is collecting money, for which charity and why. Possibly to encourage people to help with donations, the report ends by printing the devastating facts related to the problems of Africa: over 2 million killed because of AIDS, and so on.

The first text makes exaggerated claims, but the second text is more sober and serious. When opinions are used, they come from Graham, talking about the unfairness in the world and how charities can change 'this injustice'. He makes presumptions about other people ('the problems … are hard for us even to imagine'), and lays the blame on 'chronic poverty' and 'recurring drought'. It is interesting that he does not criticise governments and policies – but perhaps that would stop some people from donating.

In conclusion, the texts are very different, but suitable for their contexts. The *Inside Soap* article is full of exaggerated opinions, to attract viewers; the newspaper is just reporting, factually, what Graham and Chris Lingard are doing, and allowing Graham to voice his concerned opinion.

page 13

Grade A

The writer fears he is becoming old. He misses *Top of the Pops*, and realises he is heading towards the final stage in his life. While he complains about the axing of *Top of the Pops* and how it has been replaced by channels like Kiss, there is an understanding that this is bound to happen. In contrast, his son is there to show how young people think and act.

The text is structured around a conversation between the two of them. Much of the text is about how pop music on TV has changed but, rather than just explaining how age changes us as well, the writer demonstrates it. He is 'aghast' at the television, while his son just shrugs: 'So?' The 'semi-naked girl' affects the writer's blood pressure, yet at the same time he feels happier with his 'memories of Tony Blackburn'; but the son never bats an eyelid. Contrast is used a lot as a technique for showing the difference between then and now. For example, the *Top of the Pops* DJ was 'friendly, reliable, old', as opposed to the 'semi-naked girls faintly disguised as pop artists'.

There is humour ('No drier in the toilet?'), but overall the text has a serious message. We are led to the rhetorical question we all have to face: 'What comes after that?' This thought makes the writer appreciate what he's got now, 'while I still can'.

page 17

Grade A

The text is from a holiday magazine, so it is trying to attract people to visit the island of Capri. The audience must be quite intelligent, because the first sentence is very long and the names could be quite confusing ('Sorrento, Positano, Salerno and Amalfi'). The particular audience targeted seems to be people who like the idea of a romantic, beautiful and historic holiday destination, because it is these aspects of Capri that are emphasised in the article.

The writer uses several linguistic devices to make the idea of a holiday on Capri seem exciting. There are two similes ('mythological statues sit like sentinels' and 'like a satellite') which conjure up powerful pictures in your mind's eye. The town of Anacapri is made to seem special by describing it as a 'Garden of Eden'; this is the paradise garden in the Bible, so we are meant to think of a holiday paradise. Powerful verbs and adjectives are used throughout to stir up interest: clouds don't just move but 'flee across the sky', and the alleyways are a 'labyrinth'. So the writer makes Capri special but also manages to make it seem easy to get to. It is 'just' 20 minutes from Sorrento, and then there is just a 'short ride' by railway to Capri town.

The advertisement is successful, because it uses a mixture of geographical detail, exaggeration and emotive description to paint a picture of a holiday destination that almost anyone would love to enjoy. It 'sells' Capri by describing it as a place of sights (the 'gaze' in the title) and relaxation ('laze').

page 20

The pull-quotes summarise the key points that the interviewees are making. For example, the cleaner's quote is 'I work hard because I have no choice', a harsh view of life which contrasts with the easier attitudes of the two people on either side of her.

page 23

Grade A

The report comes from a popular newspaper and is against the arrival of the ship. The way it is presented, looking grey, grim and dangerous, and the way a metaphor is used in the headline to describe it ('a toxic rust-bucket'), make the reader feel immediately that this is undesirable. The word 'protest' in the strapline reinforces this impression – it is something that people are up in arms about.

The report is very short, with just one sentence in each paragraph, which makes it easy to read. There is far more space given to the photo and the headlines. A serious newspaper would have gone into much more detail. This is simple reporting for those with little time or who would not be interested in more complex details. However, it packs a lot into a short space. The first paragraph gives the main details in a way that makes you want to read on: it is a 'rusting ghost ship' and the protesters are 'angry'. The next few paragraphs give vital background details, and the last paragraph gives the final words to a protester.

page 25

Grade A

In the *Times Educational Supplement* extract the language is inspiring: 'he discovered … the power'. This is, after all, to 'celebrate' his birthday. He is made to seem heroic: 'Stop a riot with a ballad', and an example to others, since the boys were 'transfixed'. The language, though, seems exaggerated.

By contrast, the language in Text 2 is unpleasant: 'misery', 'thugs'. Frank is pictured as a metaphorical prisoner. This is an estate plagued by 'stones', 'excrement', 'gangs' and fear. The final, matter-of-fact statement from the police seems cold and unfeeling, making us sympathise with the old people even more.

The ordinary reader will recognise the images in the newspaper article and will be upset by them – which is what the writer intended – whereas the image of Causley's children seems to come from a different age. They are 'unruly', which suggests just naughtiness, and they are not bad enough to require punishment. Teachers reading the obituary will feel admiration for him, but an ordinary reader might suspect his pupils were not evil if he found 50 or 60 of them easy to 'quell'.

Reading poems from different cultures and traditions

page 29

There are no 'correct' pairings: any pairings are acceptable, as long as you have a clear idea about how both poems focus on the given themes. All the poems below come from Cluster 1 of the Anthology, but you can compare poems from either cluster in your exam answer. Also, you will probably be able to think of other themes apart from those suggested here. This list is just a starting point for your revision.

Suffering

Limbo – slavery
What Were They Like? – contrast between peaceful life and war
Others possible: *Night of the Scorpion, Blessing, Nothing's Changed*

Poverty

Night of the Scorpion – family living conditions
Blessing – lack of water
Others possible: *Nothing's Changed, Two Scavengers in a Truck*

Inequality

Nothing's Changed – contrast between whites and blacks
Two Scavengers in a Truck – totally different lifestyles
Other possible: *Limbo*

Man and Nature

Vultures – linked through love and evil
What Were They Like? – what the war did to the country
Others possible: *Blessing, Night of the Scorpion, Island Man*

Contrasting cultures

Island Man – differences between past and present
Two Scavengers in a Truck – the rich and poor
Others possible: *Nothing's Changed*, any contrast between the cultures presented in the poems

page 31

Extract from a Grade A* response

People living in alien societies have to come to terms with their surroundings and learn to cope in their new world. In *from Search for My Tongue*, Bhatt reveals one major problem, a metaphorical loss of her mother tongue, but indicates it is not insurmountable; whereas in *Presents from My Aunts in Pakistan*, Moniza Alvi appears to be lost in unending turmoil, as if she will never feel comfortable and settled.

Bhatt's problem is, on the surface, one of language. Because she is using a foreign tongue, she feels as if her native one is dying in her mouth. Of course, this represents her whole culture, whilst the new culture is still strange to her. She feels as if she has:

> 'lost the first one, the mother tongue,
> and could not really know the other,
> the foreign tongue.'

A mother nurtures and protects us. It is a sense of safety that Bhatt fears she has lost.

Alvi is in a different position. She does not feel as if she has lost her culture, because her past in Pakistan is still a reality for her, represented by the clothes, memories, articles around her like the camel-skin lamp, and her visions of Lahore. At the same time, though, she has adopted western traits, and longs for some western culture, represented through clothes again:

> 'I longed
> for denim and corduroy.'

Such western styles are, no doubt, what her friends wear, and are very different from 'each satin-silken top' or the 'apple-green sari', the lovely but traditional clothes of her family, in which she feels uncomfortable:

'I could never be as lovely
as those clothes.'

She is torn between worlds.

She feels 'alien' because she does not fit in at all and seems trapped in her house, excluded as if 'behind fretwork at the Shalimar Gardens'; whilst Bhatt ultimately has a more positive experience, because she knows her original culture will always be a part of her, which is a relief. Right at the end, she says her native tongue:

'blossoms out of my mouth'
which suggests beauty and growth and a sweetness that will continue into her future …

page 35

Extract from a Grade A response

The poem is set in a hot country, where the people are poor and there is little water. When the pipe bursts and water shoots out, they become excited and rush out to collect it in anything they can. The children, meanwhile, play in it, delighted at the unexpected shower.

The poet has sympathy with these people, understanding their plight and stating simply:

'There never is enough water.'

She describes the effects, as skin 'cracks like a pod', and shows how they dream of water, so that we can almost hear it:

'Imagine the drip of it'.

She understands how important it is to them, because she describes it in religious terms ('kindly god', 'blessing'), while the people are like a 'congregation', in a way worshipping the water and what it represents in such a land. In fact, the water is seen as 'fortune', 'silver' and 'liquid sun', it is so valuable.

The message of the poem is that 'sometimes' things can be better. Of course, the way the people fight for the water shows how desperate they are; and though the children are happy when the water 'sings' over them, we finish with an image of their 'small bones' and know that soon there will be no water again.

Yet this is still much more positive than the message in *Not my Business*, where the suffering has no break. *Blessing* presents a vision which has joy, if not long-term hope; *Not my Business*, in contrast, reveals violence in a society where the enemy is human but is faceless and grim. And whereas Dharkar sees the problem as one of climate and a lack of water, Osundare focuses on the evil of mankind.

page 37

Extract from a Grade A* response

The poem is set out in two sections: the first asks a series of numbered questions about the people of Viet Nam; the second has numbered responses. The questions can be read together, as rhetorical queries; the responses also offer consecutive ideas. The questions offer a vision of the Vietnamese as artistic people:

'Did they use bone and ivory,
jade and silver, for ornament?'
Also, they seemed happy (with 'quiet laughter'), soft and musical:

'Did they distinguish between speech and singing?'

The responses present unpleasant answers, as 'light hearts turned to stone'. Each numbered response shows how their life and culture were destroyed:

'Sir, laughter is bitter to the burned mouth.'

The poem moves towards a bleak end – apparent extermination – as their traditions and happiness have all gone:

'It is silent now.'

The poem is structured in this way to make the reader remember all the qualities of life in Viet Nam before the war, then to reflect on the effect of the war on the country. The questions and responses are aimed to challenge readers and give them pause for thought: if this is the result, can such wars be justified?

The structure is effective, because the questions reveal a beautiful world, which is culturally distinctive and in which the Vietnamese are happy, at one with their environment:

'Did they hold ceremonies
to reverence the opening of buds?'

Then, the second section shatters the vision and violent language is introduced to shatter the peace: 'killed', 'burned', 'charred', 'smashed', 'scream'. In the silence, we are told there is just an echo of what went before – it seems to have faded as the poem has developed …

page 41

Extract from a Grade A response

Whereas Dharker's poem is positive, with vivid images of improvement, Alvi seems trapped. In *This Room*, chairs 'are rising', but Alvi 'couldn't rise up': the house, symbolising Dharker's life, is being re-born but Alvi is not like a phoenix, and it seems that although her clothes are colourful, she is just being metaphorically consumed by her existence: 'I was aflame'.

After the initial metaphors of hatching ('breaking out' and 'cracking'), Dharker introduces a list which offers openness: 'space, light, / empty air'. Then, we have 'lifting' and onomatopoeia and the use of 'c's, producing a climax with the alliteration of 'crash through clouds'.

Alvi, though, is describing a life which lacks that rush of optimism. Using alliteration, she contrasts the softness of the Pakistani clothes ('satin-silken') with the more basic British clothes she really desires: 'denim and corduroy'. The words themselves sound modern and western. The presents are more exotic but she explains in a simile she 'could never be as lovely as those clothes'. Between two cultures, she feels out of place and seems out of hope …

page 45

Extract from a Grade A response

Both *Half-Caste* and *from Search For My Tongue* concern people who are uncomfortable in the society where they live. John Agard is angry because he does not feel 'half' of anything, and sets out to prove he has as much right to be seen as a complete person as anyone else; Sujata Bhatt is worried because she thinks she is losing her mother tongue, through speaking English all day.

Agard demands an explanation for the way people speak to him: 'Explain yuself'. The problem is that if he is seen as 'half-caste', that is demeaning, and reduces his worth and standing. Because he does not want to be seen as 'half-caste', he produces a number of examples of how colours are mixed – in works by Picasso and Tchaikovsky and in the weather. Since none of these items are thought of as half-caste, why should it happen to him?

Bhatt's problem, though, is her own. She is uncomfortable handling two languages, which represent two cultures, and since she speaks in a foreign tongue she thinks her mother tongue could die, like a flower. She believes it dies and rots, and she spits it out and thinks she is left with only the new language.

Since she uses the metaphor of a flower to talk about her language, it shows she thinks it is delicate and beautiful. However, the metaphor is expanded and she reveals that in reality the tongue, like a plant, grows back in the night whilst she dreams. Indeed, it seems to be the superior language, because she says 'It ties the other tongue in knots'; and she sounds delighted at the end, when the mother tongue 'blossoms'. It is as if summer has come back into her life.

Agard, meanwhile, is sarcastic:
> 'Excuse me
> standing on one leg
> I'm half-caste'.

By making ridiculous statements, he is mocking those who label him. Bhatt's tongue comes back in a dream – but Agard says that he only dreams 'half-a-dream' and is not even a complete human being. Making fun of those who label him, he demands they come back as whole people to see him:
> 'wid de whole of yu ear
> and de whole of yu mind'.

It is as if they are the ones with limitations. Then, he says, they will learn he is a whole person:
> 'an I will tell yu
> de other half
> of my story'.

These final lines are in a stanza on their own, to highlight Agard's cynicism and anger. We are never allowed to forget the poem is about his bitterness about the idea of 'halfness', a concept that usefully frames the poem, as it is introduced in the first three lines. His use of colloquialism, lack of formal punctuation and use of speech patterns successfully help to identify him as of mixed race, but that never suggests he lacks intelligence: the references to Picasso and Tchaikovsky, and his use of words like 'consequently', in addition to the cleverness of his ideas, reveal the quality of his mind.

Bhatt's feelings are also shown successfully. Her mother tongue is used in the poem to show us what she dreams; it also shows us how problematic it must be to live with a difficult second language. What is clear, though, is how relieved Bhatt is when her tongue survives, and this is cleverly shown as it grows from a rotten leftover, to a stump, up to a bud, then a flower which blossoms. The poem begins with her unhappiness at having lost her tongue, but ends with its recovery and the relief of the poet.

Writing

page 51

Your answer is likely to be based upon your own experiences. It is important, though, that you have developed the main ideas: at least three or four details should be included in each section. Having first produced a quick spider diagram, your more detailed ideas might be:

1 Teams
Develop skills, fitness, teamwork
Football: all ages, each evening, matches at weekends, all welcome
Rugby: currently only for older students but could be extended, growth sport in the country, school matches all over the county
Hockey and netball: teachers enthusiastic, school has won lots of matches

2 Clubs and societies
Convenient: most held during lunch break and lunch time, really popular (e.g. ICT and dance – modern, not 'Men in Tights'); plays performed recently

3 Trips
Just this year: History to the Somme, Geography field trip, England international, French exchange, visit to German market, Spanish holiday – chances to escape lessons without digging a tunnel

4 Final positives
Results in a Record of Achievement – useful when applying for jobs, and a way to unwind.

page 55

We knew nothing about the plans because the intelligence services, which are very secretive, told us nothing. It is all very sad because we could have issued warnings. We apologise and we wish we could turn back the clock, though that is simply not possible.

page 57

At home, Uncle Tom spends acres of time in his study. And this isn't because he delights in the piles of grubby school books that he has to mark. No, it's to escape from the dreaded Aunt Sylvia. Which also explains why he works long hours in school, a grim post-war building complex 3 miles down the road.

page 60

(Grade A*)

The problem for most single parents (men and women) [1] is that they have so little time to do anything but care for their children and work. Days are all the same: [2] make what seem like endless meals; [3] clean and tidy the house; work in an

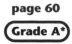

attempt to pay for next week's **4** food; and get as much sleep as possible. It's **5** a limited existence! **6**

But what can be done? **7** There must be ways that these people can make their lives a little easier.

'As far as I am concerned,' **8** said Mr Grayson, **9** who works for a government agency, ' **8** all we can do is make clear the benefits they can claim and offer, **10** wherever possible, support workers to help them through. Then it depends how the individual reacts …' **11**

Locally, **12** a considerable amount of money has been put into the system to help single parents – **13** over £500,000 – but it does not seem to have done the trick. Every single parent I spoke to was struggling. Perhaps Mr Grayson needs to come up with some more ideas? **14**

Comments

There are rules to be followed when punctuating, but writers have some flexibility. Often slightly different punctuation produces a different emphasis. The answer above, therefore, shows some possibilities.

1 The brackets here are used to add information about 'single parents'. They could be replaced by commas or by dashes.

2 The colon is being used to introduce a list.

3 Semi-colons are used to separate the parts of the complicated list.

4 An apostrophe is needed because the phrase means 'the food of next week'.

5 Another apostrophe is needed here, but in this case it is an apostrophe of omission ('It is …').

6 The exclamation mark is used here to give emphasis. It would, however, be perfectly acceptable to keep the full stop, which would make the statement more matter-of-fact; or an ellipsis could be used to make the statement fade away, almost like the existence itself seems to make people fade away.

7 A question mark is essential to complete the rhetorical question.

8 The speech marks go around the words actually spoken. The first part of what Mr Grayson says ends with the comma; then, when he continues the same sentence, we use a comma, speech marks and a lower case letter.

9 Commas go around the additional information about Mr Grayson. Brackets could also have been used, but that would not have been ideal if they had already been used in the first sentence.

10 Commas go around the phrase 'wherever possible', which Mr Grayson uses to qualify what he says.

11 The ellipsis implies there is more to be said. It could be replaced with a full stop or an exclamation mark, if the writer wanted Mr Grayson to sound more 'up-beat', or to imply that seeing how people react can be quite exciting. Speech marks conclude what Mr Grayson said.

12 'Locally' adds information to the main clause, which follows it. It is usual to use a comma to separate an adverb used in this way from the main sentence.

13 The dashes lend emphasis to the sum of money. Again, they could be replaced by commas or brackets here.

14 The rhetorical question ends the article. A full stop could have been used, but then the writer would have been making a statement, rather than questioning more directly Mr Grayson's range of ideas. An exclamation mark would have given the final sentence a more lively ending.

page 65

Grade A*

Almost everyone who lives in Horbury will tell you it's a good place to live: 'It's grand here. Smashing little place.' It is quiet, green and safe; the little shops sell us everything we might need, the shopkeepers have smiles, a cheery word and time to look after us properly; and it is even perfectly situated for travel around the north of England, close to the motorways and a main-line railway station. In many ways, it is West Yorkshire at its best. Who, then, could ask for anything more?

In all honesty, many Horbury folk would like to see improvements. People are full of ideas about what could be done to make our haven much better, despite the generally positive feelings about the town. We pay our council taxes, so perhaps the council should listen to our concerns?

First, more senior residents need some sort of centre to visit and spend time with friends. The cafés are too expensive for them, and most do not want to spend all day in the pubs. My grandfather will sit in Boons' Pub nursing a pint for over an hour, but he would prefer to be elsewhere. All that he and his friends need is a warm building with tea-making facilities and a few comfortable chairs. They must have earned that in their lifetime.

Meanwhile, their children, the parents of the town, repeatedly complain about the state of the park. They want things for their children: a skate park without vandals; playing fields without dog excrement; a safe environment for even the youngest toddlers. The council should invest in a park warden and should ensure the police are visible to prevent any problems. A community constable on the beat would produce massive improvements.

Finally, there are the teenagers. What do they want? Only a theme park, multiplex cinema, Hollywood Bowl … Of course, they currently complain there is nothing for them but street corners, bus shelters and windswept fields – and they are correct. If they do not want to stay at home and lose themselves in video games, they have no alternative but to linger outdoors and annoy others by their very presence. The world has moved on and the young expect to have entertainment close at hand. A theme park is rather optimistic, but they would be more content if they even had a coffee bar or club to head for in the evenings.

We only live once and we all have a right to enjoy our time here. Horbury is excellent, but not perfect. 'Still, it wouldn't really take much to make it even better, would it?' said one old man. And he was right.

page 69

Grade A*

We take so much for granted in our lives. What we have, we hardly notice; what we lack, we desire. And yet we are the fortunate ones: we have a stable society, social care, heat and light, sanitation and houses, transport and employment, wages and pensions. If only everyone in the world could enjoy the standard of living that makes Britain such a comfortable place to live for almost all its citizens. And if only we in Britain would recognise our good fortune and begin to give more back to those in so much need.

What better way do we have to show our humanity than to become involved in charity work? It has its own rewards; we can reap our own benefits.

What is more, the organisations which look after the needy are crying out for volunteers and fund-raisers, and perhaps you could lend a hand. You could be the one the old lady smiles at when her meal arrives; or the one giving clothes to people who have a life on the streets and little more; or packing parcels to be distributed in any number of trouble spots around the world; or simply running a marathon to help research into cancer or Parkinson's disease.

Last Christmas, I took a step into the unknown and worked in a hostel for the homeless. It was grim, and the men who stayed there were broken. But they were grateful for a bed and some warmth and for just a few days they could escape the hell of their lives on the streets. I was part of making that happen – only a small part, but I would not have missed it for the world. And I know that other hostels need other volunteers, and there is always a role for you, if you are prepared to give rather than just receive.

The simple fact is that, whether you want to be directly involved or simply raise money, every charity will welcome your interest. But don't wait for tomorrow to contact someone; do it today. Later, you might forget. Later, you might have changed your mind. 'Later' can sometimes mean 'never', which can mean a baby dies in Africa or a dog continues to be mistreated in Aldborough or a teenager cries in Altrincham.

Why not enrich your life by helping to make the world a better place and giving some of your energies to the world of charity? You can move clouds aside for others, see the sun shine down and feel its power in your own world too. It is an opportunity that is too good to miss!

page 73

Grade A*

Dear Miss Knowles,

I am sure you will have no shortage of advice about what our £100,000 windfall should be spent on. On behalf of Year 11, however, I have been asked to summarise our views on this matter, and we hope they will be of some interest to you. We have been in the school for five years and are aware of exactly what it needs most; and, in addition, many of our students have attended other schools in the past, so they have experience of how particular facilities and improvements can be of enormous benefit.

It will come as no surprise that our priority is a Year 11 Common Room. That deserves financial support because it would remove some current and serious problems: foolish behaviour on the corridors by the troublemaking few; congestion in the yard; and students leaving the premises because there is nowhere for them to settle within the campus. To provide decorations, furniture and the conversion of the old gym, you will need to spend up to £20,000 on this development, but it will be money well spent.

Next, we strongly advise you to invest in sports equipment as this is in a chronic state. We can no longer play tennis using racquets with holes in them, or football without proper posts

and nets. Our sporting results are already good, but improvements could make us the leading sports school in the area, and that would prove an uplift for the whole school – just remember the reaction in England after the Rugby World Cup. It is likely that the less academically inclined will respond really positively to these sports improvements. I am certain this advice will be supported by the PE and Special Needs Departments, as well as the main body of the school.

The remainder of the money can be put towards the new minibus – which should mean we will be able to buy it before the end of the year – and into computers for the library, which will help all those who go to the homework club each evening.

We feel that it is better to put significant sums of money into relatively few projects, so that the impact is considerable, rather than spreading it thinly across a multitude of different good causes. We are confident that this makes good sense and hope that you will listen to our advice. Others will make suggestions to you, but we in Year 11 have experienced five years in this school; we know which problems are the most important to address.

Yours sincerely,

page 77

Grade A*

Both in school and outside, I spend most of my spare time on drama of one kind or another. These are not the everyday dramas of teenage relationships and forgetting homework – though I have some experience of those too – but the more serious kind: acting, performance, productions.

I attend a drama group twice weekly, audition locally and appear in at least two major productions each year. I have appeared on television too, which means I now have an agent and am hoping to get an Equity card in the near future: that will show I have been accepted as a professional actor and it guarantees me proper rates of pay!

My drama group does not put on productions. It exists to teach skills and allows us to improvise and empathise. The advanced class has been together now for almost four years. We know each other well and that means we trust each other, and can open up emotionally without fear or embarrassment. Jude, our teacher, says, 'It's all cathartic,' which means it helps us get frustrations out of our systems. I think she's right, and I always get back home feeling much happier about life.

While the group ticks on smoothly, the productions just keep coming along too. There are always advertisements for people to audition for serious plays and musicals, and I have landed some challenging parts. I've been in Osborne's *Luther* and Friedrich Durrenmatt's *The Physicists*; and I've 'Doh, a deer'-ed in *The Sound of Music* as well as being a sailor in *HMS Pinafore*. My friends sometimes laugh at me about my passion for drama but, apart from the constant thrill I get from assuming a persona other than my own, acting allows me to meet so many girls that I think I am the one who should be laughing.

People at school certainly sat up and took note when I was on television last year. I auditioned for a part in a documentary, and made my television debut in a re-enactment scene. The programme was called *Premature Burial* and was about what happens when someone is diagnosed 'dead' but is really still alive. I played a Russian boy whose uncle was run over by the secret police but survived. Mine was only a small part, but it helped me attract an agent, who has since got me various auditions for advertisements. Performing in these can be very lucrative so now I have another reason to develop my acting skills: my aim is to be rich and famous by the age of 21!

While I am waiting for fame to call, I shall keep on doing what I have been doing because it seems to be my whole life. At times, I lose interest in other school work, but I have to persevere because I shall almost certainly want to go to stage school or drama college, and the GCSEs will be essential.

Of course, if I am picked for the next Coca-Cola advert, I shall have to think seriously about paying someone to do the exams for me …

page 81
Grade A*

Problems rarely have a simple solution, and that has been true of the main difficulties that I have had to face in my life. Looking back, I can identify two situations which caused me heartache and sleepless nights. Both of them were important because they concerned not only my own happiness, but also that of others.

Firstly, I had to cope with a grandmother who was living with us, and dying. She did not have a disease the doctors could cure; rather, she seemed to give up the will to live after a fall that rendered her unable to walk, and she just faded away, over the course of almost two years. She also developed cataracts that she refused to have treated and she eventually just about stopped eating. I had to be bright and cheerful around her and, increasingly, try to forget about her when I was studying or trying to sleep. It was the only way to survive, to support my parents and continue to care for my grandmother. I somehow managed to keep on top of my schoolwork and helped my parents by doing many of the things they no longer had time for, like gardening. This also kept me occupied, and my mind engaged.

It seems cruel, but when she died I could relax, because I knew I had survived. I loved my grandma but, by the end, I was getting through the ordeal by treating her as a problem, rather than as a person.

The second major problem was when one of my friends, Alicia, died in a car crash and my best friend blamed herself for what had happened. She had allowed Alicia to go home with her boyfriend, even though he had been drinking, and he crashed his motorbike: neither of them survived. My friend had a terrible few weeks, crying and saying it was all her fault. All I could do was be there for her. I felt close to despair at times but I listened, and tried to make her see Alicia had made her own decision – she should not blame herself.

Gradually, I persuaded her to go out again. I even arranged a date for her with my cousin and this was a starting point. She re-entered the real world. I did not feel proud but I felt relieved and glad that her improvement was partly down to something I had done.

I know that I have come through two testing times, but it is never possible to feel secure, is it? There will always be another problem, another decision to make, another person needing help. Then we have to start dealing with it all again.

page 85
Grade A*

Many places in which we spend a good deal of our time offer little of real interest: the local shops, the city centre, the bus shelter at the end of the road. We tend to think of our everyday environment with a shrug and, although we know these places have features, we often no longer register them because we know them so well. However, when you also spend a good deal of your time somewhere very different, that place can seem to exist in more vibrant colours and offer more distinct impressions. This is the case for me with Croyde in North Devon.

My family and I do not only go to Croyde because it has such a beautiful beach, although that is one of its attractions. The sand stretches soft and long and yellow around the bay, and the sea lures surfers from all over the country. We love the crashing waves, the grasses rustling in the sand dunes and the water courses running down from the hills, across the beach and into the sea; but there is more to Croyde than the beach …

At the end of the road to the coast lies Ruda, a camping and caravan park like no other. It is spotlessly clean, and it includes a leisure complex that should be a template for other such sites around the country. There are numerous bars, entertainment daily for both children and adults, and restaurants bursting with exotic menus.

Beside it, the Ruda Pool is cheap to enter and exciting. The smell of chlorine hovers around the immediate area, but that is hardly surprising because it opens from the conventional tropical inside onto a sunshine area outside; and it has a slide, waves and two giant racoons parading around and enlivening the holiday for children. It is open until late in the evening, and screams are still coming from the building at nine o'clock at night.

Back up the road lies Croyde village: once sleepy, no doubt, but now pretty and old and offering good food and the finest ice-cream shop this side of the Atlantic. Miraculously, the village rarely jams with traffic and rarely tastes of exhaust fumes. Instead, it is sunny and green and full of richness. The houses are of stone, animals are within metres of the village centre and, despite the visitors that flood the area in summer, it continues to embody a rural life that we usually have to read about in old books.

It is because of these things that we love Croyde and travel there so often. It is the sort of place that gets inside you and stays there; it spices your dreams when you are away and welcomes you when you return. The thought of going back can make even the local shops, the city centre and the bus shelter more bearable.

Index

Collins Revision

GCSE
English
Exam Practice Workbook

FOR AQA A

Written by Keith Brindle

How to use this workbook

This exam practice workbook is designed to help you develop your exam skills and test how well you are doing. Hopefully, it will show you are 'on the right lines' as well as pointing out some areas that you might be able to improve.

It deals with the final exams only because your coursework has to be completed before the exam period.

It links closely to the pattern of the AQA A GCSE English exam:

English Paper 1	Final exam: 1 hour 45 minutes	Section A: 1 hour Reading media and non-fiction texts 15% of final marks	Section B: 45 mins Writing to argue, persuade, advise 15% of final marks
English Paper 2	Final exam: 1 hour 30 minutes	Section A: 45 mins Poems from different cultures and traditions 15% of final marks	Section B: 45 mins Writing to inform, explain, describe 15% of final marks
Coursework	Produced during the course	4 written assignments 20% of final marks	3 speaking and listening assignments 20% of final marks

There are five major sections in the exam practice workbook:

Paper 1: Reading media and non-fiction texts (pages 100 – 123)

Paper 2: Poems from different cultures and traditions (pages 124 – 161)

The skills required for Section B (Writing) responses (pages 164 – 173)

Paper 1: Writing to argue, persuade, advise (pages 174 – 181)

Paper 2: Writing to inform, explain, describe (pages 182 – 189)

As you work through the book, you can check how well you have done by referring to the Answers further on in this book or by visiting **www.collinseducation.com/easylearning**. Here you will find full mark and grade guidance given in a **free** easy-to-download format.

How to use this workbook

Work through the tasks provided in the different sections and then mark your own work to find how well you have done. This will test your ability to respond to the requirements of each part of the exam.

Paper 1 Section A: Reading media and non-fiction texts

The same skills are tested in the exam each year, so you can aim to maximise your performance by practising the essential skills. The exercises allow you to check how well you can follow an argument, comment on presentational devices, and so on.

Paper 2 Section A: Poems from different cultures and traditions

There are double pages on each of the set poems, so both Clusters are included. There is a final section which gives the opportunity to practise the skill of comparing poems, using exam-style questions.

Skills for Section B responses

The Writing skills for both papers have much in common so you can practise planning, writing effective openings and endings and using high quality features such as quotations and anecdotes, as well as a range of punctuation and functional skills.

Paper 1 Section B: Writing to argue, persuade, advise

You have the opportunity to deal with each kind of writing in the triplet, as well as combining their requirements, in the sort of question that blends these forms in the exam itself. At the end of each section, there is another title for you to tackle, to help you improve your performance.

Paper 2 Section B: Writing to inform, explain, describe

This section follows the same pattern as the previous one, but focuses on the forms of writing which feature in Section B of Paper 2.

Paper 1 Section A: Reading media and non-fiction

Responding to the questions

Section A of Paper 1 should take you one hour to complete. The exam paper will contain two or three texts. You will have to read them and then answer questions on them. There are likely to be just two questions broken into smaller parts so you will probably have to offer four, five or six answers.

The questions will focus on the following assessment objectives:

(i) *read, with insight and engagement, making appropriate references to texts and developing and sustaining interpretations of them;*

(ii) *distinguish between fact and opinion and evaluate how information is presented;*

(iii) *follow an argument, identifying implications and recognising inconsistencies;*

(iv) *select material appropriate to their purpose, collate material from different sources, and make cross-references;*

(v) *understand and evaluate how writers use linguistic, structural and presentational devices to achieve their effects, and comment on ways language varies and changes.*

These may seem very difficult and confusing but they mean that when you examine the texts, you will be writing about how the writers:

- use fact and opinion
- construct their argument
- use language
- use presentational devices and, possibly, structure.

You are also likely to have to say how successful the writers have been; and will probably have to make a comparison of some kind between the texts. You will be expected to support your ideas with appropriate references. This means that whatever you say should be linked to the purpose and audience of the texts.

Although nothing is absolutely certain, the first set of questions might be about fact and opinion, argument and the texts' purposes and audiences. The second set of questions is likely to focus on the media aspect of one text or both texts and you will probably be asked to write about presentation and language in that part.

When answering the questions, you should consider the following advice:

1 Notice how many marks are available for each question, and use your time appropriately. You should spend about two minutes per mark, since there are 27 marks for Section A

2 Look closely at the question and make sure you are producing exactly what is required. Do not just write about the texts in general terms. If necessary, underline the important words in the question, so your attention is focused

3 Offer evidence for any ideas you give, either by referring to something in the text or by quoting directly. Remember that the PEE technique (point/evidence/explanation) is the best approach.

The paper will look like this:

Paper 1 consists of two sections. Only Section A of the exam paper is given here.

Paper 1 Section A: Higher Tier

In addition to this paper you will require:
- Text 1: *Need a break? Want a change? Why not try Bognor …?*, from a weekend magazine
- Text 2: *Ancient art of relaxing*, from the *Sunday Express*

These are the texts that you will be given in full in the exam. They are both media texts. They are not reproduced here.

READING: NON-FICTION AND MEDIA TEXTS

Answer all the questions in Section A.
Spend approximately 60 minutes on Section A.

Remember to spend up to 10 minutes of this time reading the texts carefully, before answering the questions themselves.

This question is asking you to identify the purpose and audience of Text 1 – not to write about the text in general.

1 Re-read Text 1: *Need a break? Want a change? Why not try Bognor …?*

  a) What is the intended purpose and audience for this text? Give your reasons. *(5 marks)*

  b) How does the writer try to convince us of his argument? Explain:
  - the main points of his argument
  - how fact and opinion are used
  - how other techniques are used. *(9 marks)*

This refers to any persuasive techniques that the writer uses, such as anecdotes, statistics or humour.

This question is asking you to show how well you can follow, and evaluate, the argument. Make sure that you cover all the bullet points in your answer.

2 Next, re-read Text 2: *Ancient art of relaxing*.

  a) Why have the presentational devices been included? To what extent are they appropriate for the text? *(5 marks)*

Finally, compare the two texts.

  b) How does each writer use language? *(8 marks)*

Total: 27 marks

This question is asking you to think about the use of such devices as headlines, photos, graphics, bullet points, use of colour and design and to comment on their effectiveness.

Note how many marks are awarded for each question, and allocate your time accordingly.

The final question usually asks you to compare the texts. In this case, you are being asked to compare only their use of language. To compare, you will need to use material from both texts, and make cross-references between them.

Purpose and audience

Why are purpose and audience important?

You might be asked to write about the purpose and audience of a particular text.

If that does not happen, the purpose and audience are still key considerations, because each element of the texts you will be looking at are chosen for a particular purpose.

Purpose

1 Why has the writer written this text? You might wish to offer alternative ideas but try to support what you say with quotations from the article.

_____

_____

_____

_____

_____

_____

_____

_____ *(4 marks)*

Hero beats the Atlantic – now for GCSEs!

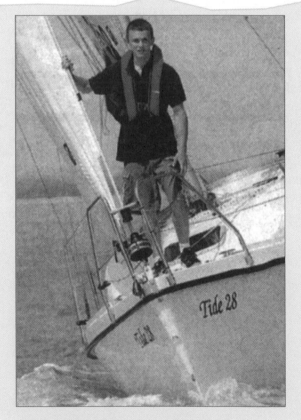

Michael Perham is fourteen years old but has his name in the record books. He sailed single-handedly across the Atlantic, alone for six whole weeks. He faced gales, 25 foot waves, danger from larger ships, loneliness and sharks. But back on dry land, he now has to face the ultimate test: his GCSE examinations.

Michael seemed very calm after arriving in Antigua, and was looking forward to returning to his home in Hertfordshire. However, the small matter of GCSE exams stand between him and his next voyage, a non-stop round-the-world trip he is planning.

He has a great deal to do before he can set out again. After all, he only took some RE work with him this time, yet did not find a moment to start on that, even with six watery weeks on his hands. He might well be a hero to his classmates, but his teachers will just see him as someone who needs to catch up!

Michael on his yacht, sailing back to his studies.

Sunday Times, 21.01.07

Audience

2 Below, there are some extracts from texts. Say:
- who you think they were written for
- why you have come to that decision.

Extract	Audience	Reason for decision	Marks
'For the woman in your life: "Erotique", the new fragrance by Henri.'	————		2
'Throughout the nineteenth century, nurses continued to do as they were told by doctors. They knew their place.'	————		3
'Discipline your children. No longer can they be allowed to do exactly as they wish.'	————		3
'Investors in Sun Life Assurance of Canada rejoiced earlier today, as share values reached unprecedented heights.'	————		3

Audience and purpose

3 What is the purpose of this text, and how does it appeal to its audience?

Continue on lined paper if necessary. (6 marks)

Selecting relevant information

What information do I have to select?

In Section A of Paper 1, you are being tested on your ability to locate precisely the right details to answer the questions correctly. You might have to comment on the information as well.

Read this report.

Tiny Stanningly Village has never seen a night like last night – and may never do again!

For a top rock band to agree to play for an audience of just 100 people is unusual enough. For such a band to play for free, for nearly two hours, is probably unprecedented. Yet that is what Silver Snake did, last night, on the Stanningly village green. And it was all designed to help a little girl enjoy the final days of her life.

When Silver Snake heard about seven year-old Jodie Graham, who has terminal cancer but adores the Snakes and their music, they got in touch immediately. The concert was planned in matter of days. Jodie, her friends, family and neighbours were all invited whilst the remainder of the village could just sit in their garden and listen as well!

'They were fantastic,' said Jodie. 'It's been a dream come true.'

For the Snakes, their manager, Chrissie Hallett, said, 'The guys heard about Jodie, and were pleased to do all they could. She's a great little kid.'

The manager chatted to Jodie for an hour and presented her with a signed copy of the band's latest CD, T-shirts and posters.

'They have brought joy into her heart,' said Jodie's mum.

1 List five things that made Jodie's life happier.

_____

_____

_____

_____

_____

_____

_____

(5 marks)

2 What detail in this report might suggest that the band could have done more?

_____

_____

_____

(2 marks)

This is a letter, sent to a newspaper, about a young man who was shot as a deserter in the First World War.

It is difficult to find words to express my sadness at the attitudes of the villagers of Shoreham who feel unable to include the name of Private Jack Brown, shot for desertion, on their war memorial.

Brown was a boy of 19 when he experienced the horrors of the battles of Mons and Le Cateau in World War I. Many were sent insane by the experience. Private Brown cracked and ran away.

I was on active service at the age of 18: I didn't undergo 1 pc of this lad's experience, but I'm not ashamed to admit that I was scared when I was fired on. Only a fool would not be. The desire to run away becomes over-whelming in any normal human being.

So, Shoreham, put this boy's name on your memorial. Let him at last rest in the peace he deserved.

P SMITH, Maidstone, Kent

3 What do we learn about Private Jack Brown? Write down four facts.

_____

_____

_____

_____

_____

_____

(4 marks)

4 What sort of person is writing the letter? Quote to prove what you are saying.

_____

_____

_____

_____

_____

_____

_____

(6 marks)

This is another letter on the same topic.

Some of those executed during World War I were guilty not of desertion, but of murder and rape. Others had already been warned for disobeying orders or neglecting their duties.

Without a painstaking examination of every case, we run the great risk of putting such people's names on war memorials alongside those of heroes who conquered their fear and died doing their duty.

B JONES, Bournemouth, Dorset

5 In your own words, say why this writer has a different viewpoint.

_____

_____

_____

_____

_____

_____

(4 marks)

Developing interpretations

What does this mean?

Think about moving beyond the obvious and try to decipher what a writer is trying to say about a person or a situation. This development becomes clearer as you link ideas and possibilities.

This is a programme preview from a television magazine.

Little Britons in the Sun

Benidorm : ITV

A couple of years ago, I went on the worst holiday of my life – a package deal to Turkey for about the price of a pint. It was the week of 9/11, but the holidaymakers in Marmaris seemed unfazed. As long as they could tan their skin red, take full advantage of the all-you-can-eat buffet, and drink themselves into oblivion, all was well. I might have thought *Benidorm* was the stuff of fantasy had I not experienced Marmaris.

This new comedy is set in the Solana resort in Spain. Not that it makes any difference, as no one moves from the pool. Here, going abroad is not about the experience of a new culture. It's about bringing Britain with you.

All the usual suspects are here – family from Hell, complete with racist, chain-smoking granny, middle class couple who couldn't be any less enamoured with their surroundings, or indeed, each other, pub quiz champion and his mother. My 'favourites' are Jacqueline and David, the husband and wife who enjoy crosswords.

In places, this is very funny. But there's also something deeply depressing about *Benidorm*, which has more to do with the subject matter than the quality of the writing. There are those within Britain who are fairly intolerant of cultural differences. Rather than laughing my way through the programme, I found myself thinking that these kinds of holidays might go some way to explaining (though not excusing) some racist behaviour we witness. If going abroad means actively seeking segregation from other cultures, perhaps the traditional British package holiday is more damaging than we realise.

Nicole Jackson
The Observer Television Magazine, 01.02.07

1 What worries does the writer have about package holidaymakers?
Make close reference to the text in your answer.

(5 marks)

This is an extract from a longer text.

Even amongst those who knew him well and might call him a friend, Anthony Jaggers was a person to be handled with care. According to the movie director who set out to chart Jagger's life, the man was simply evil. Those who did not have the luxury of escape across the Atlantic have usually been more guarded in their assessments, though many regarded him with absolute terror.

Strange, then, that someone like Miranda Stanbridge should speak fondly of him after his death. To hear her obituary for him, you might think the man had spent much of his life in church and all his spare time working for charities and the environment. On national television, she spoke of his kindness and compassion.

Had she misjudged him totally; or were there two sides to the man once labelled 'The Dark Avenger'?

There can be no doubting the fact that he attended church regularly, though whether that influenced his life for the better is less sure. Similarly, he was seen at charity events in the Home Counties, but the size of his contributions to good causes has never been revealed. He was also a loving son to his mother, who doted on him. She seems to have overlooked the fact that he was imprisoned in the 1970s for battering to death his cousin, who was just fifteen at the time …

2 To what extent does the writer balance the different views of Jaggers' personality?

_____

_____

_____

_____

_____

_____

_____

_____ *(4 marks)*

3 What do you think is the writer's opinion of the man, and how is it made clear to the reader?

_____

_____

_____

_____

_____

_____

_____

_____

_____

_____ *(4 marks)*

Fact and opinion

Is it enough to be able to spot facts and opinions?

No. It is almost certain that you will have to write about *how* facts and opinions have been *used* by the writer. You might, for example, be asked to find two facts and two opinions and say how they support the writer's argument and whether the argument is convincing.

This is an extract from a blog produced by a scientist based in Antarctica.

22 December

We are all working hard and checking temperatures, air quality and the thickness of the ice on a regular basis. However, with Christmas approaching, we seem to have a little more spare time, and I have been able to enjoy some of the delights that this incredible white expanse has to offer.

I've been out on a boat, and a huge pod of Orca whales swam past. Fantastic! I've even seen young elephant seals sunning themselves through the day, and Weddell seals and some nesting skuas, which fly at you if you go near. The penguins are just crazy: and I mean they are not very bright at all. On land, they rush towards you, then panic when they notice you are not a penguin, and try to run away and fall over. Yesterday, one of the stupid birds actually leapt out of the sea and into our boat for a few seconds. Then he shook his head and leapt back into the waves. Maybe he had thought we were a taxi?!

The best thing yet has been our transparent glacier ice. We brought it back from a trip to see some small crevasses that are opening up on the glacier. It's not like normal blue glacier ice. We keep it in the fridge and put it into our drinks. Imagine having ice that is thousands of years old with your gin and tonic ...

1 Find five facts about what the scientist has been doing and five opinions that show his attitude towards what has happened.

Facts	Opinions

(5 marks)

2 What is the scientist's attitude towards her life in the Antarctic? How does she use facts and opinions to show her attitude?

_____

_____

_____

_____

_____

_____

(6 marks)

Continue on lined paper if necessary.

This is an article from a magazine.

Jennifer Aniston: happier than ever!

People keep feeling sorry for Jennifer Aniston – but goodness only knows why. 'Tragic Jen' or 'poor Jen' seems to be how the media see her: yet we have to ask why. She is a beautiful, talented multi-millionairess; seems to have recovered remarkably quickly from her two splits from Brad Pitt and Vince Vaughn; and, surely, won't be single for long.

Approaching 40, she looks as good as ever, and the world's favourite ex-*Friend* is still one of the hottest properties in show business. She has much to thank the show for. She was paid an incredible million dollars an episode for the later series, has been nominated for an Emmy five times and been on the cover of *Vanity Fair*. And then there is her hair: it makes the world's hairdressers go weak at the knees.

She has, recently, appeared in a number of movies, and TV shows, to rave reviews (*Friends with Money*, *The Break-Up*, *Dirt*), has been talking about adopting a baby boy, following the lead of Angelina Jolie, and must, surely, be looking for a new and more lasting partner. 'I don't make plans,' she says – but the woman who has regularly topped polls for the 'world's sexiest' must have pretty limitless options.

As far as she is concerned, as long as she is happy, that is all that matters.

Sunday Express Magazine, 28.01.07

3 How are facts and opinions used to create a positive image of Jennifer Aniston? Is the writer successful in her aim?

_____

_____

_____

_____

_____

_____

_____

_____

_____

_____

_____ *(8 marks)*

Follow an argument

What will I have to do?

There will always be one question that requires you to read through a text and show you understand how the writer has put across the argument. You are likely to have to explain the main points and write about the techniques used in the text, for example, the use of contrast, quotation, examples and so on.

Read this extract.

Last night, I was re-reading ...

Isn't it incredible how so few educated people refuse to admit they read so little? 'What do you think of Plato's *Republic*?' you ask them. 'Oh, very grand, very grand ...', they reply. Of course, if you ask what they found grand about it, they make a rapid exit. Almost certainly, they have never even used the book to stand their coffee on, never mind as late-night entertainment, as they sip their hot cocoa. But why don't they just say: 'I've never read it. When I do read – mostly on the beach – I prefer books with lots of killing/romance/humour/romping in. Philosophy is deadly'? Because they would feel shown up, that's why. Life is too competitive, even when you leave the playground.

There seems no end to the pressure, because those who do read regularly over-state their qualities. Instead of 'I've just been reading *The Da Vinci Code* and ...', they regale us with: 'I was <u>re</u>-reading it recently and ...' Intellectual snobbery again – 'I am better than you because I read more, <u>and</u> re-read extensively.'

This is all so strange. Yes, we should read to enrich our lives; but what is there to brag about? Like those who give to charity or secretly eat Smarties in front of *Casualty* every Saturday night, we should keep our private life to ourselves. There is nothing wrong with recommending a book that has given you great pleasure, but never sneer at those who prefer *Coronation Street* or *Eastenders*. They too have their wisdom.

A friend of mine is a doctor and the way ardent readers peer down their noses at him frustrates him greatly. He has always loved the sciences but to be accepted in so much society he is expected to have a close working knowledge of literature and the arts. 'I am supposed to have read all the great novelists and poets,' he sighs, 'but my friends who studied English at University are not expected to know how to transplant kidneys, or to quote the latest research statistics dealing with Alzheimer's disease. The world isn't logical.'

Indeed it isn't. But I tell him it would be better if only Plato were in charge. He nods, and tells me the *Republic* is a grand book.

1 What is the writer saying about our attitude to reading? Explain in your own words, but quote to prove your points.

_____

_____

_____

_____

_____

_____

_____

_____

_____

_____

_____   *(6 marks)*

2 How does the writer make the argument convincing and interesting?

Write about:

- the opening
- the ending
- the range of techniques the writer uses.

_____

_____

_____

_____

_____

_____

_____

_____

_____

_____

_____

_____

_____

_____

_____

_____

_____

_____   *(8 marks)*

Language

Yes, but there will also be a question about the language used in at least one of the unseen texts. Obviously, you cannot analyse the whole text, so try to focus on the most striking examples of language usage: perhaps a simile, a metaphor, a short sentence, complex phrasing etc. Always say what effect is being created, and why.

Below is the opening paragraph from a review of Shakespeare's *The Tempest*. It has been broken into sections. Examine each part, saying what is interesting about the language used.

1 Let's face it, modern productions of Shakespeare are not always everyone's cup of tea.

_____

_____

_____

_____ *(2 marks)*

2 Last night's performance, at the Grand Theatre, left most of the audience wondering whether they should have stayed at home and watched even *Big Brother*; because there you have control and can switch off if you wish. In the privacy of your own home, you are safe from the modern directors who deal with the Bard's verse as if it were a rejected script for *Eastenders*, to be spat out, rushed and mutilated – obscene and best not heard.

_____

_____

_____

_____

_____

_____ *(3 marks)*

3 Nothing was as it should be. Prospero, Shakespeare's final great creation, was perverse and perverted; Ariel was deranged; Caliban was hideously naked.

_____

_____

_____

_____

_____ *(3 marks)*

4 (This was a set of foul freaks. Shakespeare's last play deserves better.

_____

_____

_____

(1 mark)

Read this extract.

> What never fails to astonish me, on my travels, is the behaviour of young people abroad. How can it be that teenagers who have never come anywhere near a school uniform have not turned into mass murderers? Why aren't they drunk all the time? Why aren't they like young people in Britain?
>
> British schools work so hard – but with what success? It's like trying to cork a bottle of beer: pushing, forcing squeezing, just to see everything spill over. The government insists on 'higher standards', and head teachers wield their metaphorical rods of iron, yet when the school gates are unlocked and the children tumble out, the neighbourhood has to be braced.
>
> First, there is likely to be the tugging and name-calling. Bustle and noise. Then the ball games, smokers, shrieks ... And later comes the alcohol, some drugs ... Passing the local park can be as dangerous as passing the pub doors at 11.00 pm, when the elder siblings leave the bars and head for the takeaways and taxi ranks and more disputes and nights in the cells.
>
> If it doesn't happen in France, Italy, Portugal, Greece, why does it happen here?

5 How is language used by the writer?

_____

_____

_____

_____

_____

_____

_____

_____

_____

_____

_____

_____

_____

(6 marks)

Structure

What will be asked about structure?

You might be asked about how a text has been put together and/or why particular features have been placed in a particular order or position.

1 Re-read the text on the previous page. How does the writer structure the passage?

_____

_____

_____

_____

_____

_____

_____

_____

_____

_____

(6 marks)

2 This advertisement is aimed at teachers looking for promotion. How has it been structured?

Write about:

• the order in which you notice things, and why

• the order of the details in the text.

_____

_____

_____

_____

_____

_____

_____

_____

_____

_____

_____

_____

_____

(6 marks)

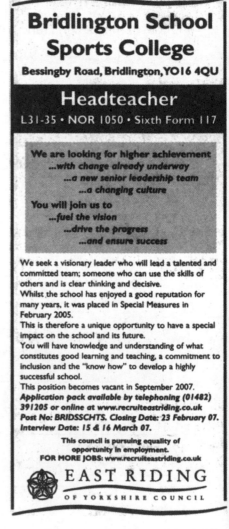

Bridlington School Sports College

Bessingby Road, Bridlington, YO16 4QU

Headteacher

L31-35 • NOR 1050 • Sixth Form 117

We are looking for higher achievement
...with change already underway
...a new senior leadership team
...a changing culture

You will join us to
...fuel the vision
...drive the progress
...and ensure success

We seek a visionary leader who will lead a talented and committed team; someone who can use the skills of others and is clear thinking and decisive.

Whilst the school has enjoyed a good reputation for many years, it was placed in Special Measures in February 2005.

This is therefore a unique opportunity to have a special impact on the school and its future.

You will have knowledge and understanding of what constitutes good learning and teaching, a commitment to inclusion and the "know how" to develop a highly successful school.

This position becomes vacant in September 2007.

Application pack available by telephoning (01482) 391205 or online at www.recruiteastriding.co.uk

Post No: BRIDSSCHTS. *Closing Date: 23 February 07.*

Interview Date: 15 & 16 March 07.

This council is pursuing equality of opportunity in employment.

FOR MORE JOBS: www.recruiteastriding.co.uk

EAST RIDING OF YORKSHIRE COUNCIL

Education Guardian, 06.02.07

Look at this newspaper extract.

BEATLEMANiA

£500m-a-year bonanza as Fab Four set to go on download

PLAY JUDE
We give classic Beatles album over the iPod treatment

EXCLUSIVE

By GRAHAM BROUGH

THE Beatles are poised for a huge revival after a deal yesterday paved the way for their songs to be downloaded for the first time.

iPod makers Apple Inc settled a 25-year trademark battle with Beatles record company Apple Corps over the use of the name.

It means massive hits such as Hey Jude and Yesterday may soon be legally downloadable – sparking a wave of Beatlemania worth £500million a year.

FULL STORY: PAGE 10

Daily Mirror, 06.02.07

3 How is it structured to gain maximum impact?

_____

_____

_____

_____

_____

_____

_____

_____

(4 marks)

Presentational devices

What are presentational devices?

This term covers items such as photographs, diagrams, text boxes, headings and sub-headings. You will be expected to explain how these devices have been used in the text. There will always be a question about presentational devices.

Read this newspaper extract.

Sunday Mirror,
28.01.07

HOW TECHNOLOGY COULD HELP

One idea is to use aircraft to pump reflective dust into the atmosphere to block sunlight

Scientists have suggested sending giant mirrored dishes into orbit to reflect sun's rays

Let's block sun with smoke and mirrors

Rapped... Exxon site

AMERICAN experts have come up with a bizarre solution to global warming and climate change – putting giant mirrors in orbit round the earth to bounce sunlight back into space.

They also want to use jet aircraft to pump reflective dust into the atmosphere and send up thousands of shiny balloons to block sunlight.

The US wants the radical ideas adopted by the Intergovernmental Panel on Climate Change (IPCC) as "insurance" against rising levels of carbon emissions and other greenhouse gases, for inclusion in a long-awaited UN report.

Scientists reckon reflecting less than one per cent of sunlight back into space could make up for man-made greenhouse gases over 400 years.

Meanwhile Esso's owners ExxonMobil – the world's biggest oil firm – were yesterday accused of peddling climate-change propaganda to schoolchildren on a website it funds. MPs say the Energy Chest site featuring "Joules the Robot" questions whether global warming is man-made.

Lib Dem spokesman Chris Huhne MP branded the firm's bosses "Toxic Texans" and "climate-change deniers". He added: "ExxonMobil is behaving in a thoroughly irresponsible manner, doing itself and its shareholders no favours by failing to recognise reality."

1 Read the text, then explain how the presentational devices:

- attract the audience
- support the article.

_____

_____

_____

_____

_____

_____

_____

_____

_____

(6 marks)

Look at this advertisement.

2 How are presentational devices used in this advertisement?

_____

_____

_____

_____

_____

_____

_____

_____

(4 marks)

3 What different effects would be achieved if the background colour were:

- orange
- silver?

_____

_____

_____

_____

(2 marks)

Making comparisons

You will have to compare some part or parts of two texts. This is something you do in Paper 2, when you compare poems (see pages 158 – 161); but you are also likely to have to make comparisons in Section A of Paper 1.

You might be asked to compare any aspect of the texts.

JAMES MORRISON ON EATING, DRINKING AND £1000 A HEAD MEALS

When you're a musician, you flip between eating stuff to just fill you up, or eating at amazing restaurants. Before I got signed, I was taken to a few posh restaurants by different labels. There was one, called Silks, where the bill was over £1000 – £30 for a bottle of beer! I went to get one at the bar and they were like, 'we'll get it.' I was like, 'thank God'. I'm not from a very privileged background, so any food I can eat, I'm glad of. Last year on tour I had incredible sushi in Tokyo and amazing soups and fried prawns in Holland. But our rider used to be just sandwiches and beer – before I'd really sold any records it was cans of Carling. Then we got Becks. Now we get Corona! Selling a million albums means on the next tour I'm getting backstage catering. A roast now and then would be brilliant.

I could cook a roast but I burn most stuff. My mum came up from Cornwall recently, and cooked this Moroccan dish – bulgar wheat, lamb and red wine. She's an amazing cook; we never had lots of money but she made sure we had great meals.

I don't drink before a show. Beer's bad for your voice – the bubbles give me claggy stuff in the back of my throat. Or I get gassy. It's all right for Liam Gallagher, but that's his style, isn't it?

The Observer Food Monthly, 01.07

WaterAid UK site

Waterborne diseases kill thousands every day

Access to water is a basic human need and a fundamental human right. Yet over a billion people in the world still live without safe, clean water to drink.

Millions of women and children spend hours every day walking miles to collect water. But, the water they work so hard to collect doesn't come from a tap – but will come from a river, pond, or simply from dug out holes in the ground, often shared with animals and polluted with waste and excrement. The diseases that result kill 5000 children every single day.

Known and feared round the world, **cholera** is an acute intestinal infection spread through contaminated water.

While **giardia** normally produces a mild bowel infection, its effects can be much worse in developing countries, leading, in some cases, to death.

Rotavirus causes severe diarrhoea and vomiting and is estimated to kill around 600,000 children under five every year in developing countries.

Around 200 million people worldwide are affected with **bilharzias**. This parasitic worm penetrates the skin. Fever, malaise, nausea and diarrhoea follow with liver failure and even death if left untreated.

Despite the clear need, water and sanitation are not high on the political agenda. They are almost so obvious they are forgotten.

WaterAid website

Compare the texts on page 118 by answering the following questions.

1 How does each text deal with drinking?

_____

_____

_____

_____

_____

_____   *(2 marks)*

2 What are the purposes and audiences for these two texts?
Explain your ideas.

_____

_____

_____

_____

_____

_____

_____

_____

_____

_____   *(4 marks)*

3 Compare the use of facts and opinions in the texts.

_____

_____

_____

_____

_____

_____

_____

_____

_____

_____

_____

_____

_____   *(6 marks)*

Skills test: Paper 1 Section A

Should this be treated like part of the actual exam?

Yes. Remember to produce answers of an appropriate length and to refer to precise detail wherever possible to support your ideas.

Write your answers on lined paper.

Read both texts carefully and then answer all the questions.

Spend about an hour on your responses.

Text 1: An article from a national newspaper

Need a break? Want a change? Why not try Bognor ...?

According to government figures, 5.5% of the UK's carbon dioxide output comes from aviation fuel. Air travel is feeding our destruction. At the same time, with global warming all too apparent, Britain is getting pleasantly warmer whilst southern Europe is falling into the grip of heatwaves that look set to kill thousands. Catastrophic water shortages will no doubt be next. Under the circumstances, it is hard to work out why it is that millions of Britons take to the skies each year, seeking rest and some form of relaxation. It would be so much more sensible to stay at home.

For centuries, the lure of the exotic has been tempting, but now we have seen it all. Television in the 21st century brings Ancient Rome, the Steppes, even the lunar landscape into our living rooms. What more is there to see? Simultaneously, the Mediterranean is becoming increasingly polluted, the beauty of backwaters is being overwhelmed by MacDonalds, and it is no longer cheap to live in Spain or Greece.

The bargain days are over. It costs relatively little to get abroad – in terms of cash, and if you forget the ozone layer – but, having arrived, you are back to grim reality. Bread and milk have to be paid for.

Meanwhile, Britain retains its history, its glorious beaches (think of Croyde in Devon, the vast stretches in Northumberland, Morar in the Highlands) and its charm. Nothing on the continent has more mystery than Stonehenge. Staithes in North Yorkshire is every bit as fascinating as Hydra in the Aegean, and to get there does not require a choppy sea crossing on a boat long ago deemed unsafe to work across the Channel. It is as easy to be pampered in Bognor as it is in the Bahamas. A night out in Manchester offers as much as Berlin or Munich.

Flights abroad will have to become a thing of the past if the world is to survive. Our future summers will have to be spent in our green and pleasant land, but that is no great loss when the whole of Wales opens its arms and thousands of hidden nooks around our coasts are waiting for us to call. As Hamlet would have put it: 'Tis a consummation devoutly to be wished.'

Ancient art of relaxing

After a hard day's sightseeing in Athens, there is no better place to be than the hotel Grande Bretagne. JANE MEMMLER checks in to soothe her weary limbs.

ACROPOLIS NOW: Take in heady views from the hotel's rooftop restaurant

MANY VISITORS to Greece bypass Athens, its dusty capital, and head straight to the islands. What they're missing is a place with a wealth of history and fabulous shopping. So take a detour and spend a few days in this frenetic yet exhilarating city.

If you're looking for class, look no further than the Hotel Grande Bretagne, one of the world's classic hotels. Its location, right on the city's central Syntagma Square, is perfectly placed for exploring the old area of Plaka and Monasteraki and is close to Athens's defining monument, the Acropolis. The imposing Parliament buildings are directly opposite and worth a visit just to see the guards in their funny pompom shoes and flared skirts.

At the Grande Bretagne, prepare to be overwhelmed. Grecian columns, miles of marble and ornate gilt furnishings make you feel as if you've stepped into an old palace.

CALM WATERS: The pool area provides a sea of tranquillity

Passing through the revolving doors come dozens of men in suits, ladies in crisp business-wear and heels and the odd casually-dressed tourist. The smart liveried doormen hardly bat an eyelid and are eager to help you find your way.

Best of all, are the views from the roof. Sweeping across to the Acropolis and the old Olympic Stadium, at night these illuminated landmarks are truly spectacular against the twinkling lights of Athens.

THE ROOM

Continuing the theme from the lobby, the rooms are grand yet cozy. A large ornate mirror, elegant table lamps and highly-polished bureau make up the busy, yet uncluttered room. Heavy swathes of Regency curtains, in burnt gold and claret, give the room a Louis XVIth feel. The beds are covered in crisp linens and have loads of squishy pillows. The bathroom, in true Grecian style, is clad in floor-to-ceiling marble, with a large shower and luxuriously deep bath.

THE SPA

The award-winning GB spa is a tranquil respite from the hustle of Syntagma Square. Comfortable white sunloungers are lined up along white marble walls surrounding the pool. Individual relaxation areas are scented with uplifting essential oils.

My therapist, Dimitri, who had the hands of a god, bathed my feet before giving me a body massage. When I showered it off, I'd felt as if I'd been cleaned by a tube of toothpaste.

THE NOSH

There is a selection of restaurants to choose from within the hotel. You can push the boat out in GB Corner on the ground floor with such dishes as oven-baked shrimps with pan-fried grouper to something a little lighter in the rooftop bar and restaurant, such as grilled steaks and salads, while you soak up the views of the sprawling city.

THE DAMAGE

EasyJet (0905 821 0905/www.easyjet.com) offers return flights from Gatwick to Athens from £52.

Luxury Hotels (00 800 3254 5454/www.luxury collection.com) offers doubles at Hotel Grande Bretagne from £190 per room per night (two sharing), room only.

Sunday Express, 28.01.07

Re-read Text 1: *Need a break? Want a change? Why not try Bognor ...?*

1 a Why does the writer think it is good to take holidays in Britain? Answer using your own words. *(6 marks)*

b Which do you think are the writer's best two points, and why? *(2 marks)*

c How does the writer try to make us agree with him?
Write about:
  • the uses of fact and opinion
  • other techniques he uses to make us agree with him. *(6 marks)*

Now, re-read Text 2: *Ancient art of relaxing.*

d Who do you think this text has been written for? Explain your opinion. *(4 marks)*

Finally, look at both texts together.

2 How do the texts try to interest the reader?
Write about:
  • each writer's use of language
  • presentational devices in *Ancient art of relaxing.* *(9 marks)*

(Total: 27 marks)

Re-read Text 1: *Need a break? Want a change? Why not try Bognor ...?*

1 a What is the intended purpose and audience of this text? Give your reasons. *(5 marks)*

b How does the writer try to convince us of his argument?
Explain:
- the main points in his argument
- how fact and opinion are used
- how other techniques are used. *(9 marks)*

Next, re-read Text 2: *Ancient art of relaxing.*

2 a Why have the presentational devices been included? To what extent are they appropriate for the text? *(5 marks)*

Finally, you must compare the texts.

b How does each writer use language? *(8 marks)*

(Total: 27 marks)

Paper 2 Section A: Poems from different cultures and traditions

How to respond to the questions

Section A of Paper 2 should take just 45 minutes to complete. The exam paper will offer you a choice of two questions. You will have to answer one of them.

One question will be on the first Cluster of poems:

- *Limbo* – Edward Kamau Brathwaite
- *Nothing's Changed* – Tatamkulu Afrika
- *Island Man* – Grace Nichols
- *Blessing* – Imtiaz Dharker
- *Two Scavengers in a Truck, Two Beautiful People in a Mercedes* – Lawrence Ferlinghetti
- *Night of the Scorpion* – Nissim Ezekiel
- *Vultures* – Chinua Achebe
- *What Were They Like?* – Denise Levertov

The other question will be on the second Cluster:

- from *Search For My Tongue* – Sujata Bhatt
- from *Unrelated Incidents* – Tom Leonard
- *Half-Caste* – John Agard
- *Love After Love* – Derek Walcott
- *This Room* – Imtiaz Darker
- *Not My Business* – Niyi Osundare
- *Presents from my Aunts in Pakistan* – Moniza Alvi
- *Hurricane Hits England* – Grace Nichols

Each question will name a poem from the Cluster. You choose one poem to compare with it.

The poems are all from different cultures and traditions, so you will be expected to write about those cultures in your response. However, that need not be a concern for you because by answering the question that is set, you will automatically write about the cultures and traditions in the poems.

You will be marked according to how well you respond in writing in these three areas:

1 the ideas, feelings and attitudes in the poems
2 comparisons, including appropriate details from the poems
3 the presentation in the poems: language and structure.

Make sure you are including these features as you answer the question.

The practice questions in this book focus on the ideas and the presentation. There is a separate unit to allow you to compare the poems.

There are different ways in which you can write your essay in the exam. You should always begin with an **introduction** which demonstrates how you will answer the question. Rather than just repeating the question, try to say something about the poems and how you intend to deal with the task:

> I am going to compare Presents from my Aunts in Pakistan with another poem of my choice and say what we learn about the people in the poems and how the poets present their ideas. ✗

> In Presents from my Aunts in Pakistan, we are introduced to a girl who is torn between two cultures. The poet reveals to the reader what is in the girls' mind and her apparent unhappiness. However, in Hurricane Hits England the situation is slightly different ... ✔

In the **main body** of your response, you might choose to compare the poems by writing about their comparable features. Or, you might respond to one of the poems in detail and then deal with the second, pointing out ways in which it compares with the first one at that point.

Either:

Method 1:   point from Poem 1/ point from Poem 2, as comparison
                  point from Poem 1/ point from Poem 2, as comparison and so on

or

Method 2:   all points from Poem 1 then points from Poem 2, making comparisons with Poem 1 as you go.

Finally, add a **conclusion** which sums up the main points you have made.

Throughout, you should be using the **PEE** technique:

- make your <u>point</u>
- give an <u>example</u> to prove it
- <u>explain</u> your idea.

As with any other element in an exam, the more you practise these techniques, the better!

Limbo
by Edward Kamau Brathwaite

What is the poem about?

Like all the poems from different cultures, it presents a cultural situation to the reader. In this case, it centres on slaves being transported to America. It tells of their suffering and has the rhythm of the limbo dance. The ending could be interpreted as optimistic or pessimistic.

1 What is happening in the poem?

_____

_____

_____

_____

_____

_____

_____

_____

_____

_____ *(6 marks)*

2 What effect is created by these lines:

> *stick is the whip*
> *and the dark deck is slavery* ?

Comment in detail on the words used.

_____

_____

_____

_____

_____

_____

_____

_____ *(4 marks)*

3 Why is there a repeated refrain:

> *limbo*
> *limbo like me* ?

_____

_____

_____

_____

_____ *(3 marks)*

4 How are rhythm and rhyme used in the poem?

_____

_____

_____

_____

_____

_____

_____

_____

_____ *(6 marks)*

5 Is the ending optimistic or pessimistic?

Make your opinion clear by referring closely to:

* the final section (from line 40 onwards)
* the rest of the poem.

Try to refer in detail to the language and structure of the poem.

_____

_____

_____

_____

_____

_____

_____

_____

_____

_____

_____

_____

_____ *(8 marks)*

Continue on lined paper if necessary.

Nothing's Changed
by Tatamkhulu Afrika

Do I have to know about South Africa to understand the poem?

It is enough to be aware of the fact that there used to be a system called apartheid in South Africa, where the white people were in charge and considered themselves superior. In the poem, apartheid has ended and Tatamkhulu Africa revisits District 6, an area which black people had been forced to leave.

1 How does the reader react to the opening stanza?
Write about:

- the words used
- how the words are organised in lines.

_____

_____

_____

_____

_____

_____

_____

_____

_____   *(6 marks)*

2 Why does the poet make the comparison between the *'whites only restaurant'* and the *'working man's café'*?
Include:

- details of the comparison
- an explanation of the effect that is created.

_____

_____

_____

_____

_____

_____

_____

_____

_____

_____   *(6 marks)*

3 How is the poem structured?
Consider:

- the order in which ideas are placed
- how the order gives structure to the poem.

_____

_____

_____

_____

_____

_____

_____

_____

_____ *(4 marks)*

4 What do we learn about the feelings of the poet?
Write about:

- his anger and how it is shown
- the ending of the poem.

_____

_____

_____

_____

_____

_____

_____

_____

_____

_____

_____

_____

_____

_____

_____

_____

_____

_____

_____

_____ *(10 marks)*

Island Man
by Grace Nichols

Will we be expected to write about such a short poem?

This poem is relatively short and it simply captures the moment when a man wakes up. However, there are important points to make about his background and his emotions, as well as the contrast between his home in the Caribbean and his life in London. These points offer much to consider.

1 What happens in the poem and how does the man feel about it?

_____
_____
_____
_____
_____
_____
_____
_____
_____
_____
_____

(6 marks)

2 How is the contrast between the Caribbean and London presented?

_____
_____
_____
_____
_____
_____
_____
_____
_____
_____

(6 marks)

3 Comment on the effect of the following:

the steady breaking and wombing	
he always comes back groggily groggily	
Comes back to sands of a grey metallic soar	
island man heaves himself Another London day	

(6 marks)

4 Why are the opening and ending of the poem appropriate, considering the poet's message?

_____

_____

_____

_____

_____

_____

_____

_____

_____

_____ *(5 marks)*

5 How do the layout and punctuation of the poem contribute to its message?

_____

_____

_____

_____

_____

_____

_____

_____

_____

_____ *(5 marks)*

Blessing
by Imtiaz Dharker

How religious is this poem?

The poem presents a third world country in which the people are poor and water is scarce. When the municipal pipe bursts, it is like a miracle and is seen by the poet in religious terms. The people, of course, are elated.

1 How is the lack of water shown at the start of the poem?

_____

_____

_____

_____

_____

_____

_____

_____ *(5 marks)*

2 How are the ideas of religion brought into the poem?

_____

_____

_____

_____

_____

_____

_____ *(4 marks)*

3 Which words show the value of the water? Explain their effect.

_____

_____

_____

_____ *(3 marks)*

4 Why is there such a long sentence to end the poem – beginning *'From the huts …'*
(line 11) and ending *'over their small bones'*?
Write about:

- how the mood of the people is shown
- the language used
- the punctuation
- the stanza break.

_____

_____

_____

_____

_____

_____

_____

_____

_____

_____

_____

_____

_____

_____

_____

_____

_____

_____

_____

_____   *(10 marks)*

5 Why is the title of the poem appropriate?

_____

_____

_____

_____   *(2 marks)*

Two Scavengers in a Truck, Two Beautiful People in a Mercedes by Lawrence Ferlinghetti

What is there to say about the culture in this poem?

What happens in the poem probably seems very close to our own experiences because it is set in America. However, the experience is one that is tied by the poet directly to America and it is presented as something with particular significance within that culture.

1 What do we learn about the garbagemen?

_____

_____

_____

_____

_____

_____

_____

(5 marks)

2 What do we learn about the *'elegant couple'*?

_____

_____

_____

_____

_____

_____

_____

(5 marks)

3 How are the two sets of people contrasted?

_____

_____

_____

_____

_____

_____

_____

_____

_____

_____

_____

_____   *(6 marks)*

4 Why is the poem set out as it is on the page?

_____

_____

_____

_____

_____

_____

_____   *(3 marks)*

5 What is the message at the end?
Comment on:
- the ideas
- the language used.

_____

_____

_____

_____

_____

_____

_____

_____

_____

_____

_____   *(6 marks)*

READING POETRY

Night of the Scorpion
by Nissim Ezekiel

What is different about this poem?

Unlike most of the poems, this one offers a narrative. As well as an impression of the culture, we are also given the story of what happens when the poet's mother is stung.

1 What sort of narrative technique does the writer use?

_____

_____

_____

_____

_____

_____

_____

(4 marks)

2 What are we told about the setting of the poem?

_____

_____

_____

_____

_____

_____

_____

(3 marks)

3 In what ways is the structure of the poem effective?

_____

_____

_____

_____

_____

_____

_____

(4 marks)

4 What do we know about the people who try to help the mother?
Write about:

- what they do
- what they say
- how language is used to show what they are like.

_____

_____

_____

_____

_____

_____

_____

_____

_____

_____

_____

_____

_____

_____

_____

_____

_____

_____

_____

_____

_____

_____ *(12 marks)*

Vultures
by Chinua Achebe

Will we be asked about this poem, when the language is so difficult?

You are allowed to pre-prepare poems in the Anthology, which means the question could be about any of them. If this poem seems particularly tricky, you need to have an overview of what it is about and you must be able to write about the different sections.

1 In your own words, explain briefly what each section of the poem is saying.

_____

_____

_____

_____

_____

_____

_____

_____

_____

_____

(6 marks)

2 What is the mood of this poem, and how is it created?
Consider:

- the opening of the poem
- any other details that you find relevant
- the long sentences.

_____

_____

_____

_____

_____

_____

_____

_____

_____

_____

_____

_____

(10 marks)

3 How are we supposed to feel about the vultures?

_____

_____

_____

_____

_____

_____

_____   *(6 marks)*

4 How are we supposed to feel about the Commandant?

_____

_____

_____

_____

_____

_____   *(4 marks)*

5 What is the poem telling us about love?
   Quote to support your ideas.

_____

_____

_____

_____

_____

_____

_____

_____

_____   *(6 marks)*

What Were They Like?
by Denise Levertov

Will we be asked about the structure of this poem?

You will never get a question just about structure. However, you will want to explain how the poem is structured because that is likely to be relevant to almost any answer on this poem.

1 How is this poem organised, and why?

_____

_____

_____

_____

_____

_____

_____

_____ *(4 marks)*

2 Why does the poet include: *'Sir ...'* ?

_____

_____

_____

_____ *(2 marks)*

3 What does the poet suggest life was like before the war?

_____

_____

_____

_____

_____

_____

_____

_____

_____

_____

_____

_____

_____

_____

_____

_____   *(8 marks)*

4 How are peace and war contrasted in the second section of the poem?

_____

_____

_____

_____

_____

_____

_____

_____

_____

_____

_____

_____

_____

_____

_____

_____

_____   *(10 marks)*

5 How does the ending affect the reader?

_____

_____

_____

_____

_____

_____

_____

_____   *(5 marks)*

from Search For My Tongue
by Sujata Bhatt

Is the whole poem metaphorical?

It is all based around an extended metaphor. In this way it deals with ideas about cultural identity, how the poet copes in another country and who she really is.

1 What is the main message in this poem?

_____

_____

_____

_____

_____

_____

(4 marks)

2 *'I have lost my tongue'* introduces the central image. How is it extended through the poem?

_____

_____

_____

_____

_____

_____

_____

_____

_____

_____

_____

_____

(8 marks)

3 Why is the Gujerati included?

_____

_____

_____

_____

(3 marks)

4 Consider the style of the poem. How does the reader become involved in what the poet has to say?

_____

_____

_____

_____

_____

_____

_____

_____

_____ *(4 marks)*

5 How is the poem made to seem positive in the final 8 lines?

_____

_____

_____

_____

_____

_____

_____

_____

_____

_____

_____

_____

_____ *(8 marks)*

from Unrelated Incidents
by Tom Leonard

Might we have to translate this poem into standard English?

No. You need to understand what the poet is saying but it will be presumed you know what it all means. Any question is likely to be about his attitude or what he believes in; and about how he expresses himself and how the poem is structured.

1 What does the speaker think about BBC news presenters?

_____

_____

_____

_____

_____

_____   *(3 marks)*

2 What does the speaker think about people's attitudes to those with regional accents?

_____

_____

_____

_____

_____

_____

_____   *(4 marks)*

3 In your own words, sum up what he is saying about *'trooth'*.

_____

_____

_____

_____

_____

_____

_____   *(4 marks)*

4 In what ways is this a poem from a different culture?

_____

_____

_____

_____

_____

_____

_____

_____

(5 marks)

5 How is the poem structured, and why?
Include comments on:

- how it is set out on the page
- the beginning and ending.

_____

_____

_____

_____

_____

_____

_____

_____

_____

_____

(6 marks)

6 What point is the poet trying to make by using such unusual spelling and such limited
punctuation? Quote from the poem to support your opinions.

_____

_____

_____

_____

_____

_____

_____

_____

_____

(6 marks)

Half-Caste
by John Agard

How serious is John Agard in this poem?

You can assume he is making a very serious point, but you might have to write about how he puts across his opinion. The other priorities are how the poem uses language and how it is structured.

1 What is the poet's message in this poem?

_____

_____

_____

_____

_____   *(4 marks)*

2 Why has the poem been written in this style? Explain in detail.

_____

_____

_____

_____

_____

_____

_____

_____

_____   *(4 marks)*

3 Why is there so much repetition in the poem?

_____

_____

_____

_____

_____   *(4 marks)*

4 How is the idea of being *'half'* of something used by the poet?

_____

_____

_____

_____

_____

_____

_____

_____

_____ *(6 marks)*

5 There are no full-stops in the poem. How has it been punctuated, and why?

_____

_____

_____

_____

_____

_____ *(4 marks)*

6 What is the effect of the final 7 lines?

_____

_____

_____

_____

_____

_____

_____

_____

_____

_____ *(5 marks)*

Love After Love
by Derek Walcott

Since there does not seem to be a different culture in the poem, how do we handle it?

The poems in the selection are from different cultures and traditions, but are not necessarily about them. In this case, Walcott's poem offers a universal message which is not tied to a particular setting.

1 Why is the poem called 'Love After Love'?

_____

_____

_____

_____

_____

_____

_____

_____ *(4 marks)*

2 How does the poet speak to the reader?

_____

_____

_____

_____

_____

_____

_____

_____ *(4 marks)*

3 What is the effect of the short sentences?

_____

_____

_____

_____

_____ *(3 marks)*

4 How does the poet create a sense of place?

_____

_____

_____

_____

_____

_____

_____

_____ *(4 marks)*

5 What is the mood of the poem? Comment on how it is created by:
- the opening
- the ending
- the poet's use of language.

_____

_____

_____

_____

_____

_____

_____

_____

_____

_____

_____

_____

_____

_____

_____

_____

_____

_____

_____

_____ *(12 marks)*

This Room
by Imtiaz Dharker

Is this another poem with no clear sense of location?

Imtiaz Dharker comes from India, but the poem could be set anywhere. The most important elements are what the poem has to say about an emotional time and how it says it.

1 What picture is created in *'This Room'*?

_____

_____

_____

_____

_____

_____ *(4 marks)*

2 How is an atmosphere established in the first two stanzas?

_____

_____

_____

_____

_____

_____

_____

_____

_____

_____ *(6 marks)*

3 Read lines 10 – 17 and explain how the poet has used:

- metaphor – when something is not literally true
- onomatopoeia – when words create sound
- enjambement – when there is no punctuation at the end of a line.

_____

_____

_____

_____

_____

_____

_____

_____

_____

_____

(6 marks)

4 How is a sense of *'excitement'* sustained by the poet throughout the poem?
Explain:

- what happens
- how language is used.

_____

_____

_____

_____

_____

_____

_____

_____

_____

_____

_____

_____

_____

_____

_____

_____

_____

(10 marks)

5 The poem ends: *'my hands are outside, clapping'*. What is the effect of this line, and what
is the final impression presented to the reader?

_____

_____

_____

_____

_____

(4 marks)

Not my Business
by Niyi Osundare

Will we need to focus on each separate incident in the poem?

In some ways this is an 'easier' poem because it breaks into clear sections and the 'different culture' is obvious. However, you will need to be aware of the particular details, and the overall message we take from what happens. Of course, as ever, the poet's methods are important.

1 What happens to the people in the poem?

_____

_____

_____

_____

_____

_____

_____

_____

(4 marks)

2 How has the poem been structured?

_____

_____

_____

_____

_____

_____

_____

_____

(4 marks)

3 How does the speaker react at each stage in the poem and how does he feel at the end?

_____

_____

_____

_____

_____

_____

_____

_____

_____

_____ *(4 marks)*

4 Why is the refrain *'What business of mine is it ..?'* repeated?

_____

_____

_____

_____ *(2 marks)*

5 How are we expected to react to the following lines?

- *Beat him soft like clay*
  And stuffed him down the belly
  Of a waiting jeep
- *Booted the whole house awake*
- *No query, no warning, no probe*
- *The jeep was waiting on my bewildered lawn*
  Waiting, waiting in its usual silence

_____

_____

_____

_____

_____

_____

_____

_____

_____

_____

_____

_____

_____

_____

_____ *(7 marks)*

Presents from my Aunts in Pakistan by Moniza Alvi

This is the longest poem in the selection: should it be avoided?

You should be prepared to answer on any of the poems you have studied. There are so many things to say about culture in this poem that it certainly deserves close study.

1 What is the girl's problem? Explain in detail.

_____

_____

_____

_____

_____

_____ *(4 marks)*

2 What does she feel about her Pakistani culture?

_____

_____

_____

_____

_____

_____

_____

_____

_____

_____

_____

_____ *(6 marks)*

3 To what extent does she feel British?

_____

_____

_____

_____

_____ *(4 marks)*

4 How is her Pakistani culture brought to life in the poem?
Comment on:

- the details
- the language used.

_____

_____

_____

_____

_____

_____

_____

_____

_____

_____

_____

_____

_____

_____

_____

_____

_____

_____

_____ _(10 marks)_

5 Why is the ending important in our understanding of the girl's feelings?

_____

_____

_____

_____

_____

_____ _(4 marks)_

Hurricane Hits England
by Grace Nichols

How can this be from a different culture, if it is set in England?

Like some other poems in the selection, this poem is about someone who is having to come to terms with a new culture. The culture of her original country is very different from the one in which she now finds herself. The poem is about her state of mind.

1 What has happened to make the poet consider her situation and what are her reactions?

_____

_____

_____

_____

_____

_____

_____

_____

_____

_____

(6 marks)

2 How are her emotions revealed to the reader? Refer closely to the text in your answer.

_____

_____

_____

_____

_____

_____

_____

_____

_____

_____

_____

_____

_____

_____

(8 marks)

3 What connection does she find between the two cultures?

_____

_____

_____

_____

_____

_____   *(4 marks)*

4 How does she feel at the end? Explain.

_____

_____

_____

_____

_____

_____

_____   *(4 marks)*

5 What do we learn about her original culture?
Consider:
- the details she includes
- the language used.

_____

_____

_____

_____

_____

_____

_____

_____

_____

_____

_____

_____

_____

_____

_____

_____   *(10 marks)*

Comparing poems

Are there any rules about which poems we compare? Do they have to be from the same cluster?

There will be two questions, from which you choose one. Which ever question you choose, you will always have to compare two poems. One poem is always named but the one you select can be from either cluster. Just be careful not to use one of the poems that are studied for Literature!

CLUSTER 1

Question: Compare *Night of the Scorpion* with any other poem of your choice. How do the poets present relationships in the poems?

1 Write your opening paragraph.

_____

_____

_____

_____

_____

_____

(3 marks)

2 Find points of comparison in the poems. Try to compare the ideas and the techniques.

Point of comparison	Reference: *Night of the Scorpion*	Reference: chosen poem	Comment/explanation

(12 marks)

3 Write your concluding paragraph.

_____

_____

_____

_____

_____

(3 marks)

4 You have already written an opening and ending. Now write the central section, the remainder of your response.

_____

_____

_____

_____

_____

_____

_____

_____

_____

_____

_____

_____

_____

_____

_____

_____

_____

_____

_____

_____

_____

_____

_____

_____

_____

_____

_____

_____

_____

_____

_____

_____

_____

_____   _(21 marks)_

Continue on lined paper if necessary. Only spend 30 minutes on this task.

CLUSTER 2

Question: How is language used to reveal the speaker's situation in *Not My Business* and in any other poem of your choice?

1 What is the speaker's situation in *Not My Business*?

_____

_____

_____

_____

_____

(3 marks)

2 Which language might you comment on in *Not My Business*?

Quotation	Comment

Continue on lined paper if necessary.　　*(6 marks)*

3 What is the speaker's situation in your chosen poem?

_____

_____

_____

_____

_____

(3 marks)

4 What language might you comment on in your chosen poem?

Quotation	Comment

(6 marks)

5 Write the whole response, comparing the situations and the use of language.

_____

_____

_____

_____

_____

_____

_____

_____

_____

_____

_____

_____

_____

_____

_____

_____

_____

_____

_____

_____

_____

_____

_____

_____

_____

_____

_____

_____

_____

_____

_____

_____ _(27 marks)_

Continue on lined paper if necessary.

Paper 1 and 2 Section B: Types of writing and Writing skills

How to respond to the questions in Section B of both papers

While Section A on both papers tests your Reading ability, Section B assesses how successful you are at Writing. You will have 45 minutes to produce your response.

Section B of Paper 1 requires you to write to:

- argue
- persuade
- advise

or

- produce a mixture of these styles of writing.

Section B of Paper 2 requires you to write to:

- inform
- explain
- describe

or

- produce a mixture of these styles of writing.

Ideally, your response will be about 1½–2½ sides long. Remember that you will be assessed on the quality of your writing, not on how many sides of paper you can cover. It is better to write slightly less and to do it well.

You are likely to have to write a letter, an article, a speech, an advice sheet or a more traditional essay. Whatever the task, the basic requirements and the mark scheme will be the same.

You will be given two marks by the examiner:

1 for organisation and communication – 18 marks

2 for accuracy – 9 marks.

If you do well on one particular set of skills, it can compensate for a lower mark elsewhere.

You will be offered four questions and you must choose just one to answer. You only have three-quarters of an hour to write your response so it is essential that you choose the question that you feel is best for you and stick with it. There is not enough time to begin one essay then decide it might have been better to do another and change at that point.

The exam paper advises you on the basic approach that is best:

- plan your response
- write (aim for about 2 sides)
- check and improve your work.

Planning

The planning stage should take you 5 – 10 minutes. Aim to produce a detailed plan because if you include a good deal of detail it makes it easier for you to write a better essay. You can then concentrate on paragraphing, punctuation, vocabulary and expression because you have already decided what to write.

You might like to consider sequencing the ideas in your plan so that you have a 'route map'. You will then know where you are starting, what sections you will move through, and where you will finish:

Paragraph 1:

Paragraph 2:

… and so on.

Writing

The mark you are given for organisation and communication will be based on:

- how well you address the purpose and audience
- how interesting it is
- the quality of paragraphing
- the choice of vocabulary.

Your accuracy mark will be for:

- sentences
- spelling
- punctuation.

Checking

You should spend five minutes reading through your work, correcting and improving it. Try to read it slowly, focusing on each word. There are no marks for neatness, so change anything which is not as good as it should be but ensure that it is still readable!

Planning

Do we need to plan our written responses?

You are advised to plan your writing. Plotting your essay's development makes it develop more logically. Without planning, ideas tend to come in a random order and paragraphing can also be less effective.

Write a newspaper article in which you argue **either** for **or** against the idea that exams should be done away with and grades should be awarded for coursework alone.

1 Collect your ideas.

_____
_____
_____
_____
_____
_____
_____
_____   *(5 marks)*

2 Produce a detailed essay plan.

_____
_____
_____
_____
_____
_____
_____
_____
_____
_____
_____
_____
_____
_____
_____
_____
_____   *(10 marks)*

Continue on lined paper if necessary.

Describe a park in summer.

3 Collect your ideas.

_____

_____

_____

_____

_____

_____

_____

_____   _(5 marks)_

4 Produce a detailed essay plan.

_____

_____

_____

_____

_____

_____

_____

_____

_____

_____

_____

_____

_____

_____

_____

_____

_____

_____

_____

_____   _(10 marks)_

Continue on lined paper if necessary.

High quality features

What are 'high quality features'?

When the examiner reads through your Section B response, there are certain things which grab his attention. These make the writing more interesting and, as a result, you are more likely to be rewarded with higher marks. These features are included in the mark scheme used by the examiner.

Rhetorical questions

Rhetorical questions challenge the reader, to involve them in the ideas: e.g. 'Can this be right?'; 'Is there no other way to ..?'

1 Write the opening paragraph of an article for a national newspaper, to persuade readers that young people should be give the vote at the age of 16. Begin with rhetorical questions.

_____

_____

_____

_____

_____

_____

_____

(6 marks)

Quotations

Quotations help to convince a reader, because they come from a different source. Usually, the quotation is from a person whose views might carry some weight (possibly the Prime Minister, a teacher, or a grandparent, depending on the topic).

2 Write the ending of a speech, in which you argue that the government should spend **either** more **or** less money on the armed forces.
Include at least one quotation.

_____

_____

_____

_____

_____

_____

_____

_____

_____

(6 marks)

Examples, facts and figures and anecdotes

You can make what you are saying more convincing by using examples, facts and figures and anecdotes (brief stories, to illustrate a point). Because you do not have access to research materials in the exam, you will have to call on personal knowledge; or you might wish to invent details to support your views.

3 In a letter, you are informing a pen friend about what your school is like. Write a paragraph in which you include some relevant examples.

(6 marks)

4 Write a further paragraph, in which you include some facts and figures about exam performances in your school.

(6 marks)

5 Write a final paragraph, which includes an anecdote that shows what life is like for you at school.

(6 marks)

Similes and metaphors

Similes and metaphors make your writing more interesting. They help the reader interpret your ideas. Similes make a comparison, using 'like' or 'as'. Metaphors say something which is not literally true

6 Complete this description of your best friend.

Whenever I need help, she/he is like _____

Of course, at other times, she/he can be as _____

as _____

In general, though, she/he (use a metaphor here) _____

_____ *(3 marks)*

7 Explain why you particularly enjoy a hobby or pastime. Try to include at least three or four similes or metaphors in your answer.

_____

_____

_____

_____

_____

_____

_____

_____

_____ *(6 marks)*

Emotive language

Emotive language touches the emotions, perhaps making us feel sympathy, happiness, or whatever: e.g. 'Try to imagine what it is like to be without food and water for days at a time …'

8 Write a paragraph in which you advise a relative to give some of their money to a charity of your choice. Use some emotive language.

_____

_____

_____

_____

_____

_____

_____

_____

_____ *(6 marks)*

Humour

Humour should be used carefully: too much humour might not be the best approach. However, if you can make the examiner smile, that is rarely a bad thing. For example, you might wish to poke fun at someone or something, and exaggeration is often a useful tool.

9 Complete this paragraph which describes school meals, continuing the sarcasm.

The meals themselves would not have been out of place in a Siberian camp for mass murderers, train spotters or maths teachers. The mashed potato _____

_____

However, that was positively delicious, compared to the gravy: _____

_____

As for the meat and vegetables – well, they _____

Then, there was the pudding! _____ (4 marks)

10 Write part of a sales sheet, to persuade people to buy your house. Make the house seem attractive, but try to end with a humorous remark.

_____

_____

_____

_____

_____

_____

_____

_____ (6 marks)

The unfinished sentence

Using an ellipsis (...) shows that the sentence has not been completed, and allows the reader to imagine what might have come next. This too can produce a smile: 'And as for the contents of his pockets ...'

11 As the ending to an argumentative piece of writing about why we should **or** should not eat more healthily, finish with an ellipsis.

_____

_____

_____

_____

_____

_____

_____

_____

_____ (6 marks)

Paragraphing

Paragraphing is a significant part of the Writing mark scheme. If you can vary your paragraph lengths effectively, you will receive a higher grade.

12 Write a section of a response which advises young people to choose their friends carefully. Try to write:

- a paragraph of about 8 – 10 lines which explains why it is wise to choose friends carefully
- a longer, descriptive paragraph, to describe the kinds of 'bad friends' you can attract
- a short, punchy paragraph to make your feelings about such people very clear.

_____

_____

_____

_____

_____

_____

_____

_____

_____

_____

_____

_____

_____

_____

_____

_____

_____

_____

_____

_____

_____

_____

_____

_____

_____

_____

_____

_____

(18 marks)

Continue on lined paper if necessary.

Punctuation

You will impress the examiner if you include a variety of punctuation (e.g. full-stops, capitals, commas, exclamation marks, question marks, quotation marks, colons and semi-colons …)

13 Re-write this paragraph, introducing more varied punctuation. Try to stay as faithful to the original as possible, concentrating on altering the punctuation, rather than the words.

The desert is cold at night. All the animals and insects seem to come to life. Overhead the moon beams down. Anyone lost and wondering feels like crying. What can I do? Where can I go for rest and safety? Such are their cries. Yet the desert is merciless and does not give any sign of hope or rescue. There is piercing cold. There is howling wind and shifting sand. There is just hopelessness.

_____

_____

_____

_____

_____

_____

_____

_____

(5 marks)

14 Write the opening paragraph(s) of a response in which you inform readers of a magazine for teenagers about how to prepare a quick meal for their friends. Make the punctuation as varied as possible.

_____

_____

_____

_____

_____

_____

_____

_____

_____

_____

_____

_____

_____

_____

(8 marks)

Opening and concluding paragraphs

Are the start and the ending particularly important?

There are no specific marks for those paragraphs, but you are likely to benefit if you impress the examiner with your beginning; and the final paragraph is the last thing he reads before putting a mark on your work.

Write a letter to advise your cousin about what to do with the rest of his/her life, since he/she is about to leave school.

1 Write the opening paragraph. Remember that high quality features will make your writing more distinctive.

_____

_____

_____

_____

_____

_____

_____

_____   *(6 marks)*

2 Write the final paragraph.
   Try to make it:

   • memorable

   • link with an idea or ideas in your opening.

_____

_____

_____

_____

_____

_____

_____   *(6 marks)*

Write a section for a school brochure, to explain to new students how to avoid problems with teachers at school.

3 Write the opening paragraph, making it serious in tone.

_____
_____
_____
_____
_____
_____
_____
_____   *(6 marks)*

4 Write an alternative opening, which is more light-hearted.

_____
_____
_____
_____
_____
_____
_____
_____   *(6 marks)*

5 Write the concluding paragraph to either of the openings you have produced.

_____
_____
_____
_____
_____
_____
_____
_____
_____   *(6 marks)*

Writing to argue

What is the most important thing to remember when writing to argue?

It is vital that an argument includes alternative viewpoints. These do not have to be balanced, but there can be no argument unless there is something to argue against.

Argue that more help should **or** should not be given to people who regularly break the law.

1 Make a list of points for and against the idea that more help should be given.

For	Against

(6 marks)

2 Read this opening paragraph. Totally re-write the paragraph, maintaining the point of view but including:

- an appropriate topic sentence
- more variety in the language and sentences
- at least one high quality feature.

> My family has had lots of trouble with people who break the law. We shouldn't help them. I think a lot of the punishments are great. Some people want to be nice to criminals. I think they are mad. One man in the paper spent nearly all his life in prison. He kept breaking the law. He needed to be punished.

_____

_____

_____

_____

_____

_____

_____

(6 marks)

3 Write a paragraph in which you balance two opposing points of view about how criminals should be treated, but end the paragraph by supporting one of the viewpoints.

_____

_____

_____

_____

_____

_____ *(6 marks)*

4 Write a paragraph supporting your own opinion, in which you use a convincing example, anecdote, quotation and/or statistic(s).

_____

_____

_____

_____

_____

_____

_____ *(6 marks)*

5 Write a paragraph which follows from the one you have just written. Make sure you:

- link them effectively
- offer an opposing viewpoint
- end the paragraph by returning to your original opinion.

_____

_____

_____

_____

_____

_____

_____

_____

_____

_____ *(6 marks)*

Practice essay title

Write an article for your local newspaper, arguing that there is too much pressure upon teenagers and that they should be allowed to enjoy 'the best years of their lives'.

Writing to persuade

What is the difference between writing to argue and writing to persuade?

Sometimes, we persuade by arguing effectively. It is also possible to persuade by presenting just one point of view and often a range of techniques is used, such as emotive language, convincing examples and appropriate anecdotes.

Write a letter to the Prime Minister to persuade him to give a large sum of money so that part of your school can be rebuilt.

1 List at least five convincing reasons why you need the money.

_____

_____

_____

_____

_____

(5 marks)

2 Write a paragraph explaining one of the reasons, using an anecdote (something that has happened) to illustrate your point.

_____

_____

_____

_____

_____

_____

_____

_____

(6 marks)

3 Write another paragraph, about a different point, this time including emotive language to convince the Prime Minister. (Emotive language touches the emotions.)

_____

_____

_____

_____

_____

_____

_____

(6 marks)

4 Write another paragraph. In this case, include humour or exaggeration.

_____

_____

_____

_____

_____

_____

_____

_____ *(6 marks)*

5 Write your concluding paragraph. Sum up your reasons for asking for the money and try to make an effective final plea.

_____

_____

_____

_____

_____

_____

_____

_____ *(6 marks)*

Practice essay title

Either:

Writing as a celebrity chef, produce a newspaper column to persuade parents to encourage their children to eat healthily.

Or:

Writing as a famous sports personality, produce a newspaper column to persuade parents to encourage their children to lead a healthier lifestyle.

Writing to advise

What is the key to effective advice?

Advice needs to appeal to the reader's sense of logic in order to be accepted. Careful planning is essential if the reader is to be convinced. The ideas can be supported by evidence or anecdote, as well as emotive touches, rhetoric and so on.

As an agony aunt who offers advice to readers in a daily newspaper, give advice to a mother who has written to you because her teenage son or daughter seems to be out of control.

1 Produce a list of problems with the teenager; and brief notes about what your advice will be to remedy the problem.

Problem	Advice

(5 marks)

Advice is sometimes placed together, after the problem or problems have been outlined. In this case, though, offer the advice in stages:

2 Select one of the problems and write a paragraph which explains what the problem is and how to remedy it.

Use a brief anecdote to support your solution.

_____

_____

_____

_____

_____

_____

_____

_____

_____

_____

(6 marks)

3 Deal with another problem. This time, use evidence and emotive language to convince the audience.

_____

_____

_____

_____

_____

_____

_____

(6 marks)

4 Select another problem, but this time use humour in your response to it.

_____

_____

_____

_____

_____

_____

_____

_____

(6 marks)

5 Write your concluding paragraph. Remember to finish with an approach designed to make the reader follow your advice.

_____

_____

_____

_____

_____

_____

_____

(6 marks)

Practice essay title

Write an article for your local newspaper, to advise residents how to protect their homes against burglars.

Combining skills on Paper 1 Section B

How do we write in different styles?

It is not really a question of writing in totally different styles. After all, arguing, persuading and advising are sometimes very closely linked. However, an option on Section B will be to write a response which involves more than one kind of writing. You might be asked to argue and persuade or you might be faced with another combination.

Write an article for a local newspaper in which you **persuade** readers to help with charity fundraising. **Argue** that the cause you are supporting is one of the best, and **advise** readers about how they can get involved.

1 Plan your article in detail, making sure that you will be persuading, arguing and advising.

_____

_____

_____

_____

_____

_____

_____

_____

_____

_____

_____

_____

_____

_____

_____

_____

_____

_____

_____

_____

_____

(6 marks)

2 Write a persuasive first paragraph, in which you include a quotation and some statistics. You can invent the material, but make sure it sounds convincing.

_____

_____

_____

_____

_____

_____

_____

_____ *(6 marks)*

3 Write two other paragraphs which:

- are well linked
- are designed to argue, persuade and advise
- use a range of appropriate techniques.

_____

_____

_____

_____

_____

_____

_____

_____

_____

_____

_____

_____

_____

_____

_____

_____ *(12 marks)*

4 Write your conclusion, making it effective.

_____

_____

_____

_____

_____

_____

_____ *(6 marks)*

Practice essay title

Write a letter to advise a relative about how to spend money they have inherited recently and persuade them to spend some of it on other members of the family.

Writing to inform

Isn't it easy to simply present information?

It can be relatively straightforward, but the examiner will still be looking for a wide range of skills: structure, paragraphing, accuracy and high quality features, as well as variety in the language itself. In addition, the response must be appropriate for the purpose and audience.

Write a section for a guide book for visitors to this country, to inform them about what Britain has to offer.

1 Write a list of significant features or areas of interest that you intend to discuss in detail. Aim to include a range of ideas.

_____

_____

_____

_____

_____

_____ *(3 marks)*

2 Write the opening paragraph. Aim to interest the reader.

_____

_____

_____

_____

_____

_____

_____

_____

_____ *(6 marks)*

3 Write the next paragraph, including relevant facts or statistics and a related quotation. Facts, statistics and quotations can be invented, so long as they sound convincing.

_____

_____

_____

_____

_____

_____

_____

_____

_____

_____ *(6 marks)*

4 Write the final two paragraphs, including a touch of humour if possible. Remember you
need to:

- appeal to your target audience
- interest the reader
- round off your response effectively.

_____

_____

_____

_____

_____

_____

_____

_____

_____

_____

_____

_____

_____

_____

_____

_____ *(12 marks)*

Practice essay title

There has been some bad publicity in the press about the area in which you live. Write a
letter to your local Member of Parliament, to inform him or her about the good things that
happen in your area.

Writing to explain

What is the difference between 'informing' and 'explaining'?

When you write to inform, you give facts and opinions about the subject of your essay. When you explain, you are saying why something happens, or how a situation arises. You move beyond the obvious, to give reasons for things.

Explain how to stay healthy.

1 Produce a spider diagram of ideas.

(6 marks)

Now, structure them into a logical sequence.

Main ideas for staying healthy e.g. cycle regularly	Explanation of 'how' e.g. buy new bike, find necessary time …
1	
2	
3	
4	
5	
6	

2 Write about your first idea, saying why it is the most important.

_____

_____

_____

_____

_____

_____

_____

_____

(6 marks)

3 Write another paragraph of your choice, including facts and figures (which you can invent) and an emotive appeal (touching the reader's emotions) about why this way of staying healthy is so important.

_____

_____

_____

_____

_____

_____

_____

_____

(6 marks)

4 Conclude your essay, summarising your ideas.

_____

_____

_____

_____

_____

(6 marks)

Practice essay title

Write an essay for a magazine for teenagers, in which you explain how teenagers can be fashionable. You might wish to write about clothes, music or lifestyles.

Writing to describe

What sort of description will be required?

It is unlikely you will be expected to produce a story. The question will probably ask you to describe a person or place. If that is the case, avoid the temptation to write a narrative.

Describe the most unusual person you have ever met.

1 Write an introductory paragraph, in which you describe the person in general terms and make clear why he/she is unusual.

_____

_____

_____

_____

_____

_____

_____

_____   *(6 marks)*

2 List three similes and three metaphors which you can use in your description.

Similes

- _____
- _____
- _____

Metaphors

- _____
- _____
- _____   *(6 marks)*

3 Extend your description, by writing further paragraphs which use your similes and metaphors and give an indication of what the person looks like and how he or she behaves. You might also wish to include incidents in which the person has been involved, speech, others' opinions of the person, and so on. If necessary, continue on lined paper.

_____

_____

_____

_____

_____

_____

_____

_____

_____

_____

_____

_____

_____

_____

_____

_____

_____

_____

_____

_____

_____

_____

_____

_____

_____

_____

(15 marks)

4 Write a concluding paragraph, to sum up your feelings about this person.

_____

_____

_____

_____

_____

_____

(6 marks)

Practice essay title

Describe a scene in winter.

Combining skills on Paper 2 Section B

Is this the same as on Paper 1?

It is exactly the same situation. One of the essay titles offered will ask to inform and explain, to explain and describe, and so on.

Some students are arriving from another country, on an exchange trip.
Write a handout sheet to inform them about things they need to know about this country; and to explain the most important laws.

1 Things they need to know about this country

_____

_____

_____

_____

_____

Important laws

_____

_____

_____

_____

_____ _(6 marks)_

2 Write a brief and welcoming first paragraph.

_____

_____

_____

_____

_____

_____

_____

_____ _(4 marks)_

3 Write three paragraphs which give information and explanation. Remember to:
  • be precise and detailed in your information
  • explain how the laws work and why they are necessary.

_____

_____

_____

_____

_____

_____

_____

_____

_____

_____

_____

_____

_____

_____

_____

_____

_____

_____

_____

_____

_____ _(12 marks)_

Continue on lined paper if necessary.

4 Conclude your sheet in a way that is appropriate for the purpose and audience.

_____

_____

_____

_____

_____

_____

_____ _(6 marks)_

Practice essay title

Describe your favourite television programme and explain why you enjoy it.

Revision advice

Working through the sections in this book will have helped you to focus on the important elements in each part of the exam.

You can extend your revision and preparation in various ways.

Section A Paper 1

Try to spend five minutes each day examining a text. For example, if you have a newspaper, decide how the writers have set out to influence their purposes and audiences.

You might adopt this sort of routine:

Day 1: how presentational devices have been used in a text

Day 2: how an argument has been constructed

Day 3: how facts and opinions have been used in an article

Day 4: how language has been used in a report

Day 5: how successful a particular writer has been and why

and so on.

Section A Paper 2

It is relatively easy to read through all the poems from different cultures and traditions, but that is not necessarily the best way to prepare for your exam.

Instead, try working on one poem each day. Read a poem and make sure you know:

* exactly what the poet is saying (ideas, feelings, attitudes)

* how the poet says it (language and structure).

Choose a different poem the next day, and make the same decisions. In addition, decide in what ways it is the same as the other poem, or different. Deal with the other poems in the same way.

Section B responses

The more you practise the vital skills, the better you are likely to perform in the exam.

Consider:

* setting your own titles and producing detailed plans

* writing sections of the essays, which include high quality features

* producing responses in 45 minutes

* checking your work for errors and making appropriate improvements.

Remember to check your answers for free online: **www.collinseducation.com/easylearning**

Reading media and non-fiction answers

Most of the answers that follow are not 'the correct answers' but should help you to see the sort of answer you would need to write in order to get a top grade. As a reminder, here is an outline of the skills you need to show at different grades at GCSE:

Grade	Skills demonstrated
B/C	• clear attempt to answer question • organised response • selects details and comments on them • a variety of information and comment
A/A*	• a full understanding of what is required • material fully understood and used to answer the question • references to text blended into what is being said • details combined to produce a complete answer to the question

Pages 102–103

1

The writer is producing a news story which sets out to show the heroic nature of Michael Pelham ('his name in the record books'); the article illustrates all the difficulties he has faced, listed for effect ('He faced gales, 24 foot waves…'); then introduces humour by suggesting that his biggest test is yet to come, when he sits his GCSEs – as if they were anything like as terrifying! We are meant to learn about Michael and see him as someone who is really not so different, in some ways…

2

Extract	Audience	Reason for decision
'For the woman in your life: "Erotique", the new fragrance by Henri.'	Probably men (1 mark)	Any suitable comment on 'For the woman in your life' (1 mark) **Or** any comment on 'Erotique', suggesting romantic involvement (1 mark)
'Throughout the nineteenth century, nurses continued to do as they were told by doctors. They knew their place.'	Those learning about history, or the history of medicine (1 mark) **Or** general readership interested in medical/ historical matters (1 mark)	Appropriate comment on historical nature of material (1 mark) Appropriate reference to 'doctors' and 'nurses' (1 mark)
'Discipline your children. No longer can they be allowed to do exactly as they wish.'	Parents (1 mark) Looking for or needing advice (1 mark)	'Your children' (1 mark) (Strict) tone: 'discipline', 'No longer can they…' (1 mark)
'Investors in Sun Life Assurance of Canada rejoiced earlier today, as share values reached unprecedented heights.'	Possibly readers of business news (1 mark) **Or** newspaper readers (1 mark) **Or** investors (1 mark) **Or** relatively educated audience (1 mark)	Subject matter deals with finance ('share values') (1 mark) Apparently newsworthy content ('Investors… rejoiced earlier today…') (1 mark) Relatively complex language ('unprecedented heights') (1 mark)

3

The text is intended to attract visitors to Paris; but, importantly, it sets out to persuade them to travel with Leger Holidays. The speech bubble makes the positive impression seem genuine, because the couple look normal and happy; and the vocabulary used is similarly designed to impress: 'wonderful' and 'so easy'. This all seems like a proper holiday. The work 'easy' is repeated at the beginning of the block of text, for effect – but 'romance' is now an important addition to the appeal. The audience is expected to respond to the word, because it sums up the traditional image of Paris; and it is reminded of what the famous city has to offer: 'the Eiffel Tower, Arc de Triomphe and Champs Elysees'…

Pages 104–105

1 Any <u>five</u> from:

- top rock band played
- played free for nearly 2 hours
- Jodie – and everyone she knew – was invited
- it was a dream come true
- manager chatted to Jodie
- she received gifts from band

2 'The manager chatted to Jodie for an hour': the group did not!

3 Any <u>four</u> from:

- shot for desertion
- name not on Shoreham war memorial
- fought at Mons and Le Cateau at age of 19
- he 'cracked'
- and ran away

4

'The writer has every sympathy for the young soldier and what he was suffering:

'The desire to run away becomes over-whelming…'

He asks the villagers for understanding because he, too, has faced the horrors of war:

'I was scared when I was fired on.'

Now, he seems thoughtful about the experience and can reflect on what happened:

'It is difficult to find words to express…'

Maybe this is because the true horrors of war can only be understood by those who have been there, who know about 'the horrors', being sent 'insane' and being terrified: 'Only a fool would not be'…

Pages 106–107

1

The writer thinks package holidaymakers represent much that is bad about Britain. She identifies the stereotypical figures who feature in the programme ('family from Hell… racist, chain-smoking granny…') and, by her description, identifies their flaws. They are the sort of people who will get sunburn ('tan their skin red'), eat too much ('take full advantage of the all-you-can-eat buffet') and become drunk – and, we suspect, obnoxious too. However, she is not just criticising them as individual people. She is pointing out that because we, as a nation, group together on package holidays, this is part of the reason why the British as a whole can be so racist in their outlook…

2

From the first sentence, the writer shows the two sides of Jaggers' personality: even friends handled him with care. The review of his life balances the apparent contradiction in him. Miranda Stanbridge 'spoke fondly of him' as if he worked for charities and the environment; yet the director says he was 'simply evil' and he was called 'The Dark Avenger'. A word like 'fondness' does not mix, usually, with 'dark' and 'evil'. The writer is positive about Jaggers by saying he went to church and gave to charity but is careful to point out that no one knows how much he gave – and that he battered his cousin to death. The reader is bound to think that is not very charitable!

3

Even though some people may have supported Jaggers, the writer does not seem to think he is a good man. He mentions Stanbridge's assessment, which implied he was a church-goer and so on, but always gives more weight to Jaggers' evil. Three of the four paragraphs end with a note of criticism and the final fact is especially powerful – 'imprisoned for battering to death his cousin'. This makes him sound brutal. It seems to answer the rhetorical question he asked earlier: 'were there two sides to the man?' Maybe there were, but his opinion seems to be that one side is more important…

The writer appears to give a balanced view of Jaggers' personality, but his sarcasm convinces the reader that he views Jagger with something approaching contempt. As readers, we do not warm to Jaggers just because his mother loved him; and the implication that Jaggers did not actually give anything to charity ('the size of his contributions to charity has never been revealed') makes us view him with suspicion. When mentioning Standbridge's obituary, he makes it seem like a work of fiction ('To hear her obituary…you might think the man had spent much of his life in church…'). Importantly, too, the extract both begins and ends with a focus on Jaggers' villainy…

Pages 108–109

1 Facts and opinions include:

Facts	Opinions
checking temperatures etc	white expanse is 'incredible' and provides 'delights'
has had more spare time	whales were 'Fantastic'
has been on a boat and seen whales	penguins are 'crazy'/'not very bright'
has seen seals and skuas	penguins 'panic'
has seen penguins	birds are 'stupid'
was in boat when penguin dropped in	'maybe he thought we were a taxi'
collected glacier ice	'best thing yet' is the ice
kept ice in fridge then put it in drinks	'It's not like normal blue glacier ice'

2 **Extract from a Grade A* answer**

Although the writer is a scientist, she seems very excited by the natural world around her. The facts are given to us: things like how the team are spending their time 'checking temperatures, air quality…'; but that all seems to be in the background, because she is more interested in how she has spent her free time. In factual terms, she has been out on a boat, seen lots of whales and birds, and has collected some ice from a glacier. However, the writing comes to life because of the way she reacts to all this. For example, the penguins seem almost human as they 'rush towards you'… and her opinion is designed to make us laugh: 'Maybe he had thought we were a taxi?!'…

3 **Extract from a Grade A* answer**

From the beginning, the writer presents a positive opinion of Jennifer Aniston. She mocks those who are of the opinion she should be seen as 'Tragic Jen' or 'Poor Jen': in her own opinion Jennifer Aniston is 'a beautiful, talented multi-millionairess'. It is certainly a fact that Aniston is rich (another fact we are given is that she earned a staggering one million dollars an episode to appear in 'Friends'), but the writer successfully builds a picture of Aniston as rich in opportunities too, blending facts about her life ('the woman who has regularly topped polls') with opinions (she 'must have limitless options') right up to the end of the article…

Pages 110–111

1 Main points in the argument:

- Many educated people read little but will not admit it:
- 'refuse to admit they read so little'
- They pretend because they do not want to be 'shown up':
- 'Life is too competitive, even when you leave the playground'
- Even those who do read exaggerate:
- 'I was re-reading it recently and…'
- We should not think that only people who read are wise:
- 'They too have their wisdom'
- People who do not read can have many other talents which are just as valuable, though they can be overlooked:
- 'The world isn't logical'

Each point needs to be supported by a relevant quotation. Those given are merely examples.

2 **Extract from a Grade A* answer**

The writer is very critical – and tries to make us accept his opinions and interest us by making us smile but also by peppering the argument with persuasive techniques.

He begins with a rhetorical question with which it is hard to disagree, then moves straight into an example, to prove the point. In case we might be tempted to disagree with his ideas, he immediately mentions Plato's 'Republic' and the average reader might well accept his point of view simply because he is presenting himself as someone who is, clearly, well-read. He pours scorn on those who pretend to read ('they have never even used the book to stand their coffee on'); looks down on them, not just as pretenders, but also as lovers of 'killing/romance/

humour/romping'; and dismisses them with patronising abruptness:

'Because they would feel shown up, that's why'.

He imagines his superior attitude will win the day; but although he is presenting an argument about reading, he engages the reader with his conversational style, beginning sentences with connectives like 'But' and 'Because' and beginning: 'Isn't it'. He is, simultaneously, taking the role of a more common man…

Pages 112–113

Other answers would be acceptable for these questions, as long as they make sense and are clearly explained.

1 • A conversational opening: 'Let's face it' – to attract a wide audience.
   • Use of a cliché (metaphor): 'not always everyone's cup of tea' – for same purpose, not appearing too intellectual.

2 • Exaggeration for effect: 'left most of the audience…' – to criticise the show and make the disapproval seem unanimous
   • Mention of Big Brother and Eastenders – once more, to appeal to a wide, everyday audience
   • Mention of Shakespeare as 'the Bard' – showing the writer is educated
   • Violent vocabulary to show how badly the play was produced: 'spat out, rushed and mutilated' – shows emotions of writer
   • Play on words: 'obscene and best not heard' (changed from 'Children should be seen and not heard') – to add a touch of humour and, again, suggesting intelligence in the writer.

3 • Simple statement: 'Nothing was as it should be' – which seems indisputable.
   • Contrast between traditional view ('Shakespeare's final great creation') and this version, made to seem cheap and sordid ('perverse and perverted')
   • Characters seem mad and unpleasant: 'deranged' and 'hideously naked' – putting further personal interpretation on the performance.
   • Descriptions of characters make them seem like characters out of a mad house.

4 • Alliteration used: 'foul freaks' – frightening/unpleasant 'f' sounds.
   • Simple statements again, making straightforward points which, it seems, cannot be contradicted.

5

The writer uses language to try to make us agree with his opinions about young people and how they behave. He starts with some rhetorical questions, to gain our attention: 'Why aren't they drunk all the time?' He is exaggerating and trying to make us laugh.

Then, when he compares British schools to a bottle of beer – which is a simile – he makes it seem like the children might be almost drunk, so they are hard to control. Then, the headteachers looking after them are like riot controllers, with 'rods of iron'. This makes them sound tough, and makes us think they need to be.

The language used when the kids come out of school is very busy and rushed ('Bustle and noise') so we can imagine the scene…

The writer is offering a critical view of Britain, its teenagers and its society. She challenges us to offer an explanation for what goes on, using rhetorical questions ('Why aren't they like young people in Britain'), but also using sarcasm ('How can it be that (they) have not turned into mass murderers?'). She praises schools' efforts, yet criticises the results ('but with what success?'); and puts 'higher standards' in inverted commas, to indicate that they are not being achieved. When she compares children and their behaviour to 'beer spilling over', there is even the suggestion that it is as if the pupils are associated with drugs, and that their surges cannot be stopped…

Pages 114–115

1

The writer opens and closes his text with the same idea – that young people behave much better abroad. The central section examines that theory: first, by asking pertinent questions about behaviour; then by moving on to look at what happens in school and after school.

Throughout, the writer gives the idea that this is a pressing problem by using concentrated detail. He begins with a list of questions and uses lists as a technique throughout the text. For example, the children appear to be 'pushing, forcing squeezing' and late there is 'tugging and name-calling. Bustle and noise'. It is as if there is concentrated and on-going activity. There is also a sense of danger in the writing. We have mention of beer and later drugs and pubs. These ideas help to link the parts of the overall message…

2

The layout of the advertisement is certainly not exciting – but it is aimed at teachers looking for promotion, so it is efficient rather than exciting. The name of the school heads the text, since the location will be a significant element in anyone's search for a new job. The post itself follows, white on black, to give added impact: indeed, it leaps out of the advertisement, giving it special significance. The box underneath, in the main body of the advertisement, is filled with grey – again, offering a different look, to attract the eye – and the box explains what the school is seeking to achieve and, in general, what sort of person it is looking for. The reader is being led, logically, through the information. Next come the specific requirements the school has for a new headteacher…

3

The text aims to capture readers' attention, so the front page is dominated by the faces of the Beatles. To show that they were around a long time ago, it is in black and white; and to develop this theme, the remainder of the page is also in black and white. In case anyone did not recognise the singers, the headline is very clear: 'Beatlemania'. That is bound to get attention, because it suggests everyone is going crazy about the Beatles. The size of the word suggests the size of the reaction.

As your eyes move down the page, there are more details. The sub-heading continues the attractiveness of whatever is happening ('£500m-a-year' and 'bonanza'); the text box offers us an 'Exclusive', whilst to end, there is a joke ('Play Jude' – a reminder of the Beatles' song 'Hey Jude') and, finally, a couple of words to lure us on for more ('Full story Page 10').

It all works well because the first sentence in the text box says, 'The Beatles are poised for a huge revival', and as we look at them, it is as if they are all in the modern age and set to be big all over again…

Pages 116–117

1

The text comes from a tabloid newspaper, and it treats the whole idea of global warming like science fiction. We are initially attracted by the top heading:

'How technology can help'. This is in block capitals, to make it seem important and serious. However, the effect is undermined below, where it says: 'Let's block the sun with dust and mirrors' – which makes it seem like a game we can all join in. Even before we start to read the article, therefore, we suspect we will not be taking the ideas seriously; and the picture could be from a comic. At first glance, the illustration seems scientific, but then we realise that the scale is impossible. No reflectors could be that big and no aeroplane is that size. The insert from the Exxon site further adds to the ridiculous impression…

2

The advertisement is obviously aimed at teenagers and children, so the presentational devices are appropriate for that audience. The central figure, a figure out of nightmares – or comics! – dominates the page. His grin suggests he is relishing something – just as, perhaps, the reader will relish the novel that is being advertised (and shown in the advertisement too, with the same figure on the cover, to aid product recognition). Is the figure rubbing his hands together in satisfaction, or clapping in triumph? In either case, since the book is about 'The end of the world?', the gestures seem fitting and make the reader want to know more about him and the world's finish. There are also ghostly figures wandering behind him…

3 Possible answers include:

Orange: impression of fun … maybe reminding us of an orange drink … a summery colour … bright ('in your face') colour, to attract young readers … making the book seem not too serious

Silver: cold and more frightening … like steel … or the coldness of stars … clinical … lifeless, in a way…

Pages 118–119

1 James Morrison: only drink mentioned is beer – and it's all very casual (£30 a bottle; Carling, Becks, Corona; beer has a bad effect on your throat or makes you gassy)

In contrast:

WaterAid website: water is a matter of life and death – and the problems caused by dirty water are listed

2 James Morrison

- Purpose: to entertain or inform
- Support will select appropriate detail about James Morrison's lifestyle

- Audience: likely to be casual reader or fan
- Support likely to focus on the 'lightweight' nature of the text – there is nothing of any real importance here

WaterAid:

- Purpose: to inform about the conditions and, perhaps, at the end, suggest that politicians should do more to help (It is never stated, but perhaps, because of the nature of the material, they are hoping to gain support for their cause)
- Support might identify the most serious diseases, significant detail or the final paragraph, as relevant
- Audience: web-surfers, those who are seeking information, supporters of WaterAid
Support likely to mention it is from a website and/or precise details of diseases and close focus on the water situation

3 | Extract from a Grade A* answer

Both texts use facts and opinions, though James Morrison is talking about trivia: the facts of his materialistic life and how he responds to the food and drink with which he is provided. WaterAid, meanwhile, is dealing with the facts of life and death, and opinions are used to direct readers to the seriousness of the situation and express the charity's opinion of how the world responds to peoples' needs.

Morrison gives facts about the ridiculous price of eating and drinking in Silks and the beers they drink or have drunk on tour. He gives the opinion that since everything is prepared on the road, 'A roast dinner now and then would be brilliant'. In contrast, WaterAid gives the fact that 'Around 200 million people worldwide are affected with bilharzias' and explains what this does to the body. The contrast is glaring.

So, too, is the difference in the opinions in the two texts…

Page 123

1a | Extract from a Grade A* answer

To understand the full argument, the reader would have to be reasonably intelligent. The text deals with details about potential disaster for the world, with foreign destinations and places in Britain: the audience, presumably, would already be aware of these things. In addition, the audience will be the sort of people who have the funds to travel widely,

because this argument would be wasted on those earning low wages who cannot afford holidays to begin with. The text is intended to make the readers think about their behaviour and its possible repercussions – for the world itself, which is faced with a frightening future and even 'catastrophic water shortages'…

1b | Extract from a Grade B answer

The writer offers a logical argument. She says that we must stay at home, otherwise the world will become over-polluted. However, that is no hardship, because Britain is as good as the continent and we can see everything we need to on television. It is also as cheap to stay where we are.

The text itself is full of facts and opinions. The facts are things like 5.5% of Britain's carbon dioxide coming from aircraft fuel. This is bound to make the reader think. She also offers opinions like 'Air travel is feeding our destruction'. It sounds like we are feeding an animal that will destroy us…

2a | Extract from a Grade A answer

If you are advertising a hotel, it would be foolish not to include pictures. They are the most likely device to attract readers – and, potentially, visitors. In this case, the reader's eye is immediately attracted to the picture of the Acropolis. It is a sight known across the world. And in case the reader did not recognise it, the name is put in bold and in capitals beneath. It looks like one of the wonders of the world, and especially so when directly beside a heading like 'Ancient art of relaxing' – the 'ancient' nature of the place is stressed here and stands out. The caption beneath the picture links the view to the hotel and is again in bold, so as not to be missed…

2b | Extract from a Grade A* answer

The writer of 'Need a break' begins with rhetorical questions; but if they do not challenge us enough, adds a touch of apparent sarcasm; 'Why not try Bognor..?' We are, presumably, expected to be amazed or chuckle, then read on. We are hooked.

In contrast, the writer then becomes much more formal and factual. The use of government figures and a statistic is meant to appeal to our logical and practical sensibilities; and the short, punchy sentence hammers home an immediate message: 'Air travel is feeding our destruction.' The metaphor is meant to be frightening…

Reading poetry answers

Answers to many poetry questions may be a very personal response, so there is rarely a right or wrong answer. The grid below shows you the sort of skills you need to show at each GCSE grade – what the examiner will be looking for when he or she marks your paper. The points that follow indicate the most likely points that answers to different questions would contain. Some questions also have an extract from a sample answer. Visit www.collinseducation.com/revision for more guidance about marks and grades.

Grade	Skills demonstrated
G	• simple comment • reference to some detail • able to say something simple about how the poet has written the poem
F	• some simple supported comment • reference to appropriate detail • simple statement on two or more aspects of presentation e.g. 'The poet uses a simile'
E	• some simple extended comment, joining ideas together • appropriate quotation to support points made • simple comments on aspects of presentation e.g. 'The simile makes us think that …'
D	• able to mention feelings or ideas or attitudes in the poems • range of supported comments • comments on how things in the poem affect the reader e.g. 'This makes us feel sad, as "…"'
C	• understanding of feelings or ideas or attitudes – clearly explained • range of extended supported comment • some detail of what the poet intended to do and how he achieved it
B	• able to explain the feelings or ideas or attitudes • effective use of textual detail: the right quotations used in effective ways • understanding of a variety of the poet's techniques and purposes – clearly supported from the poem
A	• exploration of and empathy with writer's feelings, attitudes and ideas: a range of interpretations • references integrated into response so it all flows effectively • analysis of how the writer achieved effects: in depth, looking at layers of meaning
A*	• consistent insight and convincing imaginative interpretation: candidate understands everything about the poet's intentions and how the effects are achieved • close textual analysis

Limbo

Pages 126–127

1 Answers are likely to include:

- Slaves being transported to America
- Slaves singing/dancing
- Slaves being treated harshly
- Desperation of slaves on the ocean
- Possibly interpretation of 'knees spread wide'
- Interpretation of the ending; salvation or further misery on solid ground

2 Answers are likely to include:

- Onomatopoeia – 'stick' and 'whip' and what the sounds suggest
- The repetition of the sound
- Alliteration – 'dark deck' and what the sounds suggest
- Metaphor – 'dark deck is slavery': what this suggests about slavery

3 Answers are likely to suggest:

- Song that the slaves are singing, and why
- It is repeated, maybe to suggest length of voyage and their suffering
- 'limbo' set under 'limbo', to show the way they go down
- Interpretations of 'limbo': such as the dance, the state between heaven and hell, as something that keeps them going, something they are made to do, showing how they are being forced down…

4 Answers are likely to cover ideas such as:

- To create the rhythm and sound of the dancing on the ship
- Italicised sections might have a different emphasis – maybe as they are chanted by all
- Explanations of line such as:
- 'long dark deck and the water surrounding me'
- long dark deck and the silence is over me'
- Maybe: the chanting sounds dismal and depressing because of the repetition, the alliteration and the words themselves
- Explanation of rhymes like 'ready' and 'steady' which words sound solid and settled – as the slaves are sorted out by the beatings
- Explanations of rhymes like 'praising' and 'raising': uplifting at the end
- The way the rhythm slows with 'up up up' and particularly 'hot slow step' and what this suggests

5 Answer are likely to refer to:

- 'sun coming up' and 'out of the dark'
- how we interpret 'the dumb gods' and their acts
- whether the slaves are rising out of the ship or out of this life
- whether they are arriving in a better place or not
- whether they have been tricked and are in a place that is no better or whether they have actually been saved
- 'hot slow step' and what that suggests
- 'the burning ground' and what it is
- the importance of the full stop at the end and what it suggests
- and how this re-enforces or changes how we read the rest of the poem
- whether this is continuation of their suffering or, finally, relief from it

> **Extract from a Grade A* answer**

The ending of the poem is undoubtedly optimistic. After all their suffering when they were beaten by the 'whip' and the 'stick', the slaves at last reach salvation. In one way, this is just reaching landfall, America, and escaping the hell of the boat (which was the 'limbo' between hell and heaven); but in another way it is as if they have been saved. Their gods might not have been able to do anything for them on the voyage (they are described as 'dumb gods', in contrast to the noise of the punishments – 'stick hit sound'), but all turns out well in the end. The visions of rape, with 'knees spread wide', the horrors of the 'long dark night' and the terrors on the ocean with 'water surrounding me' are past – now, the poem moves them 'up up up', as they are lifted to a better existence: out of the hold and into the glory of somewhere better…

Nothing's Changed

Pages 128–129

1 Answers are likely to include the following:

- Opening line: short, sharp words capture sounds (onomatopoeia) as he walks, e.g. 'hard stones click'
- 'under my heels': maybe sense of being 'down at heel', i.e. poor
- Enjambements (some lines not punctuated at end), moving us on to next line smoothly/quickly, as he moves on
- 'thrust/bearded seeds' – we sense the thrust to the next line

- More onomatopoeia: 'cans, trodden on, crunch'
- Scene of desolation where there used to be life/people living
- Friendly, beautiful weeds at end: maybe like the people who lived there – you do not have to be a rich flower to be beautiful
- 'amiable weeds' all alone, for emphasis, at the end
- All lines broken up, maybe like the black people's world

2 Answers are likely to include:

- 'whites only restaurant': select, exclusive, blacks not allowed
- 'working man's café': contrast – sounds poor, shows who are the workers in the country
- Associated details:
  restaurant – amongst the weeds, like a squatter (should not be there), 'new, up-market, haute cuisine' (for the rich), 'guard at the gatepost' (to keep the unwanted out, 'crushed ice white glass' etc (elegance)
  café – 'bunny chows' (poor man's food), take away or basic tables (not for the well-off), no napkins, and likely to be spit on the floor
- The effects of each detail should be included (reader senses the injustice; responds to each description with feelings of…)
- Explanation of how the effect is achieved (e.g. how we feel about each instance of imagery)

3 Answers are likely to include:

- stanza 1: Afrika returns
- stanza 2: how he feels about District 6
- stanza 3: description of restaurant
- stanza 4: crucial statement of obvious division
- stanza 5: what is inside the restaurant
- stanza 6: contrasted with café
- stanza 7: his emotions and what he would like to do
- It is as if we move with the poet and feel his reactions at each stage
- poem begins with Afrika's trek into District 6 and the description and ends with how he feels about what he has found
- Last line same as title – a circle that continues
- 3 stanzas… 2 lines… 3 stanzas: how the two lines are made central to what is being said

4 Answers are likely to include:

- reasons for the anger
- how it is shown, e.g. repetition in stanza 2, his reaction to the restaurant, etc

- significant details, e.g. what has happened to District 6, the restaurant and the café, his emotions at the end
- close textual references, with their effects
- the ending includes quotes such as:
  - 'boy again'
  - 'small mean'
  - 'Hands burn'
  - 'a bomb'
  - 'shiver down the glass'
  - 'Nothing's changed'

Extract from a Grade A* answer

The opening stanza describes District 6 to the reader, as Afrika walks through it. We are prepared for the anger he shows later, as we are introduced to the ruin and desolation of the place: 'cans, trodden on, crunch'. The onomatopoeia lets us hear, through the emptiness, the noise his feet make. The weeds may be amiable, but we sense Afrika is not.

His anger is shown for the first time in the next stanza. He explains how his entire being recognises the district ('feet…hands…skin…') but as the lines extend, so his emotion is made more apparent. The list, linked by 'and… and…' builds, to include the 'labouring of his lungs', as he can hardly breath, then 'the hot, white, inwards turning anger of my eyes'. It is ironic that his anger is 'white': but that stresses the extreme heat as well as identifying the people who are the source of his upset. It is his eyes that witness the scene; and as he registers what has happened – or, has not happened, since 'Nothing's Changed' – the anger is channelled from his eyes throughout his body…

Island Man

Pages 130–131

1 Answers are likely to include:

- Man wakes up, in London
- Has been dreaming of his island home in the Caribbean
- We are given the images of his past, what used to be there when he awoke
- He seems unstable/only half awake
- London is very different
- We get the sounds of London
- He drags himself out of bed to face another day in the capital
- The descriptions make it sound as if he is not happy
- He would rather be back in his home

2 Answers should include (with the impression created):

- 'blue surf' – beauty, cleanness
- 'steady breaking and wombing' – sounds, waves and birth
- 'wild seabirds' - freedom
- 'fishermen' – in touch with natural world
- 'sun surfacing defiantly' – alliteration: smoothness
- 'small emerald island' – sounds like a jewel
- 'grey metallic soar' – sounds industrialised and play on words (soar/sore)
- 'surge of wheels' – sounds
- 'dull North Circular roar' – sounds again plus lack of real life (dull)

3
- *the steady breaking and wombing* – sense of calm, waves coming in, effect of 'wombing' (birth)
- *he always comes back groggily groggily* – gap shows how his mind stops for a moment;repeated 'groggily' emphasises his confusion/state of mind
- *Comes back to sands*
- *of a grey metallic roar* – contrast in two lines (second unexpected); colour and 'metallic' so unlike what an island offers
- *island man heaves himself*
- *Another London day* – effect of 'heaves': real effort; space leaves him more time to think; simple bluntness of what he faces

4 Opening:

- Beautiful impression of Caribbean
- Presents all that he has lost
- Details to be examined

Ending:

- 'muffling muffling' as if he is trying to cut out reality
- 'crumpled' unpleasant – closest he gets now to waves
- The huge effort to just get out of bed
- Dismal impression of final line

5 Answers are likely to include:

- Lines create impression of waves
- Sense of impressions coming and going, with the lines
- Effect created by space before 'groggily groggily'
- Final line isolated, for effect
- Only punctuation is capital letters – which shows starting points ('Morning', 'Comes back' and 'Another')

- And also shows the heaviness of important features: 'North Circular' and 'London'
- Lack of other punctuation allows fluidity – which might once have been the on-going motion of the waves, but is now the ceaseless sounds of the city or the endless days in London

Blessing

Pages 132–133

1 Answers are likely to include:

- 'The skin cracks like a pod' – simile - suggests dryness, people are suffering like the crops
- 'There never is enough water' – blunt statement of fact
- 'Imagine the drip of it' – onomatopoeia; and the sense that it can only be imagined – it is the stuff of dreams
- 'the small splash, echo' – onomatopoeia; and 'echo', as if the imagination keeps returning to the imagined sound
- 'the voice of a kindly god' – as if water comes from god and just a small drop would seem like an enormous gift

2 Possible ideas of how religion is brought into the poem:

- Suggested initially by 'voice of a kindly god'
- A 'roar of tongues' almost like a religious outpouring
- People rushing out for water are 'a congregation'
- The idea of a 'blessing'

3 Words and their effect:

- 'voice of a kindly god'
- 'sudden rush of fortune' – as if someone has struck gold
- 'silver' – sense of value
- 'liquid sun' – giving life
- How everyone rushes to collect the valuable commodity (details of the crowds or all that they use to collect the water, so none is wasted)
- The idea of 'blessing'

4 Answers are likely to refer to:

- sentence rushes on because the people are so excited and there is so much happening
- no stop until the end
- 'man woman child' tumble together, without even a comma

11

- listing shows enthusiasm, mood
- anything will do to collect water
- 'frantic hands'
- 'screaming'
- sense of richness for the moment
- 'polished to perfection'
- 'flashing light'
- children identified as having real fun and 'blessing sings over their small bones'

Extract from a Grade A* answer

The long sentence, which is actually more than half the poem, captures the excitement and bustle as the people rush to collect the water. There is no full stop because there is no time for them to stop. We see how they come together, almost as one ('man woman child') in a mad scramble to collect what they can. The list of their collecting vessels shows how vital it is to get the water: anything will do. We can almost hear the clash of the 'pots, brass, copper, aluminium, plastic buckets…'; and there are also the 'frantic hands' – and that is a telling adjective to use, which sums up their reactions and state of mind…

5 The title of the poem is appropriate:

- Because they feel blessed – maybe their lives have been saved
- Because of the religious significance
- Because they are likely to see it as God's doing

Two Scavengers in a Truck, Two Beautiful People in a Mercedes

Pages 134–135

1 Answers are likely to include:

- Wearing 'red plastic blazers'
- Hanging on to the garbage truck
- Up since 4 am
- Dirty but on their way home
- How the older man is described – close detail
- How the younger man is described – close detail
- They are looking down into the Mercedes

2 Answers are likely to include:

- Man very trendy – 'hip'
- Wears a suit
- Long haired, with sunglasses, appearing 'cool'

- An architect, who does not have to begin work early
- Woman young, blond, with hair that has been made to seem 'casually' got ready
- Short skirt and coloured stockings, seeming to have made herself attractive
- Apparently works with him (secretary?)
- Both seem as if out of a TV advertisement ('odourless', as if removed from reality)

3 They are contrasted by:

- Transport
- Clothing
- General appearance
- Life styles
- Younger men have things in common, but…
- Older man 'gargoyle Quasimodo' contrasts with girl, as partner of younger man
- They are a 'distance' apart
- Only together for an instant

4 Answers are likely to include:

- To show the shifting nature of society
- To show how society is broken into bits that only just manage to hang together
- To represent waves 'in the high seas of this democracy'
- To show how the vehicles are edging forwards at the lights
- And it affects how we read the poem: we break it into the units that are lines, so that, for example:
  'and looking down into
                        an elegant Mercedes'
  makes us pause, as perhaps, the garbage men pause; and our eyes drop, like theirs, as we move to the next line.

5 Answers are likely to suggest:

- The American Dream is still possible – everyone has a chance
  or
- They only meet for an instant: it is 'as if anything at all were possible', but it is not
- Answers likely to hinge on the interpretation of the 'small gulf' (which is an oxymoron – a contradiction in terms)
- There might be comment on the layout and how that suggests a coming together or drifting apart – especially looking at the final lines
  Language is likely to range across:
- 'odourless TV ad'
- 'everything is always possible'/'anything at all were possible'

- 'an instant'
- 'small gulf'
- 'in the high seas of this democracy'

Night of the Scorpion

Pages 136–137

1 Answers are likely to include:

- First person narrative, which make sit all seem real
- Chronological – in the order that it happens
- Conversational from the start, as if talking to a friend
- Quoting and describing just how it happened
- Moving to significant final three lines – which is the only time the mother speaks

2 Answers are likely to include:

- We know it is in the Third World and people are poor – 'a sack of rice'
- Rainy season
- No electric lights – 'dark room' and 'candles/lanterns'
- Mud-baked walls', so probably huts
- Sit on floor
- Insects and scorpion so somewhere hot

3 Answers are likely to include:

- Starts with statement of what happens
- Main section ends with an equally simple statement
- Ends with mother's words, as she recovers
- Takes us through chronologically, so we see the incidents in the order they happened
- Attempts to save her becoming more extreme, through neighbours' prayers to rites of holy man, to husband trying things in which he does not believe, then trying to burn the poison away

4 Answer is likely to refer to:

Peasants:
- 'like swarms of flies'
- buzzed the name of God…'
- 'with candles and with lanterns…'
- 'They clicked their tongues'
- what they said
- what they believed
- sat around mother
- more of them

Father:
- 'sceptic, rationalist'
- 'trying every…'
- the paraffin
- Holy man:
- his rites
- and incantation

Nissim Ezekiel obviously lived in a poor but very close society, so when her mother is stung, many people arrive to help.

First, there are the neighbours:

'the peasants came like swarms of flies
and buzzed the name of God a hundred times.'

As 'peasants', we know they must have been disadvantaged and must have had little money, yet they swarmed around, presumably to help. Of course, flies swarm around anything dead or going bad, which is not a positive image. Extending the idea, though, they are buzzing name of God, so they must be muttering prayers quietly and often. We are given the impression that although the poet resents their presence, just as we would not want flies around, at least they do care. They believe they could defeat the scorpion themselves, as their prayers were designed 'to paralyse the Evil One'. The poet presents them as people with a clear if simple understanding of good and evil, with both primitive beliefs and also a belief in God…

Vultures

Pages 138–139

1 Section 1

- Miserable dawn
- Two vultures on a dead tree
- Description of male
- His head 'inclined' to hers
- Yesterday they ate the dead animal
- They still kept what was left in sight afterwards

Section 2

- Contemplates the strangeness of love
- In many ways it is very 'particular'
- But will put up with dreadful things, make the most of them and even pretend they do not exist

Section 3

- This is linked to the Commandant at Belson
- Has fumes of human roast in his nostrils

- Stops on way home to buy chocolate for his 'his tender offspring'
- They wait at home for the man who is simply their 'Daddy'

Section 4

- Contemplates the contradictions
- Be pleased that even the worst have had goodness within them
- Or despair because even love harbours evil

2 Answer is likely to refer to:

- atmosphere at the start and how it is created e.g. 'greyness', 'drizzle', 'despondent dawn' etc
- the tree and the description of the male vulture
- what the vultures eat
- vocabulary like 'charnel house'
- how love is presented
- the contrasts in the Commandant's life
- the ideas in the final section of the poem
- how the long sentences run on like all the horror in this life seems to run on
- possibly mentioning enjambments, where lines run on to the next to create a particular effect e.g. 'cold/telescopic eyes' so the 'cold' and the 'telescopic eyes' are both given prominence as the phrase slows down

Extract from a Grade A* answer

The mood of the poem is dismal. From the outset the tone is utterly depressing. We are presented with 'greyness' and 'drizzle', like the worse sort of winter's morning; and the alliteration of 'd's in 'despondent dawn' hammers like a drum at a funeral. The vulture's tree is appropriately dead and although he has a mate, he is utterly unattractive with a 'bashed–in head', as if he is something like a corpse himself, a hard and insensitive 'pebble' for a head and 'gross' feathers, which are not sleek, but a 'dump'. If the description is funereal, it is appropriate for the glance we are given of the previous day – like an extract from a horror movie, the birds were picking at the eyes of a corpse which has been dead for some time and has become 'swollen'…

3 Answers are likely to include opinions based in detail upon:

- what the male vulture looks like
- what they have done and are doing
- their relationship

4 Answers are likely to include:

- A evil creation: 'fumes of human roast...'
- Even mentioning his 'hairy nostrils'
- Caring about his child/children when he is so awful to others
- Contrast: chocolate/human roast
- 'Daddy' but a monster

5 Answers are likely to include:

- analysis of the relationship between the vultures
- the love and hate that are part of the Commandant
- how love might well ignore what it finds distasteful
- it is good that even evil creatures can love
- it is tragic that even in love, there still exists evil

What Were They Like?

Pages 140–141

1 Answers are likely to include:

- 2 sections: questions and answers
- Questions present images of Viet Nam as it was
- Answers explain what has happened to it
- Poem can be read from line 1 through to the end
- Or we can read a question, then its answer, and so on: either way makes sense
- Organisation gives clear sense of how it has been transformed: then and now
- It also gives impression that people have forgotten what it was like – hence the questions

2 Answer is likely to include:

- shows respect of Vietnamese people to others
- it is as if a child is speaking to someone who should be their teacher
- it is like a soldier talking – one who has seen the reality

3 Answer is likely to refer to:

- simple and maybe artistic ('lanterns of stone')
- religious ('ceremonies')
- closeness with nature ('to reverence the opening of buds')
- peaceful and happy ('quiet laughter')
- full of beautiful artefacts ('bone and ivory...')
- lives full of poetry, perhaps ('epic poem')

- as if all their life was harmonious ('Did they distinguish…')
- answers likely to state or imply the feelings of the people and the general nature of their society

Life before the war is presented through a series of presumably rhetorical questions. The questions are listed – and the second section of the poem responds to them – but in themselves they present a picture of the rich cultural life enjoyed by the people of Viet Nam before everything was changed.

Their life was simple (they used lanterns of stone), but they were close to the seasons. Their ceremonies did not simply acknowledge 'the opening of buds' – they 'reverenced' the opening, as if worshipping nature. They were 'inclined' to laughter, suggesting they were quiet, respectful people who would not wish to disturb others; and their laughter was 'quiet': dignified, unassuming, appropriate, civilised. Their ornaments were made from precious materials…

4 Answer should refer to the fact that the answers to the questions present an alternative viewpoint and might well deal with:

- 'stone': now light hearts and lanterns forgotten
- 'buds' now no more and representing children too
- mouths now burned so don't laugh (napalm?)
- no ornaments because no joy; and bones all burned
- poetry was of an oral tradition, told by fathers to sons – but all their life was destroyed (answers should include details) so no one now knows
- image of 'moths in moonlight' – frail and soon gone; and all is silent now

The people's lives have been transformed. What was once, is no more. So, for example, where there were once 'lanterns of stone', now it is hearts that are hardened – presumably because of the devastation they have witnessed. The idea of hard hearts is cold and unfeeling, and we suppose that there are no longer 'pleasant ways' to light, and no more gardens. The stoneyness makes their world now seem unfeeling and barren. Blossom, similarly, has gone. But this section of the poem suggests more. By using the word 'buds', the poet is expecting us to associate it with both nature and young children, so we realise that nothing at all

grows after the war. The people are tied to the nature and both have been 'killed'…

5 Answers should mention the final five lines and might suggest:

- Probably a sense of depression and devastation: 'Who can say? It is silent now'
- However, there is still something of their culture, somewhere: 'There is an echo yet…'
- and the beauty of their existence: 'speech which was like a song'
- What has been lost was fragile and beautiful: 'their singing resembled the flight of moths in moonlight'
- And the reader is left to lament their passing
- And the fact that so little about them is known ('Who can say?')

from Search For My Tongue

Pages 142–143

1 Answer is likely to include:

- Identity is important
- Problems arise when you move to another country, which speaks a different language
- Even when you think you have lost it, your 'mother tongue' stays with you
- The language in this poem represents the identity of Bhatt
- The language represents her culture

2 Answer is likely to refer to:

- tongue as identity, link with past and culture
- the two tongues
- how the mother tongue struggles in a foreign land
- the rotting
- 'I thought I spit it out'
- the Gujerati
- how the mother tongue is sandwiched between the English
- the re-growth and its strength
- the blossoming
- how language is used to put across the poet's message

The extended metaphor of the tongue carries the message of the poem, as it represents the poet's culture and way of life. The poet first presents:

'the first one, the mother tongue'

on one line, and this is the culture she has been brought up with; but when the other is mentioned ('the foreign tongue') it is on a line on its own, as if to show its isolation from what she really is.

The poet's main message is that the two tongues cannot co-exist: we must be one thing or another and she fears that her mother tongue is rotting – an unpleasant image, suggesting not just death but also decay. This is particularly grim when we consider the idea that this is happening within her own mouth. When it seems the tongue must be 'spit out', that implies it will be quick, because of the sharp monosyllables, and is an action the poet might seem to want to do. However, the tongue is not removed so easily, for which she is grateful…

3   Answer is likely to suggest:

- it shows us how she spoke in her own country
- it brings to life her culture and way of speaking
- it forces its way into the poem, just as it does into her dreams
- as we struggle to read it, we understand her problems in our country
- it is stuck between English sections, just as she feels surrounded in England

4   Answers might include points such as:

- Direct opening, talking to reader
- As if part of conversation
- Rhetorical question
- Second person approach
- Conversational throughout
- We are expected to read the Gujerati

5   Answer is likely to refer to:

- repeated 'grows'
- impression created by vocabulary like 'longer', 'moist', 'strong veins'
- metaphor of victory: 'ties other tongue in knots'
- sense of opening, new beginning
- 'bud' equals new life
- 'opens' repeated for emphasis
- it is stronger: 'pushes other tongue aside'
- contrast to 'forgotten' – 'blossoms'
- idea of flowering, something beautiful growing, etc
- sense of summer

Extract from a Grade A* answer

After all her worries earlier in the poem, Bhatt leaves us with a sense of genuine optimism and wonder. The metaphor of the tongue is extended right to

the end, where it comes back like a flower and we witness its growth from shoot to bud to flower. It almost feels like spring as Bhatt stresses the idea of development:

'grows longer, grows moist, grows strong veins'

The repetition of 'grows' makes it seem to be forcing its way up and out, and the length and moistness suggest its vitality. The strong veins imply vigour and life. The fact that we have several lines with just commas at the end instead of full-stops also makes us think that there is no stopping this tongue – it is developing with no more than a pause and the poet seems breathless as she tells us what is happening…

from Unrelated Incidents

Pages 144–145

1   Answers are likely to include:

- He does not like them
- They think they are superior and speak correctly
- Their correct speech suggests to people that what they say is true
- He dislikes the idea that only those who speak correctly actually understand what is true

2   Answers are likely to include:

- They think they are inferior
- They see those with regional accents as 'scruffs'
- They think do not know what is true
- And ordinary people cannot be believed
- They think only those who write and speak correctly are to be trusted
- The speaker does not accept people's prejudices

3   Answers are likely to suggest:

- Truth is usually expected to come from people with the 'right way' of talking
- 'right tokn' and 'spellin' should not be a guide to what is true
- We each have a right to 'trooth'
- Any of us can claim we have the truth and others don't – we can claim that our truth and way of speaking is actually correct

4   Answers are likely to include:

- the language indicates a different culture from what is accepted as 'normal'
- the speaker is not part of formal English society

- he seems to be angry and frustrated by the way people judge him
- unusual spellings and analysis
- unconventional features (things that are not normally accepted) in the way it is written e.g. punctuation and even line length

5 Answers are likely to refer to:

- Like an autocue, with its link to a BBC announcer and the fact that this way of speaking is an alternative
- Opening like a news broadcast
- Change into Scottish accent
- Lack of punctuation to begin
- 'this is the six a...': contrast at end with 'thi'
- 'news' and 'nyooz'
- 'talk wia BBC accent' and 'yi canny talk right'
- Repetition, start and end
- Effect of 'belt up'

Extract from a Grade A answer

The poet is focusing the poem on the idea of newsreaders and how they speak, so the poem is set out in the form of an autocue – as if he is reading it for camera. Of course, the joke is that the language he uses is far from what is expected, so there is an irony at work as he points out that the truth is what is important, not the accepted forms.

The poem begins with a well-known phrase: 'this is the six a clock news' but the fact that the punctuation and spelling are incorrect prepares us for what is to follow. He is using the conventional form to express unconventional views …

6 Answers are likely to refer to:

- Showing that what is conventional is not actually required
- Showing that it is still fine to be different – you can still be understood
- Demonstrating a lack of respect for conventions
- Likely to illustrate all ideas with close detail from poem
- Likely to demonstrate how the accent comes through the spelling
- Likely to show how the lines in which it is written help the reader towards
- understanding, so punctuation is not always needed in any case

Extract from a Grade C answer

The spelling clearly represents the way the narrator is talking. However, there are some interesting variations. The poem begins 'this is thi/six a clock/news'. This immediately shows a certain disrespect for conventions whilst also demonstrating that the standard spelling is not necessary, because the message is still clear. At the end of the poem, we have 'this is/the six a clock/nyooz'. At first it looks as though the 'norm' has returned, but the narrator stays firm in his intent. The standard spelling goes and 'nyooz' hits home again. It is showing there is usually a perfectly acceptable alternative. When we have the concluding 'belt up' – as usual, without a capital letter to begin, maintaining the 'anarchic approach' – the spelling is exactly as the word is said, but only because it is hard to imagine any different spelling…

Half-Caste

Pages 146–147

1 Answers are likely to suggest:

- Everyone is the same, regardless of their colour
- People who us the term 'half-caste' are stupid/racist
- The term implies that someone of mixed race is only half a person, which is clearly not the case
- There are many mixes of colour in things in the world, but they are not considered 'half-caste'
- Those who see mixed race people as 'half-caste' are really the limited ones – using only half their intelligence

2 Answers are likely to include:

- To capture the way John Agard talks
- To challenge the reader
- To make it sound like an argument or conversation
- Mention of irony/sarcasm, to attack the ways people see 'half-caste' individuals

3 Answers are likely to include:

- Makes poet sound persistent ('explain', 'explain'…)
- Repeats the question because people do not seem to have an answer ('what yu mean…')
- 'mix' is repeated to stress how much mixing there is in the world, apart from mixed race people
- 'half' repeated because it is the central idea
- 'and when…' repeated to show how this involves all of his life, not just a part
- 'the whole' repeated at the end because a whole is the ideal

4 Answers are likely to include:

- He is called 'half-caste' so he reveals how other things that are mixed do not suffer the same fate
- He chooses a natural thing (England weather)
- And things of beauty (Picasso's paintings, Tchaikovsky's symphony)
- He ridicules the idea that he only perceives through 'half of mih ear' etc
- He makes fun of the fact that it might be supposed he only lives half a life
- And that he has still only told half of his story at the end

5 Answers are likely to include:

- Lines help us read the poem – they make sense of the words for us
- Capitals open sections of the poem
- Lack of punctuation generally is an indication that the speaker is not seen as the same as most people
- Shows that you can be a little different but still be of value
- Where the speaker pauses there is a /, to give us that indication
- Lack of punctuation generally shows that this problem has no natural stop – it just goes on and on

6 Answers are likely to include:

- It is as if the listener/reader is being dismissed – and should come back with a more open mind
- It is not the speaker who is 'half', but the listener
- The lack of wholeness is stressed by the repetition of 'de whole of yu…'
- And the mind is the third 'half' in the list – the most important item, because only half the brain seems to have been working
- Final lines suggest poet is still willing to educate the listener, once the listener opens his mind
- Final joke – there are two halves to his story

Love After Love

Pages 148–149

1 Answers are likely to include:

- Presumably a relationship has failed ('whom you ignored for another')
- So now he has to learn how to love again

- Only this time it is how to love himself and what he is
- This true self has been a lover in the background, throughout life
- This love and understanding of self is what has been forgotten through the relationship and is the 'love after love'

2 Answers are likely to include:

- Enthusiastically
- Directly: 'you'
- Like someone encouraging the reader to be positive
- As someone offering advice, instruction: 'Sit. Feast on your life.'
- As someone offering a brighter future

3 Answers are likely to include:

- They are very direct – commanding
- They make all the advice seem very simple
- 'Give wine. Give bread': the echo of Christianity, perhaps
- 'Sit. Feast on your life': like the owner of a restaurant, welcoming diners.

4 Answers are likely to refer to:

- A house: 'at your own door, in your own mirror'
- Friendly place: 'each will smile…'
- Ideas of what has happened here: 'love letters from the bookshelf'
- There has been a history: 'The photographs, the desperate notes'
- A place that is rich in life: 'Feast on your life'

5 Answers are likely to refer to:

- choice of vocabulary: 'elation', 'greet', 'smile', 'welcome'
- long sentence to open – enthusiasm
- friendly welcome and offer: simple and kind: 'Eat.'
- importance of 'love again'
- religious vocabulary; wine and bread
- returning to original love: 'Give you're your heart'
- sense of change at the end – removing what is past and changing to optimism
- final line: sense of relish, as 'Eat' has changed to 'Feast'

Extract from a Grade A* answer

This is a most positive poem. From the start, the vocabulary gives a sense of delight: there is the joy

18

of 'elation' and the 'smile' of welcome. The paradox of:

'You will greet yourself arriving'

manages to maintain the impression as 'Greet' suggests nothing less than pleasure; and there is also the suggestion of true homecoming, with all the happiness which that implies because you feel comfortable with what you know around you:

'your own door… your own mirror'

Walcott allows no contradiction. He says what must be done: 'Eat', and is in no doubt that 'You will love again the stranger who was your self…'

This Room

Pages 150–151

1 Answers are likely to include:

- A room representing delight and life
- Sense of things expanding, tearing apart
- Uplift
- Celebration
- Excitement
- Joy

2 Answers are likely to include:

- Verbs: 'breaking', 'cracking through'
- Enjambements, as the lines run on to emphasise excitement
- Idea of moving onward, upward to a better place: 'in search of space, light…'
- Bed shifting form nightmares, presumably into dreamland
- 'dark corners' left behind
- Chairs are 'rising up'
- This is an exciting escape; 'crash through clouds'

3 Answers are likely to include:

- 'daily furniture of our lives stirs'
- 'pots and pans bang together'
- 'clang past'
- 'the crowd of garlic, onions, spices'
- 'a' sounds
- How the enjambements give emphasis to the words that begin the next line

4 Answers are likely to refer to:

- details within the house
- what happens to the items in the house
- nightmares and dark corners gone

- positive verbs – often of sound and movement
- cluster of impressions, movement, bustle
- onomatopoeia
- enjambments
- 'excitement' at end – and growing from what has come earlier e.g. 'This is the time and place to be alive'
- 'clapping' – applause for what has happened

Extract from a Grade A* answer

The whole poem is full of scintillating detail. It is about escaping the depression of life and moving up to wonderful freedom. There is a sense of chaotic movement and joyous abandon. The initial verbs, 'breaking out' and 'cracking through' set the poem in motion. The room appears to be seeking 'space, light, empty air': the list is invigorating and sweeps the reader on to the next idea – that the bed is escaping anything bad ('lifting out of/its nightmares so again there is the upward motion). Metaphorical 'dark corners' in life are being cleared as the sky is again the limit:

'chairs
are rising up to crash through clouds'…

5 Answers are likely to include:

- Happy ending
- As if everything is being pulled into exciting pieces (line separated from previous verse)
- Emphasis on final word – a verb: 'clapping'
- Which is onomatopoeia and suggests applause because something has gone well
- Sense of escape to conclude

Not My Business

Pages 152–153

1 Answers are likely to include:

- Akanni
- Danladi
- Chinwe
- The speaker in the poem

2 Answers are likely to include:

- Regular stanzas with familiar pattern
- To mirror familiar situations arising in the country
- Each situation with individuals followed by three line chorus from speaker, repeating how he is not getting involved

- Significant final stanza, as his turn comes
- Use of jeep at start and finish
- Change in situation with regard to yam at end
- His silence mirrored by jeep at end

3 Answers are likely to include:

- Knows exactly what happens to Akanni, Danladi and Chinwe
- Ignores them, to concentrate on his yam, on himself
- Repeated chorus to stress his attitude
- At end, it all changes
- His 'hungry hand' – which emphasises how he cares about his own welfare and needs –
- Is 'frozen', showing how things are about to change and showing his fear
- Presumably he, like his lawn, is 'bewildered'
- He is intimidated by the waiting jeep

4 Answers should include:

- To show how he refuses to become involved
- To show how much he is ignoring
- To remind us of his lack of care for others or fear for himself

5 Answers are likely to include:

'Beat him soft…'
- Simile: response to the idea he is beaten soft, so all bones broken, or until he is senseless/has no strength left
- 'stuffed' like something of no importance
- Jeep sounds like a hungry animal (metaphor of belly)
'Booted…'
- Violence of image
- And no way of avoiding it (metaphor – whole house wakened)
'No query…'
- Straightforward list; no way it can be changed
- Negativity: 'no'
- No rights for the unfortunate victims
'The jeep was waiting…'
- Sense of being 'bewildered' (metaphor)
- 'waiting, waiting' – patient and there will be no escape
- Silence threatening

Presents from my Aunts in Pakistan

Pages 154–155

1 Answers are likely to say things like:

- She is torn between two cultures, of 'no fixed nationality'
- She does not feel at ease with either
- The clothes illustrate the different cultures
- Has only distant memories of Pakistan
- But the items around her keep that culture alive, even if she does not feel she fits with it
- Likes English clothes, but not free to express herself fully

2 Answers are likely to include:

- The items around her represent that culture
- Clothes seem beautiful to her
- Bangles hurt her, literally and, perhaps, metaphorically
- 'alien' in the clothes
- 'couldn't rise up out of its fire'
- Camel-skin lamp: has been transformed but still beautiful
- Mother's jewellery stolen – loss of culture?
- School friend not impressed by clothes
- She admired them
- Remembers conflict in Pakistan, like conflict in herself
- Aunts – screened in their culture
- Beggars at the bottom of the caste system – and she herself feels excluded from the best, staring through fretwork

3 Some possible points:

- Doesn't feel comfortable in Pakistani clothes
- 'alien', 'couldn't rise up out of its fire'
- Longs for 'denim and corduroy'
- 'half-English'
- Maybe like the lamp, wants to be transformed

4 Answer are likely to refer to:

- the salwar kameez; colours, simile, etc
- the slippers
- the bangles
- the apple green sari
- satin-silken tops
- the lamp
- the jewellery
- the mirror-work
- memories of Pakistan
- the aunts

- the beggars
- and to comment on how the colour, imagery etc bring to life the culture for the reader

Extract from a Grade A* answer

The Pakistani culture is presented in vivid colours and precise detail in the poem. The reader's senses are excited from the start where one salwar kameez is described as 'peacock-blue' and the other, in a simile, as 'like an orange split open'. It is made to seem soft, even fragrant, and exotic, and far removed from the culture of England, which has 'denim and corduroy'. The slippers seem similarly oriental with their 'points curling', but the culture does not seem to sit comfortably with the girl: the attractive glass bangles ('candy striped', like tasty sweets) 'snapped, drew blood', as if this is a world that can hurt her…

5 Answers are likely to suggest:

- She feels like an outsider
- as shown by 'staring through fretwork'
- Mention of beggars, sweeper girls, implies, that she, like them, feels a sense of exclusion
- 'of no fixed nationality' presents her situation
- 'Shalimar Gardens' at the end: significant place in Pakistan but she can only see it from a distance
- Presents her problems

Hurricane Hits England

Pages 156–157

1 Answers are likely to include:

- She has moved from the Caribbean to England
- She has not felt settled in England
- But then a hurricane arrives
- At first she is confused about what is happening
- But it reminds her of home
- And she then realises that being in England is like being at home
- She feels freed from her worries and isolation
- She warms to life again
- And that all places are similar, all just parts of the earth

2 Answers are likely to refer to:

- first through the poet's presentation of the storm ('howling ship', etc) and her wakefulness: presumably she is worried/afraid
- then through her questioning of the gods

- her balancing of the 'illumination' and the 'darkness'
- the rhetorical questioning about what is happening
- 'unchained' – the transformation for her
- her links with the weather and what it means
- the 'frozen lake' in her has gone
- she recognises that you can live and warm anywhere: 'the earth is the earth'

Extract from a Grade C answer

From the beginning, we are given the poet's perspective. The storm is 'like some dark ancestral spectre'. This implies fear, as if the spirits of the past are returning for vengeance. However, the situation is 'Fearful and reassuring'. There is the fear, but if it is 'reassuring', we suspect it is something the poet welcomes.

When she begins to speak directly, she calls on the gods from her past: Huracan, Oya, Shango and Hattie. The storm is bringing her culture to her. It takes her back to her roots and she feels it is like a member of her family – not described as a frightening ancestral spectre now but as 'My sweeping, back-home country'. Her emotions here are positive, as she feels the link to where she came from.

She questions the storm, but not as if she is scared, but more as if she finds it all uplifting and exciting…

3 Answers are likely to include:

- The storms can come in either place
- The devastation will be the same in England as in the Caribbean
- Caribbean imagery (of ships etc) applied to English setting
- The trees falling remind her of whales
- It is as if the gods are in both places
- 'the earth is the earth is the earth'

4 Answers are likely to include:

- Relieved and relaxed
- Grateful to the storm and what it means
- Describes it as 'sweet mystery'
- Her 'frozen' nature has now gone
- Metaphorically her foundations have been shaken and she is alive again
- There is a new philosophy for her in the final line – she now knows that everywhere is part of one earth

5 Answers are likely to refer to:

- 'ancestral spectre'
- 'Huracan, Oya, Shango, Hattie'
- 'old tongues /Reaping havoc /In new places'
- 'whales'
- winds and storms

and how the concepts are presented, such as:

- 'howling ship of the wind' (onomatopoeia and metaphor)
- the 'darkness' of the ancestral spectre – suggesting evil, perhaps, and something to inspire fear
- 'My sweeping, back-home cousin' – sounding welcomed and as part of the family
- enjambement in 'old tongues…' so that each part of the sentence is stressed, giving an almost breathless sensation

Extract from a Grade A* answer

The poet's original culture seems to be one that is violent but welcomed; a culture that is based on gods and storms but which links the poet with the vital forces in the earth. Her encounter with a storm that reminds her of her life in the Caribbean changes her whole perception of life in England. She has felt alienated from England, but the hurricane transforms her. Her 'frozen lake' is melted and she can link the two cultures, recognising she can be comfortable anywhere because 'the earth is the earth is the earth'.

It is as if the gods of her homeland have arrived in England, bringing the storm. She calls upon different ones: Oya, Shango, Hattie – pleading with them to communicate with her. She repeats, 'Talk to me…' and we understand her desperation, her need to link back to her homeland…

Comparing poems answers

Pages 158–159

Cluster 1

1 An effective introduction should:

- Deal with the title – 'how' and 'relationships' and might:
  - Make at least one point about each poem
  - Involve a comparison of some kind

2 Comparisons can be found in the ideas, in the language or in the structure.

3 The conclusion might:

- Clearly re-state the main points of comparison
- And/or summarise how relationships are presented

4 The precise nature of the content will depend upon which poem you have chosen as a comparison.

The Night of the Scorpion section is likely to deal with:

- how the poet presents the mother i.e. how they relate to each other
- the neighbours and their involvement
- the father
- the holy man
- the mother's final words

Pages 160–161

Cluster 2

1 Answer is likely to include:

- he is in a country in which people are being persecuted unfairly
- he keeps himself to himself and does not get involved
- he is concerned with his own life/own appetite
- finally, though, the jeep comes for him

2 Answer should deal with the language and, ideally, link with the speaker's situation, e.g. 'my savouring mouth': he is happy just eating and focuses on his appetite rather than his neighbours' problems; his mouth is watering as they suffer. What is happening to them is a part of his situation, so comments might be based around the suffering of Akanni, Danladi and Chinwe.

3 To achieve a Grade B or above, you need to make three or more points with explanation and details from the poem.

4 You would earn one mark for each valid comment which deals with the language and, ideally, links with the speaker's situation.

5 Content will depend upon which poem you have chosen as a comparison.

The *Not My Business* section is likely to deal with:

- the neighbours and what happens to them
- the speaker's reaction to their problems
- the state of the country
- how his situation is transformed at the end

Importantly, there should also be a close focus on **how** language is used in the poems.

Writing answers

No two people will write the same answer to questions of the sort contained within this Exam Practice Workbook – or indeed in your GCSE exam. There is no such thing as a right or wrong answer, but in order to achieve certain grades at GCSE you will be expected to demonstrate certain skills in your writing.

The following grid gives you some general guidelines. If you visit www.collinseducation.com/revision, you will find grids and guidance that relate more specifically to individual questions.

Grade	Possible content
F/G	• content which has some link with the topic • unlikely to be suitable for purpose and audience • fails to interest • some accurate spelling of simple words but likely to be little accurate punctuation • unlikely to use any higher quality language features
E	• content attempts to introduce the topic effectively • attempts suitability for the purpose and audience • attempts to interest • some accurate spelling and punctuation • some attempt at higher quality language features
D	• content addresses the topic • some suitability for the purpose and audience • some interest for the reader • generally accurate spelling and punctuation • a few higher quality language features
C	• content is appropriate • acceptable for the intended purpose and audience • interests the reader • mostly accurate spelling and punctuation • uses appropriate high quality language features
B	• content is both appropriate and well organised • appropriate for the intended purpose and audience • likely to hold the reader's interest • mostly accurate spelling of a suitable vocabulary • a range of generally accurate punctuation • effective use of linguistic devices
A/A*	• content is appropriate, well organised and convincing • totally suitable for the intended purpose and audience • likely to grab and hold the reader's interest • accurate spelling of an advanced but appropriate vocabulary • a range of accurate punctuation • original and effective use of linguistic devices